THE DISCIPLINES OF VOCAL PEDAGOGY:
TOWARDS AN HOLISTIC APPROACH

To Alan

THE UNIVERSITY OF
WINCHESTER

The Disciplines of Vocal Pedagogy:
Towards an Holistic Approach

KAREN SELL

ASHGATE

© Karen Sell, 2005

Published by
Ashgate Publishing Limited
Gower House
Croft Road
Aldershot
Hants GU11 3HR
England

Ashgate Publishing Company
Suite 420
101 Cherry Street
Burlington
Vermont, 05401–4405
USA

British Library Cataloguing in Publication Data
Sell, Karen,
    The Disciplines of Vocal Pedagogy: Towards an Holistic Approach
    1. Singing – Instruction and study. 2. Voice culture – Study and teaching. I. Title.
    783'.04'071

US Library of Congress Cataloging in Publication Data
Sell, Karen,
    The Disciplines of Vocal Pedagogy: Towards an Holistic Approach / Karen Sell.
       p. cm.
    Includes bibliographical references and index.
    1. Singing – Instruction and study. I. Title.
    MT820.S466 2005
    783'.04'071–dc22   2004028164

ISBN 0 7546 5169 X

This book is printed on acid free paper.

Typeset by Saxon Graphics Ltd, Derby

Printed and bound in Great Britain by MPG Books Ltd, Bodmin, Cornwall

Contents

List of Illustrations

Acknowledgements

Illustrations 1 and 2 © Learning Methods Publications. Originally published in Gorman, David, *The Body Moveable*, Guelph, Ontario: Ampersand, 1981.

Illustrations 3 and 4 © Schirmer. Originally published in Miller, Richard, *The Structure of Singing*, New York: Schirmer, 1986.

Illustrations 5, 12 and 13 © Pearson Education. Originally published in Minifie, F.D., T.J. Hixon and F.W. Williams (eds), *Normal Aspects of Speech, Hearing and Language*, Englewood Cliffs, New Jersey: Prentice-Hall, 1973.

Illustrations 6 and 7 © Pro-ed. Originally published in Perkins, William H., and Raymond D. Kent, *Functional Anatomy of Speech, Language and Hearing*, Austin, Tx: Pro-ed, 1986.

Illustration 8 © *Scientific American*. Originally published in Sundberg, Johan, 'The Acoustics of the Singing Voice', *Scientific American*, March, **236** (3), 1977.

Illustrations 9 and 10 © CIBA Pharmaceutical Company, CIBA-GEIGY Corporation. Originally published in Saunders, William H., 'The Larynx', *Clinical Symposia*, **16** (3), 1964.

Illustration 11 © Elsevier. Originally published in Pernkopf, E., *Atlas of Topographical and Applied Human Anatomy*, Vol. 1, Munich: Urban and Schwarzenburg, 1963.

Preface

Since my objectives in this book are stated in the Introduction, it will suffice here to thank those who have inspired and assisted me in my endeavours. Over the years I have benefited greatly from the wisdom and teachings of John Taylor in England, Donald Bell in Canada and Richard Miller in the United States. To them I owe more than I can say.

This book is a revised version of my Middlesex University doctoral dissertation. Unlike many such works, however mine is not of the kind which could have been produced at or near the beginning of a career. On the contrary, it arises from many years of performing as a soprano, of teaching in educational institutions from primary to tertiary, of working in private practice at home and abroad, of lecturing to professional bodies and conducting workshops and masterclasses, and of serving as a voice consultant to members of the health professions.

I am grateful for the rigour of the committees through which my original proposal passed under the kindly administrative eye of Doreen Humm; and for the guidance and encouragement of my supervisors, Professor Michael Bridger and Professor Leon Rubin. Thanks are due also to my examiners, Professor David Howard of the University of York and Dr Peter Fribbins of Middlesex University for their subsequent comments, and for encouraging me to seek a publisher.

It goes without saying that the attempt to show the multi-disciplinary nature of vocal pedagogy has entailed considerable bibliographical effort. In this connection I should like to thank staff of the following libraries for their assistance: Acadia University, Nova Scotia; The British Library; The Library of Congress; The Hollis Library, Harvard University; The Huw Owen Library, The University of Wales, Aberystwyth; The National Library of Wales; The Open University Library and The University of Tulsa Library, Oklahoma. I have been particularly well served by the library of Middlesex University – not least by its extensive run of journals – with its tradition of music pedagogy on the Trent Park campus stretching back more than half a century.

Karen Sell

Introduction

In this study I propose to engage in scholarly research in the light of, and with a view to fostering, reflective practice in the field of vocal pedagogy. As the title, *The Disciplines of Vocal Pedagogy: Towards an Holistic Approach* implies, there is more to educating the singer than training the voice. The particular thesis to be demonstrated here is that an holistic education entailing multi-disciplinary study is essential if classical singers and vocal teachers are to be prepared adequately for singing and for their teaching role, and equipped to cooperate effectively in inter-professional relations. Singing pedagogy is a field to which a number of mutually supportive disciplines contribute and singers should be well versed in these.

Throughout the book the term 'singer' is used to include both performer and teacher. This usage recognizes the fact that many singing teachers are also, or have been, performers; and that, owing to such factors as paucity of work, family commitments, and shortness of performing career, many performers also teach. It is therefore all to the good if all singers in training master the disciplines contributing to vocal pedagogy. I shall limit my study to the disciplines of classical singing pedagogy, understanding by 'classical' the style and repertoire of Western classical music. This restriction of interest implies no elitism, but recognizes the fact that while there are, for example, physiological and anatomical factors common to all styles of singing, technique and interpretation in non-Western singing, musical theatre, popular music and jazz are studies in their own right.

By way of anchoring our study in reality, let us consider events that actually occur in a voice studio, and offer some preliminary suggestions of the writers from whom guidance may be sought, and whose works are listed in the Bibliography.

1. A potential student arrives for a preliminary discussion and possible audition. The first set of considerations is not strictly musical, but concerns the establishment of good personal relations and ethics. The most pressing question under the latter heading is, *Ought* I to enrol this student? Here the teacher's integrity is very much at stake. Suppose that the first few bars of warming up suggest that the person may have nodules, or appears to have a significant respiratory problem. Ought I to recommend a medical check-up prior to enrolment? But suppose professional performance is imminent? Here the teacher faces a clash of *prima face* obligations: the obligation to assist those who have singing career commitments on the one hand, the obligation not to do harm on the other. These are significant ethical questions, especially in the context of financial

incentive, particularly where the private teacher is concerned (Shall I take the money and run?). Voice teachers need skill in making such judgments – and all of this in addition to integrity in general business ethics, which covers a wide territory from giving good service to not poaching the students of others.[1]

2.   In making the assessment of the voice on which the ethical judgment is based the teacher will have watched closely and listened intently. Here the disciplines of anatomy, physiology and acoustics come into play. Standard works in this connection are: Warwick, Perkins, Sataloff, for anatomy and physiology; Sundberg, Titze and Howard for acoustics.

3.   Supposing that it is appropriate to enrol a student, which curriculum will best meet the student's needs? If a beginner, is the student aged eight or eighty? Here we call upon developmental psychology, which at its most basic may suggest that there is something grotesque about a child mouthing the songs of unrequited love, or a senior citizen singing about pixie dells. For developmental psychology, reference will be made to Valentine, Chosky, Hargreaves, Swanwick, Wood, Hayes, and various articles listed in the Bibliography.

4.   On the assumption that we may proceed as far as a piece of music, what do we find?

   (a) A title, which may give a preliminary clue to interpretation. Hoole suggests that interpretation as a subject cannot be taught,

   but it can be cultivated in all but a small minority. Anyone whose personal desire is to learn a musical instrument must, by the fact that they are interested, suggest at least some basic interpretational senses on which to build (1995, p. 12).

   Easthope Martin's 'Come to the fair' suggests a mood significantly different from Handel's 'He was despised' (*Messiah*). Again, we may see that the song is an operatic aria, in which case we need to know the context in which it appears and the dramatic purpose it fulfils – matters discussed by Caldwell and Kivy.

   (b) We see the names of a composer and a poet. Enter history and literature, with their attendant questions of period, style, ornamentation and interpretation. Battisti states:

   Composers, more than anyone else, understand the limits of musical notation. While many work hard to provide as much guidance and information as possible in a score, they expect the conductor to read between the lines of the music (1996, p. 14).

   The substitution of 'singer' for 'conductor' may be made here, and with the general point Greene, Lilli Lehmann, Bernac, Banfield, Thom, Pickett, and Hemsley are in agreement.

   (c) We see time, key signatures, and expression marks which open up the areas of theory and notation. In addition to the printed instructions, there are subtleties of phrase shape, phrase direction, and awareness of harmonic movement. In this connection sources include H.M. Brown, Strouse, Taylor, and Juslin *et al.*, the last of whom explore the possibility that listeners may have emotional feelings transmitted to them by the timing patterns in musical performance.

(d) The song is written in a language – and a competent singing teacher will be something of a linguist, aided where necessary by the International Phonetic Alphabet, a good ear and dictionaries. Wall, Catford, Wells, and Miller are among the reliable writers in this field.

(e) Finally, of course, there are the actual musical pitches. What is their range and *tessitura*? Can this young man with a changing voice manage this piece? Is this soprano technically secure enough to attempt this aria? Such questions are discussed by Miller and Sell.

If the initial interview is satisfactory, training will begin, and sooner or later opportunities for performance (in examination conditions or in public) will arise. This involves, among other things, the following topics:

(a) The psychology of performance, together with communication and artistry. This includes the matching of the sound with the literary content, the tone with the word, and the voice with the drama. The issue of performance anxiety also arises. Stubly presents a philosophical analysis of a 'particular relationship between musical performance, knowledge, self and culture' (1993, p. 94). Vernon Howard pursues virtuosity; Sandra R. Harris states that while the debilitating effect of performance anxiety in athletes has been recognized by mental health practitioners for many years, it is not until the last fifteen years that their findings have been applied to musical performers. Steptoe relates performance anxiety to the stresses of musicians' careers and begins to outline some coping strategies, and further relevant contributions have been made by Hartford, Miller, Sloboda, LeBlanc, Sataloff, Emmons, Senyshyn, Haid, and Picard. Dealing with an opera house with appalling acoustics raises the much-argued problem of the amplification of singers' voices, a topic discussed by Jeal and Tomlinson.

(b) The judging of performance. What disciplines enter into adjudication? First there are questions of technique involving *inter alia* physiology, anatomy and acoustics. Then there are questions of interpretation and judgement which fall within the field of aesthetics. This broad term covers criticism and philosophical aesthetics. The question of the relation of these will be discovered with reference to Osborne, Plummeridge, Kimmel, Sim, Hanfling, Senyshyn, and Rowe. The former concerns an individual's response to a performance; the latter is a second order discipline which analyses the language of criticism. Thus, for example, when I say, 'That was a beautiful performance!' do I have in mind a Platonic idea of beauty? Am I really making the subjective judgement, 'That sounded really beautiful to me', or the emotive exclamation, 'I liked that!'? And is it possible to adduce grounds for any of these judgements? Predelli opposes musical Platonism, cf. Yuktanandana. In one of its senses, therefore, aesthetics, is a branch of philosophy with which, like ethics, the voice teacher should be conversant (Edidin). Having decided what one means by what one intends to say in an evaluative statement there is still the question of the most appropriate mode of expression in practice. This is an important consideration in criticism, but it is especially so where person-to-person adjudication, whether in the studio or a festival, is concerned. For these are contexts in which the claims of honest judgement and the need to encourage singers are finely balanced. In a word, psychological considerations should suggest the manner of the saying. What other factors might influence an adjudicator? Wapnick *et al.* make a case for physical attractiveness in singers affecting adjudicators' assessment of their performance. Other arguments in the general field of the aesthetics of music and aesthetic education to be considered include those of Weatherston and Scruton.

In the light of the welter of considerations thrown up in the context of a voice studio, and on the basis of a number of years' experience as a singer, voice teacher and lecturer, I wish to show that adequate vocal pedagogy presupposes knowledge of a constellation of complementary disciplines. While, for the sake of clarity of discussion I shall, in the chapter headings which follow, preserve disciplinary distinctions, it must be understood that a measure of overlap is not only unavoidable, but will assist my case regarding the inter-disciplinary nature of vocal pedagogy. For example, psychological considerations pertain to both pedagogy and performance; questions of technique, themselves turning upon anatomy and physiology, arise in connection with both the interpretation of a song and the evaluation of a performance.

The several disciplines will be considered to the extent that they focus upon the voice, and apply to the vocal teaching and performance of all age groups, thus:

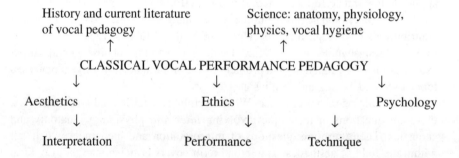

I feel that there is a great need for this book. There is at present no single work that shows the mutual relations specified in the preceding flow chart, and applies them comprehensively to vocal pedagogy for all age groups. Whereas a number of older and contemporary works cover some of the above topics in a general way, research in every field moves on. As might be expected, researchers and writers tend to concentrate on their own specialisms, or sometimes combine two or three disciplines only, for example: Sundberg, Titze, and Howard in physics, Sataloff,

Morrison, and Davies and Jahn in medicine. Thus, for example, Sundberg discusses the anatomy and physiology of the voice. He uses spectrographs to consider such things as formant frequencies, he describes how the emotional state reflects vocal sound, deals with the differences in perception of sound to the singer and the listener and concludes with a chapter on voice disorders. Titze concentrates on physics and its bearing on voice production and Howard covers acoustics and psychoacoustics from a musical and scientific perspective. As we turn to the medical researchers we find Morrison, himself an otolaryngologist, focussing on voice disorders, but including chapters by colleagues; for example, a speech language therapist, a psychiatrist, a singing teacher, and a paediatric otolaryngologist, all working with him in the Voice Clinic Team in Vancouver, Canada. Sataloff, otolaryngologist and professional singer, who has played a leading role in inter-disciplinary work, edits an expanded edition of a previous volume, in which, although mainly addressing physicians, he includes chapters on many other disciplines. Davies and Jahn contribute to a medical reference book for professional voice users.

There is often an unfortunate time lag between the completion of the research and its publication and, understandably enough, the research is only patchily applied to vocal pedagogy in private studios and conservatories. There is thus a case for a work which reviews and critiques recent contributions in all relevant fields, with a view to showing that competent vocal pedagogy presupposes knowledge of these several territories. There is a wealth of material on all the relevant disciplines which, as stated above, does not always follow through to vocal pedagogy. This is not necessarily a criticism of the specialist authors, but their findings need to be assessed and harvested for teaching. Authors of works on vocal physiology and aesthetics, for example, are not blameworthy if they do not venture into pedagogy; but the gap between theory and pedagogical practice needs to be bridged.

The purpose of this book is thus to bring all the disciplines together and to relate them to vocal pedagogy, with a view to seeing how, and to what extent, they can be drawn upon in the pedagogical situation with students of varying ages and levels of attainment from beginners to professionals.

It is not suggested that vocal pedagogy alone draws on a variety of disciplines. Winspur argues that the training of pianists necessitates an understanding of physiology and anatomy as they apply, for example, to posture, breathing, hand positions and movements. There is, nevertheless, an obvious distinction between vocal pedagogy and the teaching of other instruments in that the voice is integral to the performer in a way that no other instrument is. From the point of view of physiology this means that whereas if a violinist sits on his instrument and breaks it, it can be replaced, if the voice is seriously damaged there is no replacement. Further, from the psychological point of view, since the voice is expressive of the personality, criticism of the voice can be perceived as criticism of the person. Whereas in reviews of performance the piano is not normally adversely criticized but rather the way in which it is played (though presumably a grossly out of tune piano would call for comment), in the criticism of singing the distinction between the instrument and the way it is used is frequently not so clearly drawn.

As the following chapters show there is a considerable literature on every aspect and this will be reviewed as appropriate. The underlying question to be addressed to this body of work is: 'How do the findings of the following specialists best contribute to the pedagogical armoury of the classical singing teacher?' So to the plan:

Chapter 1 and its accompanying Appendix 1 survey, sift and critically analyse the pedagogical scene from classical and biblical times to the present day in the Western classical tradition. Important diverse roots are exposed, which yield differing and even conflicting tonal ideals. The historical study provides one element in the consideration of different singing styles, and the interpretation of songs and arias.

Chapter 2 concerns ethics and psychology. I shall first observe that ethical considerations permeate the entire pedagogical process as such, and that they concern, for example, business practice and integrity *vis à vis* the student and other members of the teaching profession. The way in which behaviour of integrity makes a beneficial psychological impression will lead us towards further contributions from psychology. Developmental psychology is examined from pre-birth to old age, taking note of the differences in opinion, for example, between the widely accepted philosophy of Piaget and the responses of Gardner. Many other aspects of psychology such as cognitive, behavioural and social psychology are drawn upon. The question of professional ethics for the singing teacher, is discussed in this chapter in view of its psychological implications.

Chapter 3 on the science concerned with the singing voice includes anatomy, physiology and acoustics which are discussed especially with a view to showing their importance for vocal health and hygiene. A common descriptive language is sought to enable coherent communication between colleagues in such related disciplines, as otolaryngologists and speech language therapists. The question how much science the singing teacher needs to know is pondered. Practical applications for teaching are proposed.

Chapter 4 is the pivotal chapter of the book, for the matters treated here are fundamental to the singer's technique, vocal health and ability to perform consistently and well over time. I shall first follow the voice through the successive stages of human development, paying attention to children's voices, the adolescent voice, and the maturing and ageing voice. Next, tonal ideals and the national schools of singing will come under review, as will voice categories and the question of incorrect classification. Against this background a variety of issues concerning vocal technique will be discussed, including impulse; the coordinated onset and release of sound; breath management; vibrato; agility; resonance; laryngeal factors; formants and the singer's formant; articulation; vowel modification; *sostenuto*; dynamic control and *messa di voce*; hearing, feeling and seeing the voice; warming up and cooling down the voice and the spoken voice.

In Chapter 5, on performance, I consider the interpretation of songs in relation to, among other things, style, historical context, and dramatic purpose. Performance is discussed in relation *inter alia* to psychology, acoustics and theatrical conventions. On the basis that every judgement passed upon the singing student's performance is an aesthetic one, I examine the nature of these judgements, with reference to such philosophers as Langer, Adorno, Sloboda, and Scruton. The ways in which the principles and techniques of aesthetics may assist teachers, adjudicators, examiners and others concerned with the assessment of vocal performance are indicated.

In the Conclusion the findings of the study are summarized, and the implications for the training of singer/teachers and for inter-professional cooperation are spelled out.

Four introductory points remain to be made. First, the purpose of this book is to show which disciplines contribute to vocal pedagogy and provide its theoretical underpinning. The primary emphasis, therefore, is upon what the voice teacher needs to know in order to proceed in a fully competent manner. While lengthy experience in the field of performance and pedagogy will be drawn upon for illustrative purposes, this is not a manual for voice teachers of the kind which offers lesson plans, practice schedules, repertoire for the several age groups, and analyses of the works proposed. But, of course, as soon as we ask, 'Why does the vocal pedagogue need to be conversant with so many disciplines?' we approach the realm of practical application. If we cannot show any pedagogical benefits accruing from knowledge of the complex of disciplines with which we are concerned, our attempts to interest voice teachers in them will be an uphill task indeed. The upshot is that we may expect a certain oscillation within this study between the analysis of the content of the several relevant disciplines and the justification of their use in the pedagogical context. In this latter connection the writing style may at times verge upon methodological advocacy, but this will be rooted in the theory and justified by reference to it. It will certainly not take the form of those theoretically ungrounded 'tips for teachers' (which range from the preposterous to the positively harmful) with which, as we shall see, too much of the literature of vocal pedagogy is littered.

Secondly, as to evidence that the holistic approach is successful we may expect at the outset that the most that can be claimed is that if pursued, effectively desirable results should follow. But the best theory in the world cannot succeed if teachers are incompetent and unable to communicate with students, and if the students themselves are unresponsive.

Thirdly, it is clear that in a multi-disciplinary work of this kind more could be said under each of the chapter headings. However it is hoped that sufficient material is provided to substantiate the main argument of the book, namely, that the several disciplines conspire to inform fully competent singer/teachers, and should therefore be covered in the training of these.

Finally, I shall from time to time use the following vowel symbols drawn from the International Phonetic Alphabet (IPA) (as reproduced in Miller, 1986, p. 298):

IPA Symbols	English	German	Italian	French
[i]	k<u>ee</u>n	L<u>ie</u>be	pr<u>i</u>ma	l<u>is</u>
[I]	th<u>i</u>n	<u>i</u>ch		
[e]	ch<u>a</u>os	L<u>e</u>ben	p<u>e</u>na	<u>été</u>, cri<u>er</u>
[ɛ]	b<u>e</u>t	B<u>e</u>tt, G<u>ä</u>ste	t<u>e</u>mpo	<u>è</u>tes, p<u>è</u>re, n<u>ei</u>ge
[ɑ]	f<u>a</u>ther	St<u>a</u>dt	c<u>a</u>mer<u>a</u>	r<u>a</u>s, <u>a</u>ge
[ɔ]	s<u>o</u>ft, <u>a</u>ll	S<u>o</u>nne	m<u>o</u>rto	s<u>o</u>mme, j<u>o</u>li, v<u>o</u>tre
[o]	n<u>o</u>te	S<u>o</u>hn	n<u>o</u>n	b<u>eau</u>x, p<u>au</u>vre, gr<u>o</u>s
[ʊ]	n<u>oo</u>k	M<u>u</u>tter		
[u]	gn<u>u</u>, f<u>oo</u>l	M<u>u</u>t	<u>u</u>so	<u>ou</u>
[ə]	(schwa) <u>a</u>head	g<u>e</u>tan		d<u>e</u>main

Notes

1   I have myself pursued some of these themes in a number of articles.

Chapter 1

A History of Vocal Pedagogy

In keeping with the overall intention of this book, my purpose in this chapter is not to provide a complete history of singing and song, but to extract from the general history material which will exemplify the historical roots and variety of pedagogical methods. Since these come to the fore from the sixteenth century onwards, this will be our point of departure.[1]

The history will reveal how singers and teachers have been challenged to assimilate stylistic and technological developments. In order to understand the various strands of contemporary vocal pedagogy it is necessary to have some knowledge of their roots. In each of the following sections I shall tell the story with special brief reference to the significant differences of approach to such matters as posture, the breathing mechanism, the vibrators, resonators and articulators, and to other interdisciplinary perspectives. As a result of this enquiry, we shall in subsequent chapters be able to draw upon the pedagogical inheritance when considering the good teaching practice to be aspired to today.

The Sixteenth Century

In 1562 Maffei (early sixteenth century; fl. 1562–73), a lutenist, singer, philosopher, physiologist and physician, produced in a letter to his employer probably the first written method of singing. As far as we know he was the first to use the terms *passaggio/passaggi*. He begins with a description of anatomy and physiology acknowledging Aristotle and Galen. His method consists of ten rules, of which the eighth reads, 'that one propels the breath little by little with the voice; and one takes great care that it does not go out through the nose or the palate ...' (cited by Timberlake, 1993, p. 24).

Zacconi (1555–1627), in his *Prattica di Musica* (1592), emphasizes the importance of physical appearance, 'The singer must be young, refined, well-dressed, not entirely ignorant, not hesitant of speech, nor sharp in speaking; but gentle, courteous, clean ...' (cited by Duey, 1951, p. 38). He goes on to say, 'Some when they cannot reach the figures in certain chords stretch their necks and arch their eyebrows, so that it is apparent that they are pulled there by force' (ibid., p. 39). The use of vibrato, which he calls 'tremoly', is recommended. 'This tremolo', he says 'should be slight and pleasing; for if it is exaggerated and forced, it tires and annoys' (cited by Miller, 1998, p. 302).

Many sixteenth century singers, including Rossetti, Frosch, Zacconi, Coclico and, of course, Maffei, most if not all of whom probably taught, placed high importance on breathing and the problems of breathing for singing. But there is no evidence concerning their actual technical instruction. The problems were very similar to those that occur in the studio of the twenty-first century. The importance of having a good listening ear was stressed. Zarlino (1517–90) wrote 'hearing when it has been purified, cannot easily be deceived as to sound' (cited by Duey, 1951, p. 40). Precise intonation, accurate singing of intervals, correct singing of what was written was required. But, again, there are no manuals to inform us how the voice was to be trained, for example, in flexibility, to cope with widely ranging intervals, ornaments and embellishments. The advice seems to have been that students should find teachers who sing well. Coclico (1499 or 1500–1562) and Maffei suggest that singers could learn to sing without any help from a teacher but by studying their singing manuals which, as we have seen, did not explain *how* to sing. Of Zacconi's *Prattica di Musica* Duey writes:

> For the most part he offers only generalities and these tell what should be done rather than what was done ... [They] ... should have a good chest for sufficient breath, vocal agility, a good ear, know when and where to perform the ornaments with good taste (ibid., p. 42).

As with Maffei *coloratura* is an ideal, and Zacconi offers the suggestion that singers should practise their exercises on all vowels in an attempt to secure evenness of tone throughout the vocal range. This evenness of tone throughout the vocal range may be the precursor of vowel modification. However Zacconi is saying very little that is different from previous writers.

As in the medieval period, vocal registers, were recognized. Three were suggested by some: high, middle and low, and two by others.[2] Much more interest was taken in the falsetto voice – about which there is much misunderstanding throughout the whole of the history of vocal pedagogy, and of which more will be said later. At this period falsetto is understood to be the feminine sound of the male singer, and it is described as emasculated and effeminate, in agreement with Raynard, Abbot of Citeaux.[3]

Music flourished widely during the Renaissance. Choirs were to be found in the courts of nobles, in monasteries and in churches. Boy sopranos were in short supply and some were even abducted to sing in choirs. It is said that Orlando di Lasso (1532–94), when a boy soprano, was abducted three times before his parents finally gave their permission for him to go into the service of the Viceroy of Sicily. Male falsettists replaced the boy sopranos who were in turn succeeded by the castrati.[4] The composer Lodovico Viadana (1564–1645) preferred the castrati to the boy soprano because, in his opinion, 'the boys sing mostly sloppily and with little grace' (cited by Günter, 1997, p. 10). Also, by the time they had learnt technique and repertoire their voices would have changed. However the falsettist's voice was unpopular because of its feeble sound.

Very little, so far in the history, has been said about the breathing mechanism. Duey quotes Caccini (c. 1545–1618) as telling us why breath control is so necessary for his 'noble manner' of singing, of which more anon: 'A man must have a command of breath to give the greater spirit to the increasing and diminishing of the voice, to exclamations and other passions as is related' (1951, p. 74).

This was all empirical teaching; the earlier pedagogues were more concerned with when to breathe rather than with Caccini's suggestions about the importance of breathing. For most teachers a light flexible voice that sang softly was the ideal. It is not until well into the seventeenth century that we have more technical detail and instruction. Most singers and teachers seemed to agree that the best way to learn was by imitating a good teacher, but without suggesting what constitutes a good one.

The Seventeenth and Eighteenth Centuries

Many scholars call this the age of *bel canto*. Whereas today some composers, most of whom are not singers, make extreme demands upon the voice, in the centuries with which we are now concerned many of the singers and teachers were also composers of vocal music and thus tended to write more sympathetically for the voice.

It was at the end of the sixteenth century that individual soloists emerged as public performers in their own right. Previously they had been mainly attached to courts or religious institutions. Although they were highly skilled, singing was mostly in ensemble form as in the contrapuntal motets of the period. With the 'birth of opera', firstly in Italy and later in France, solo vocal works began to require a more consistent and developed technique. There was a new emphasis upon vocal display, agility, dramatic ability and voice production capable of filling not just smaller chambers but large halls and theatres. These skills were called for in the music of Monteverdi, Purcell, Handel and their contemporaries, and also in works flowing down from Mozart's big showpiece arias, to those of Rossini and Bellini. Thus arose the need to discover and circulate technical principles, and to promote the discipline of vocal pedagogy. Since the castrati predominated among the teachers of the time, all voices, male and female alike, were taught to model their singing imitatively upon their practice. Four vocal qualities were demanded by the Baroque composers: perfect intonation, good breathing technique, clear diction and meaningful expression of the text – exactly what one expects from singers today.

There was considerable medical research into the singing voice during this period. Many earlier teachers looked back to Galen's theory of voice production, which describes the position of the vocal folds as elliptical, closing together as the pitch rises. In his *Syntagma musicum* (1619) the German theorist Michael Praetorius (c. 1570–1621) notes that daily vocal practice is an aid to the general health of the singer, warming up the muscles and cultivating a feeling of well being. He goes on to comment positively on vibrato: 'a singer must have a pleasantly vibrating voice'; breathing: 'some singers take too many breaths'; and, unusually at this time, on resonance: 'some sing through the nose and hold the voice in the throat; others sing with the teeth closed' (cited by MacClintock, 1979, p. 164).

Giulio Caccini (c. 1545–1618), composer/singer/teacher, was probably the earliest Baroque writer on singing. He states: 'Therefore, to proceed in order, thus will I say that the chiefest foundations and most important grounds of this art are the tuning of the voice in all the notes' (1601/2, p. 382). He goes on to write, 'a man must have a command of breath to give the greater spirit to the increasing and diminishing of the voice, to exclamations and other passions, as is related' (ibid., p. 391). Concerning diction he says: 'unless the words [are] understood', the singer is not able to 'move the understanding' (ibid., p. 378). Caccini identifies two registers – chest and head and warns against singing all songs in the same way.

In 1636 in Paris, the monk and priest Marin Mersenne (1588–1648) published his encyclopaedic work *Harmonie Universelle,* which includes a treatise on voice and singing, *Traitez de la Voix et des Chant.* A precise description of the vocal mechanism as known at this time is given, based on the teaching of Galen. The first chapter includes paragraphs on the voice, the parts that produce sound, the ear and hearing. This appears to be the first time the importance of hearing is mentioned with regard to singing. We shall see what Bacilly has to say about this when we come to his contribution. Mersenne writes about the muscles for breathing: the intercostals and the diaphragm; he observes that the source of the voice is the glottis and that the muscles and the nerves of the larynx are necessary in order to be able to sing high or low. He is very precise about articulation and writes praising Baillif, presumably a well-known singer, 'who pronounces very distinctly and sounds all the syllables instead of stifling them in the throat, as do most of the others' (cited by MacClintock 1979, p. 173). Mersenne goes on to say that the voice is as individual as the face and that one can be recognized by this vocal individuality.

Like Mersenne, Bénigne de Bacilly (c. 1625–90) underlines the importance of having a good ear. The main cause of 'bad pitch' is 'ignorance of whole-steps and half steps … a good knowledge of notes can greatly contribute to its correction' (cited by Caswell, 1968, p. 28). He describes *cadence* (translated as 'vibrato') as a 'gift of nature' that sometimes becomes too slow or too fast. For Bacilly a pretty voice, 'is very pleasing to the ear because of its clearness and sweetness and above all because of the nice *cadence* [here *vibrato*] which usually accompanies it' (cited by Miller 1998, p. 301). Bacilly continues the two-register theory and appears to give singers the choice of singing in either register: 'Some people are proud of their high voices, and others of their low tone … [some] scorn the falsetto as being too shrill … ' (cited by Caswell, 1968, p. 19). It may be that as much seventeenth century vocal music had a limited range of eleven notes, this choice was a reasonable option. On the other hand the policy may have been to avoid the diffi-culty of singing seamlessly through the registration events. This issue will recur in eighteenth century pedagogy. Other treatises of the late Renaissance refer frequently to unwanted nasality and out of tune singing. They demand beautiful tone but, again, do not suggest ways of achieving this.

Eighteenth century vocal pedagogy became the cornerstone for vocal technique, and much of today's international historic Italianate teaching of singing is based on this. Breath management was paramount, and a common exhortation was '*filar il suono*' (spin the tone), which means control the airflow emission. Writers, among them Giustiniani, Mancini, Agricola, Tosi and Burney, called this *portamento*. By *portamento* was meant the literal translation 'carrying' – the carrying of the voice. This is not a complete description; a more accurate suggestion may be that it means the blending of equally matched tone with tone, both in quality and quantity, ascending and descending. It means more than just *legato*. We use the term *portamento* today in an instrumental sense, for example, the linking of two or more intervals together.

Francesco Antonio Pistocchi (1659–1726) founded the Bolognese school about 1700. The elaborate, florid style of technique taught in this school closely vied with string playing. Antonio Bernacchi (c. 1690–1756), a pupil of Pistocchi taught two of Handel's favourite castrati, Senesino and Carestini. It seems that in the very early seventeenth century operas predominance was given to the tenor voice, but after about 1640 the castrati appeared more regularly and took the dominant roles to the end of the eighteenth century.[5]

In Naples Nicola Porpora (1686–1768), a pupil of Alessandro Scarlatti (1658–1725), was known as a great teacher rather than a great singer. He was a tenor, at a time when tenors were generally considered unimportant. Porpora founded a school and was famed for his pupils, the castrati Caffarelli and Farinelli, the female sopranos Mingotti and Gabrielli, and the composer Joseph Haydn (1732–1809). This school became internationally famous. The aims of the school were to sustain (*cantabile*) and to move the voice (*cabaletta*), anticipating the aria form (*cavatina/cabaletta*) of the nineteenth century.

Jean-Baptiste Bérard (1710–72) in his *L'art du chant* (1775) agrees with the international historic Italianate school as he discusses breathing for singing. He argues for the outwardly raised rib cage, the descent of the diaphragm and controlled breath exhalation as indispensable for good singing technique. Bérard had studied anatomy and was probably one of the first teachers to propose a specific way of breathing for good singing. Great singers into the nineteenth and twentieth centuries used this method effectively. Pronunciation and articulation are also dealt with in his treatise. He admits that it would be easier if singing involved only simple sounds but then, of course, it would sound like instrumental music that cannot express the subtleties, emotion and ideas inherent in words. Bérard considers that all that is necessary to sing well is a correct raising and lowering of the larynx and good breath management. He believes that one raises or lowers the larynx for each degree of pitch or semitone, although he is quick to point out that these measurements are not to be made absolutely strictly.

In 1723 the castrato Pier Francesco Tosi (c. 1653–1732) published his well known treatise *Opinioni de' cantori antichi e moderni, o sieno Osservazioni sopra il canto figurato* which was translated into many languages, and into English by Johann Ernst Galliard (1680–1749) in 1742. Like many before and since, Tosi was by no means happy about the state of the art of singing and complains in 1723, 'Gentlemen Masters! *Italy* hears no more such exquisite Voices as in Times past, particularly among the Women' (rep. 1968, p. 15). The treatise is mainly concerned with ornamentation but Tosi makes general references to technique, for example, problems in breath management: 'The Master may correct this Fault, in teaching the Scholar to manage his Respiration, that he may always be provided with more Breath than is needful' (ibid., p. 60). He goes on to write: 'there are Singers who give pain to the Hearer, as if they had an Asthma, taking Breath every Moment with Difficulty, as if they were breathing their last' (ibid., pp. 60–61). He also mentions two vocal registers, *voce di petto* (chest voice) and *voce di testa* (head voice) but without any suggestions as to how they were to be dealt with: 'for if they may not be distinguished; for if they do not perfectly unite, the Voice will be of divers Registers and must consequently lose its beauty' (ibid., p. 23). More is revealed about the articulators and their effect on the resonator tract. As with many in the Italianate school Tosi favours the use of lateral vowels, for example, [i] and [e] in preference to rounded vowels, for example, [ɔ] and [ʊ] in the upper range of the voice on the grounds that they were less fatiguing. This may be the origin of the bright/brilliant Italianate sound that has, over the centuries been heavily criticized. On the other hand Tosi writes, 'that the higher the Notes, the more it is necessary to touch them with Softness, to avoid Screaming' (ibid., p. 19).

Tosi is not a little disparaging concerning the attitude of singers towards their health:

> A discreet Person will never use such affected Expressions as, *I cannot sing Today*; – *I've got a deadly Cold;* and, in making his Excuse, falls a Coughing. I can truly say, that I have never in my Life heard a Singer own the Truth, and say, *I'm very well To-day*: They reserve the unseasonable Confession to the next Day, when they make no Difficulty to say, *In all my Days My Voice was never in better Order than it was Yesterday* (ibid., p. 147).

He goes on to confirm one of my introductory premises:

> It may seem to many, that every perfect Singer must also be a perfect Instructor, but it is not so; for his Qualifications (though ever so great) are insufficient, if he cannot communicate his Sentiments with Ease, and in a Method adapted to the Ability of the Scholar (ibid., pp. 160–61).

In the main, Tosi wished his singers to learn by imitation and by hearing great singers. He also stressed the importance of a good ear, and like Caccini, warns against singing all songs in the same way. However he disregards any anatomical or physiological description of the vocal organs. Although mainly directed to the castrati, Tosi used the same method with male and female voices.

It was not until 1741 that the functioning of the voice was more accurately explained. Anton Ferrein (1693–1769), a professor of anatomy, published a paper entitled 'De la Formation de la Voix de l'Homme'. Some repudiated his findings. He describes the functioning of the human larynx, stating that the vocal folds vibrate as air passes between them and that pitch rises as the folds tense at the edges. Ferrein compares them with the strings and a bow of the violin family – hence, *cordes vocal* or vocal cords. This analogy and terminology is still in use today in some circles.

Giambattista Mancini (1714–1800), a castrato soprano, was another renowned pedagogue. His treatise, *Pensieri, e riflessioni practiche sopra il canto figurato* (1774) contains mainly, as the title suggests, thoughts and reflections on vocal orna-mentation. At the time of publication of the first edition Mancini was a voice teacher at the Imperial court in Vienna. As he had been taught by Bernacchi his training would have been grounded in the traditional techniques of that period. Mancini was very concerned with resonation in relation to mouth openings:

> the rules for the opening of the mouth cannot be general, nor can they be made universally the same for every individual … Some have wide openings, some narrow, and others medium … (cited by Duey, 1951, p. 103).

Mancini goes on to describe the natural positions of the buccal cavity and the use of the smiling posture to modify the shape of the vocal tract:

> all faces differ in structure, and some are better proportioned for singing than others; nevertheless certain positions were best for a smooth, pure quality of tone, and certain positions would bring out a suffocated and crude tone (cited by Coffin, 1989, p. 8).

He even goes to the length of examining his pupils to see if they have any physical impediment or disease of the larynx, for example, that the tongue is flexible, and that the tonsils, soft palate and uvula are healthy. Duey quotes him as saying, 'Imperfect organs of voice are incurable and hence will inevitably result in imperfect singing' (1951, p. 129). Mancini devotes a whole chapter to the *messa di voce,* stressing that singers, in performing the *crescendo* to maximum strength, must not hold the throat or push breath into the tone. On the *diminuendo* the noble posture (a traditional Italianate posture for singing) must be maintained. He goes on to say that singers will become aware of how the body reacts to subtle changes of colour and dynamic. Very little is said about the technique of breath management apart from how easy it is to inhale; what is of greatest import is dealing with the inhaled air. Mancini believed that 'the Italian vowels [i, e, o, u] could be sung on each note in the position of a smile with the [o] and [u] being slightly rounded … [he felt] the [i] vowel was difficult and should be sung in the position of a "composed smile," ' (cited by Coffin, 1981, pp. 47–9). Unfortunately many teacher/singers misunderstood Mancini's smile position, hence the appearance of grinning distorted faces resulting in unpleasant sound, very often at the most inappropriate time, for example, during a funereal song or tragic opera aria. Commenting on the two registers which he calls 'chest' and 'head' Mancini says that they should be equalized naturally and never forced: 'it requires ability and such a careful use of the voice to render it equally sonorous and agreeable, that few students succeed' (cited by Duey, 1951, p. 114). Vocal agility is also an important facet in Mancini's teaching: 'A run and all kinds of agility must be supported by a robust chest, assisted by the graduation of breath, and a light "fauces" (the opening leading from the mouth into the pharynx)' (cited by Miller, 1998, p. 304).

Chiaro/scuro, a balanced 'light/dark' sound was Mancini's goal. He did not like the artificially bright *chiaro*. Good posture is said to be crucial, particularly to allow for correct head position and freedom in the neck muscles.[6] A later translation of Mancini's treatise by Pietro Buzzi (1912) is dedicated to the tenor Alessandro Bonci who commented: 'If the modern scientific discoveries would blend themselves with the old Italian Method, using the latter as a foundation, then the Art of Song would again be raised to its former high standard' (cited by Coffin, 1989, p. 7). Mancini mentions the vocal health of singers; he states that all parts of the body have to be in good health.

It thus appears from the foregoing account that the teaching philosophy of the eighteenth century was that when all the faults in the voice, such as uneven register change leading to a disturbance in the unified flow of sound, are eliminated we have tonal perfection. It is interesting to note that although Tosi and Mancini use different terminology they appear to mean the same thing. Mancini goes one step further than Tosi; he wants the singer to develop sensations of sound, a kinaesthetic approach we should call it today.[7] In keeping with a contemporary style which encouraged lavish ornamentation, both paid more attention to technical facility than to interpretation. Charles Burney (1726–1814), the music historian, met Mancini in Vienna in 1772, and was told by him that he was sure that he could transform poor voices into good voices given that he had enough time. Nonetheless, vocal insight in the eighteenth century was still mainly grounded in observation and auditory sensation, although many of the results can be substantiated scientifically today.

Vincenzo Manfredini (1737–99), although not giving any advice on how to proceed, insists in his *Regole Armoniche o sieno Precetti Ragionati per apprender la musica* (1797, p. 61) that vocal registers should be blended in order to promote the equalization of the ascending scale. Like Mancini he is very particular about posture and mention is again made of the noble posture of *appoggio* technique:

> When singing, one should always hold one's head firm and straight; neither should one make any unbefitting motions with one's shoulders, arms, or any other part of one's body; on the contrary, one should hold oneself in a noble posture (cited by Duey, 1951, p. 65).

Although Manfredini encourages, among other things, careful listening in relation to the blending of registers, he offers no contribution to the physical act of phonation.

Good health, a sensible diet, regular sleep and physical exercise were generally accepted as part of the singer's training. There were many remedies for sick throats: raw garlic under the tongue, the fluid of the crocodile root boiled in water, and benzoin dissolved in water, both to be drunk. Singers were advised not to sing too high or too low for too long, and Tosi suggests that the best time for singing is with the rising of the sun.

At the present time many teachers all over the world use similar technical exercises and the question of where they originated is often asked. In fact, most of the exercises heard in the world's studios today are from the Old Italian masters and with a competent teacher good results are achieved.

In Germany more and more musicians became voice teachers: Heinrich Schütz (1585–1672) declared that:

> [The singer] should not close the teeth together, nor open the mouth too widely, nor stick out the tongue over the lips, nor pout the lips, nor twist the mouth, nor move around the cheeks and nose like long-tailed monkeys (cited by Duey, 1951, p. 66).

Johann Mattheson (1681–1764) left a detailed, though inaccurate, account of the vocal process, but declared that:

> the first and most important abuse in singing may well be when through too frequent and untimely breathing the words and thoughts of the performance are separated, and the flow is interrupted or broken (1739, p. 265).

He went on to say, like Tosi before him:

> each singing voice, the higher it goes, should be produced increasingly temperately and lightly: however in the low notes, according to the same rule the voice should be strengthened, filled out, and invigorated (ibid., p. 266).

Mattheson pleads that a healthy voice should first be found and then maintained by taking care of it and thus preserving it. He underlines the importance of a good diet and occasionally a little medicine – prescribed by medical doctors, and of eating only a little before singing.

F.W. Marpurg (1718–95) followed mainly in the footsteps of Schütz and suggests that a singer should avoid fog, cold, heat, smoke and dust. Johann Adam Hiller (1728–1804) wrote two books, *Instructions for CORRECT Singing* (1774) and *Instructions for GRACEFUL Singing* (1780), though he did not specify how the larynx functions in phonation. George Friedrick Wolf (1762–1814), following Hiller, published *Lessons in the Art of Singing* in 1774; Johann Baptist Lasser (1751–1805) contributed *Complete Instructions for the Art of Singing* (1805). There are no exercises included by Hiller and Wolf, but many by Lasser. Hiller is very much opposed to forcing the voice, particularly during mutation. He, like

Marpurg, warns against the dangers of impure air. Lasser agrees with all of the above recommendations.

Overall, German pedagogy was based on the Italian school, but nonetheless very little is said either in Germany or France about the blending of the registers before the flautist, composer and writer Johann Joachim Quantz (1697–1773) commented upon a different practice in those countries. This was the old practice of Caccini's time where singers sang in either of the two registers, transposing the music to suit the voice, and where even the natural break was acceptable. This natural break was also accepted in the twentieth century. In an interview with Jerome Hines, Marilyn Horne says 'We know from the records we've heard from Golden Age people that they didn't bother to smooth over the break. They just broke, went into the chest, and that was it' (cited by Hines, 1988, p. 140). Vibrato, too, was discouraged in Germany and France and this has implications for later singing schools. England held fast to the Italian teaching. There was a great love of Italian opera and many Italian castrati visited London. There was also a glut of teachers in Italy, many of whom moved to England. Well-known among them were Domenico Corri (1746–1825), a student of Porpora, who wrote *The Singer's Preceptor* (1810), Gesualdo Lanza (1779–1859) who published *Elements of Singing* (1813), and Jacopo Ferrari (1763–1842) who formed a singing school in 1825. They all had a very similar method. Domenico Corri became one of the most influential teachers in Britain, particularly on account of his provision of practical examples of vocal embellishments of the period, and exercises, the first of which featured *messa di voce*. Ellen Harris quotes Corri (1810) on performance and style: '… yet true into-nation, the swelling and dying of the voice, with complete articulation of words, is essential to all' (1989, p. 99). However Corri gives no advice on how to achieve this. He is adamant that the same vocal registrations are in all categories of voices, and he requires them to be blended throughout the vocal range. In holding that the voice should increase in volume as it rises in pitch and decrease as it descends, he contra-dicts the teaching of Tosi and Mattheson and his proposal demands great skill in eliminating the registration events. If not responsibly taught this could result in vocal damage. Corri has very little to say about the physiological nature of voice production.

Lanza discovered that some of his pupils had difficulty in pronouncing Italian vowels. He invited six beautiful girls to come and demonstrate the mouth positions necessary for correct vowel posture. These mouth positions were illustrated on a page of his book, and it is interesting to note how Italians in 1813 might sing using these postures. The girls did not smile as they sang the vowels, but had 'pleasant' expressions on their faces. Lanza advised that the voice should not be strained when singing, that it should be allowed to grow slowly, and that a pupil should not sing high too frequently.

In France, the only practical early seventeenth treatise was by Jumilhac (1611–1682), *La science et la practique du plainchant* (1673). His theories of voice production are based on Plato's dicta.[8] Blanchet (1724–78) published his treatise

L'art, ou les principes philosophiques du chant in 1756. He was not a musician, but had researched the mechanism of the human voice in great detail. He was very concerned with the use that can be made of the subtleties of posture and declared that all singing teachers should be familiar with the anatomy and physiology of the singing voice.

The great composer and theorist, Jean Philippe Rameau (1683–1764) has some practical suggestions for singers in his *Code de musique practique ou Méthodes* (1760). He has things to say concerning vocal function, and is particularly keen that it should be free and easy. The German, Johann Paul Aegidius Martini (1741–1816), who worked mainly in France, has nothing new to say. Tomeoni (1757–1820), whose father was Italian, was an influential teacher of Italian methods in Paris.

The Conservatoire Nationale de Musique was founded in Paris in 1795. The authorities required that a systematic method of teaching singing be produced. A committee was formed which included, among others, two Italians, Luigi Cherubini (1760–1842), the director of the conservatoire and the singing pedagogue, Mengozzi (1758–1800). The *Méthode* was divided into three sections: 1. The principles of Singing; 2. Solfèges from the best composers; 3. Arias for all characters from older operas. It was circulated in translation in both Germany and Austria and became the model for many future publications by French singing teachers. Incidentally, these new publications had to be vetted by the Conservatoire before they could be used in other studios. Mengozzi asserts that the scales are the most necessary of all exercises and gives six rules for performing them. In 1803 the famous *Méthode de Chant du Conservatoire de Musique* appeared. It was the first book of systematic teaching to appear based on Italian principles. Mengozzi, who, it seems, was mainly responsible for this text, thinks it unnecessary to have a scientific definition of the vocal organs in the *Méthode*, but does specify the principal means of achieving good vocal function.

We now come to the much maligned term *bel canto*. Translated literally this means 'beautiful singing', but unfortunately it has come to be understood by some as a 'method'. Hence advertisements in which teachers claim to teach the magical 'Bel Canto Method', something that does not exist. Probably what they are referring to is the Old Italian style of the seventeenth and eighteenth centuries, which emphasized the tonal beauty and vocal technique of the castrati. At that time the term *bel canto*, in fact an Italian coinage of the 1860s, did not exist. It did not appear in music or general dictionaries until after 1900 (Duey, 1951, p. 11). It is interesting to note that much of the *bel canto* that is professed to be taught today is based on the sound made by the castrati – a sound which, apart from the very distorted recording of Moreschi, we have never heard. An alternative hypothesis is that the modern, well-trained falsettist may very well have a similar timbre, and certainly has a similar range to the castrati. However falsettists sing mainly without complete adduction of the vocal folds, whereas the castrati (cf., Moreschi's recording) adducted the vocal folds in their middle registration but resorted to falsetto in their higher range.

The list of contributors to the art of singing in the seventeenth and eighteenth centuries is vast; I have noted only a small sample of the most important. Several conclusions may nevertheless be drawn. During this period there was, broadly speaking, general agreement about teaching singing, something which cannot be said of singing pedagogy today. Common standards could, therefore, be maintained. Theories of vocal functioning were incomplete and often inaccurate, and played very little part in teaching, though in this regard Bérard and Blanchet were exceptions. Stress was placed on having a pleasant appearance, and on utilizing an inherent physical gift naturally. The singing teacher of note was an experienced performer whom the pupil was encouraged to imitate. Lessons began at an early age and continued, without interruption, through puberty. As far as can be seen short cuts and quick fixes did not exist. Health and hygiene advice ranged from the sensible to the nonsensical.

For all that, Tosi complained about the decadence of singing in his time. Pleasants (1983) suggests that during the eighteenth century there were two 'golden ages' of singing; one between 1720 and 1740 with Farinelli, Caffarelli, Senesino, Bernacci, and Carestini and the prima donnas Faustina and Cuzzoni; and the other between 1770 and 1790 with Guadagni, Pacchierotti, Marchesi and Crescentini and the prima donnas, Mara, Todi, Banti and Catalani. Charles Burney (1726–1814), composer and musical historian, in his *A General History of Music,* II (1789), vividly describes the singing of Farinelli, Pachierotti, and the two rival female singers, Cuzzoni and Faustina.[9] Such judgements are impossible to substantiate in the absence of auditory evidence, but the impression given is worthy of note.

During the period under review singing became more and more self-centred. Whereas agility and bravura display was originally intended to heighten drama and emotion, the emphasis was increasingly placed on stylized performance technique rather than interpretation. Singers gloried in their virtuoso ability to create special effects by, among other things, agility, the sustaining of the breath for inordinately long phrases, the creation of cadenzas of an instrumental type, and elaborate embellishments and ornamentation. Many critics considered the panache of those who elevated vocal pyrotechnics above the music itself as decadent.

The Nineteenth Century

Thus far information on vocal pedagogical method has been scanty, but in the century currently under review there is a proliferation of writing in the field. It thus becomes possible to focus in particular upon the main pedagogues, while at the same time noting specific points of continuing interest.

Once again we are met with declarations bemoaning the great decline of the art of singing. Among the reasons for this are bad teaching, change in repertoire and the advent of Wagnerian operas. However since many singers of the period were well trained in the Italian school and in the repertoire of J.S. Bach, Handel, Mozart and

Rossini, one might assume that they could adapt and cope with the change in style without damaging their voices. On the other hand, whereas some singers were able to fill large halls with sound, others had been taught always to sing gently and softly, and they would have had to modify and improve their technique. Even so, some singers, Heinrich Vogl and Lilli Lehmann among them, were singing Wagner well when they were sixty years old.

In the middle to late part of the nineteenth century there was a transition from *bel canto*/romantic to *verismo*. *Verismo*, a realistic/naturalistic kind of opera such as Mascagni's opera *Cavalleria Rusticana,* demanded a darker and heavier sound, a different tonal ideal. The larger size of orchestra and the richness of orchestration required new kinds of opera singers able to assert themselves against the unprecedented volume of orchestral sound found in Wagner and Verdi operas. 'We are still not habituated to Signor Verdi's violent music', said the music journalist Henry F. Chorley (1808–72), recollecting the year 1848 (posthumous, 1926, p. 217). He goes on to say, 'The year, in brief, in spite of every outward sign or honour and glory, was felt to be virtually one announcing decomposition and embarrassment' (ibid., p. 217). Similarly, he was moved to write, 'The year 1858 gave me yet one more opportunity of realizing the ruin of Italian music in its own country' (ibid., p. 387). Non-operatic songs were composed in a similar vein, apart from most German *lieder*. Another outcome of *verismo* was the cult of the projection of the personality. Some students of the period suggest that various singers achieved greatness by virtue of their personality rather than by the skill or beauty of their singing.

There was much more scientific investigation of the voice, and great interest in voice production. The aim of the pedagogue was the cultivation of powerful and agile voices, with an emphasis on *legato* and *sostenuto*, so that singers could deal with the long, lyrical and beautiful wealth of melodies of this period. Such composers as Donizetti and Meyerbeer often indicated vibrato for expressive purposes in opera scores. Vibrato became an issue and much was written about it. It goes without saying that in the absence of recordings we have no evidence of the results achieved. We do, however have the comments of some contemporary critics. H.F. Chorley, for example, disliked vibrato and describes it as 'the habit of trembling ... [it] became more monotonous and tiresome than the coldest placidity could have been' (ibid., p. 146). He goes on to say, '... Signor Tamberlink had contracted the habit of vibration, which always, more or less, gives an impression of fatigue and premature decay' (ibid., p. 284). Tradition has it that the vibrato of instrumental playing was a positive imitation of the singing voice. George Bernard Shaw complained that vibrato was 'sweeping through Europe like influenza' (cited by Rushmore, 1971, p. 158).

The Spanish singing teacher, Manuel del Popolo Vincente Garcia (1775–1832), who wrote the treatise *340 Exercises composés pour ses Elèves* (1868), was taught by the Neopolitan teacher Giovanni Ansoni (1744–1826), hence his training was Italianate. Garcia passed this teaching down through his own family: his son, Manuel (1805–1906), and his two daughters, the famed performers Maria Felicita

Malibran (1808–36) and Pauline Viardot Garcia (1821–1910). Before Garcia *père*, French scientists were becoming heavily involved with scientific vocal research. They were interested in the possibility that science could justify some of the precepts of Italianate teaching. Nineteenth century voice teachers became interested in these scientific writings with their implications for the improvement in singing and began to add, for better or worse, their own theories. Such teachers include Manuel Garcia II, trained in the Italian school by his father and who taught in England towards the end of his career, and the Frenchman Charles Battaille (1822–72). Not least because of the efforts of Battaille, Chorley was able to say, 'though betwixt Italian indolence and German transcendentalism ... there is increasingly good training in France' (1926, p. 399).

Manuel Garcia II had a controversial career in some ways. He performed as a baritone, but after an unusually short performing career he is said to have retired because of vocal problems. He assisted in his father's studio and therefore continued to assimilate Italian method. Garcia II mastered the workings of the vocal instrument as then understood. He had enrolled in courses at the military hospitals in Paris and had also studied the excised larynges of dead animals. In 1831 he set up his own teaching practice. Among his famous pupils were Jenny Lind, Mathilde Marchesi, Julius Stockhausen, Charles Battaille, and Charles Santley. Lucie Manèn attributes the decline of the art of singing to the younger Garcia:

> By using the vocal-cord mechanism, a singer could vary the music composed for him in respect of range and volume; but he was no longer taught to employ any of the timbres of Bel Canto (1987, p. 23).

Garcia II's important contribution to the history of singing pedagogy is his *Traité complet de l'art du chant* (1847 and 1872). This book contains exercises specifically designed to encourage the development of power and volume. These include the singing of scales with a *messa di voce* on each note. His infamous *coup de glotte* (stroke of the glottis) has caused much controversy and debate among singers, teachers and critics – especially George Bernard Shaw. However Garcia himself felt that there was a misunderstanding which some have suggested may have arisen because he was not writing in his first language. Certainly if one reads his later work carefully it can clearly be seen that he qualifies what he had been understood to say about coughing by introducing the word 'slightly':[10]

> Q. What do you mean by the stroke of the glottis?
> A. The neat articulation of the glottis that gives a precise and clean start to the sound.
> Q. How do you acquire that articulation?
> A. By imitation, which is the quickest of all; but in the absence of a model, let it be said that by slightly coughing we become conscious of the existence and position of the glottis, and also of its shutting and opening action. The stroke of the glottis is somewhat similar to the cough, though differing essentially in that it needs only the delicate action of the lips and not the impulse of the air (1911, p. 13).

A footnote on the same page, presumably added to the second edition by the editor Hermann Klein, explains the *coup de glotte* even more clearly (ibid., p. 13).

The eminent otolaryngologist used by singers at this time was Dr. Morrell Mackenzie, who was very often at loggerheads with Garcia.[11] They clash in print about the use of the laryngoscope (which, according to tradition, Garcia was said to have invented), the training of children, and the number of vocal registers. Mackenzie, although acknowledging the benefits of the study of anatomy and physiology for singing teachers, insists that to have singers learning to sing by studying the vocal organs, particularly with a laryngoscope, is as absurd as a painter learning to paint by studying the eye with an ophthalmoscope.

Throughout his long career Garcia's views strayed from his Italianate training and dangerously so, not least in what he says about the manipulation of the larynx. With reference to his *messa di voce* scale he writes:

> ... we have seen, this procedure stabilizes the larynx and contracts the pharynx. Then, without changing the position, and consequently the timbre, one will pass into chest register, stabilizing the larynx more and more to prevent it from making any abrupt movement, which might produce a hiccup at the separation of the two registers. Once in the chest register, one will raise the larynx and expand the pharynx to brighten the timbre, so that the student will begin the tone softly and in falsetto and dark timbre (cited by Timberlake, 1990, p. 27).

Cornelius Reid believes that Garcia was looking to science for shortcuts in voice training, in so far as gaining direct control over the vocal instrument was concerned. This led Garcia to introduce theories at variance with his initial Italianate training. Over such a long lifetime of teaching from such a well-known teacher these theories were bound to have a great influence. Reid blames Garcia for the demise of the 'old' school of singing. His efforts to combine science and the art of singing has made Garcia a controversial figure to this day.[12] He was, nonetheless, very highly regarded and is considered by many to have had the greatest ever influence on the art of singing. Certainly, much of what he says accords with current scientific findings. Owen Jander writes of Garcia:

> His personal teaching was in fact more influential than his *Traité* ... Garcia's method was based upon a thorough understanding of the workings of the 'instrument' known at that time (larynx, throat, palate, tongue, etc), and covered as fundamental aspects such things as posture, breath control, enunciation and the use of the three registers ('chest', 'middle', and 'head') (1980, p. 345).

Towards the end of Garcia's long life he appears to become less mechanistic and one might say he has come full circle.[13] Sterling Mackinlay's justifiable conclusion is that,

> His Method may be summed up in the doctrine that it was *not* a method – in the sense that he had no hard and fast rules, – his object always being to make each pupil sing in the way most natural and involving the least effort (1908, p. 283).

Charles Amable Battaille was a leading bass in French opera, a physician, singer, researcher and teacher. He had more professional training for performance than Garcia, resulting in a longer and more successful singing career. Bataille felt it was necessary for all singers to have a basic knowledge of the physiology of voice production. Unfortunately his books are not as readily available in translation as those of Garcia, so his work has gone largely unnoticed in the English-speaking world. He disapproved of teaching by imitation, considering it dangerous. To him efficient breathing is the bedrock of singing. Advocating much disciplined technical practice in onset, breathing and vocalizes, he maintained that voices can be improved and strengthened with technical study, but that teachers should not attempt to try to make a voice into something it can never be. Battaille insisted that every voice is different and that the teacher must adapt to individual needs. Believing that his researches have justified much of Italianate teaching he derided some of the newer methods. He made much use of the laryngoscope, improved its capabilities, and wrote up many detailed pages of his experiments that are, given the scientific knowledge of the time, both perceptive and accurate.

Neither Francesco Lamperti (1813–92) nor his son were known as performers, but both were very revered teachers. Lamperti senior studied singing at the Conservatory in Milan, taught there from 1850–75, and published his book *The Art of Singing* in 1890. He was another musician who bemoaned the decline in the art of singing and attributed it to the fact that singers were pursuing their careers on the stage before they were ready, and also to the absence of the castrati who, having left the stage, were not always being replaced. The most renowned pupils of Lamperti were Marietta Alboni, Teresa Stoltz, Italo Campanini and William Shakespeare. Lamperti emphasizes posture (the noble posture) as being all-important and demands a ringing quality of vibrato. His treatise has as its core the concept of *appoggio*, which he understands as a complex equilibrium between several sets of muscles both at respiratory and laryngeal level. He suggests that all notes from the lowest to the highest are produced by holding back the breath, *la lotte vocale* (French, *la lutte vocale)* or vocal struggle. This means that when singing, the inspiratory muscles labour against the expiratory muscles to retain the breath within the body. He goes on to say that good singing uses surprisingly little breath:

> To sustain a given note the air should be expelled slowly; to attain this end, the respiratory muscles, by continuing their action, strive to retain the air in the lungs, and oppose their action to that of the expiratory muscles, which, at the same time, drive it out for the production of the note. There is thus established, a balance of power between these two agents, which is called the *lutte vocale,* or vocal struggle (Francesco Lamperti, 1890, p. 25).

Some musicologists have suggested that the term *appoggio* was not used before the time of Lamperti. The full phrase *appoggiare la voce* means to lean on, support or sustain the voice. It thus designates 'a technique, associated with the historic Italian school, for establishing dynamic balance between the inspiratory, phonatory, and resonatory systems in singing' (Miller, 1993, p. 55). Lamperti's English translator, J.C. Griffith retains the Italian terms:

> By singing *appoggiata* is meant that all notes, from the lowest to the highest, are produced by a column of air over which the singer has perfect command, by holding back the breath, and not permitting more air than is absolutely necessary for the formation of the note to escape from the lungs (nd., p. 22).

As we have seen the noble posture (*una nobile attitudine*) of *appoggio* technique was anticipated by Manfredini in 1797 in his *Regole Armoniche.*

There are many references to the great Italian pedagogues of the past. In an attempt to unlock the mysteries of Italianate singing much of the literature of the nineteenth and early twentieth century leans either towards scientific and medical evidence, or towards a total disdain of both. However a vigorous, international dispute arose about which is the most efficient and effective way of breathing for singing. It started with the publication by the Frenchman Louis Mandl in 1855, 'De la fatigue de la voix', *Gazette Médicale.* He equated low abdominal breathing with diaphragmatic breathing, and singers began to be taught to breathe by trying to push down the diaphragm and protrude the lower abdomen, seeking to do so in a manner which was repudiated by Dr, Harry Campbell:[14]

> [Mandl] obtained a wide following, and in schools of singing most strange devices were resorted to for the purpose of fixing the ribs and compelling abdominal breathing; thus, the pupils were made to sing while lying down on mattresses, sometimes with weights, more or less heavy, placed on the sternal region; masters were even said to make a practice of seating themselves familiarly upon the chests of their pupils (cited by Lunn, 1906, pp. 32–3).

Lunn himself goes on to say: 'the evidence of evil is overwhelming, and is constantly on the *increase*, owing to the pseudo-science that prevails and the unchecked interference of unqualified persons' (1906, p. 33). To the present day many students are being taught the 'down and out' method of low abdominal breathing.[15] Let Miller make it clear:

> There will be some outward motion in the epigastric-umbilical area (between sternum and naval) but little movement in the hypogastric (pubic) area between naval and pelvis … When the lower abdominal wall is forced outward, the costal area tends to move inward, thereby inducing more rapid lung volume reduction. This proves the fallacy of lower abdominal distention as a viable "breath support" method for singing (1993, pp. 25–6).

Giovanni Battista (Giambattista) Lamperti (1839–1910) was an accompanist in his father's studio as a child and had singing lessons from his father. He went on to teach in Milan, then Dresden and later in Berlin, and published *The Technics of Bel Canto* (1905). His most famous students were Martha Sembrich, Ernestine

Schumann-Heink, and Roberto Stagno. It would seem that he agreed with his father that *appoggio* should be central to voice teaching. They both looked with gratitude to the past Italian masters:

> The act of tone production is in 'contrary motion' to that of breath-taking; the pull of the diaphragm goes parallel with the inspiration, whereas the push of the abdominal muscles is felt to oppose it … although both stand in causal conjunction. The breath pressure increases regularly as the pitch in the tone rises [sic] (Giovanni Lamperti, 1905, p. 9).

Lamperti II states that breathing efficiently is the foundation for singing and also maintains that singing should be a natural and health-promoting activity. The method for breathing which he advocates is diaphragmatic and abdominal – 'Expiration should be affected chiefly by the abdominal muscles in a gradual matter to spin out the tone' (cited by Coffin, 1989, p. 64). Lamperti was enthusiastic about the use of a mirror so that the pupil could monitor mouth openings for register changes and correct inappropriate facial expression.

All the written works of the Lampertis are essential reading for singers and teachers today. The maxims of Giovanni Lamperti, for which we are indebted to his pupil, William Earl Brown, are classics:

> In my opinion, it is not absolutely necessary for a singer to have a big voice, nor even a pretty one: if one just acquires security of breath, purity of enunciation and legato, any voice will sound agreeable to the ear (1957, p. 4).

Unfortunately professional opera singers of the twenty-first century are normally required to have 'big' voices, to 'compete' against large orchestras and dense orchestration. If care is not taken, this can lead to fatigue and abuse of the vocal mechanism. It is encouraging that one of the objectives of the present study is clearly spelled out by Lamperti II: 'In these times, when the demands of the singing art are growing vague, let us return to a study of physiology and the *older* Italian method' (ibid., p. 11).

Julius Stockhausen (1826–1906) was born in Paris and died in Frankfurt-am-Main. He trained at the Paris Conservatoire and with Garcia II in London. After a long singing career Stockhausen settled in Frankfurt and founded his own singing school, which had a great impact on German singing. His *Gesangsmethode* was published in 1884 and translated into English by his student Sophie Löwe *circa* 1886. Stockhausen was a pioneer in the linguistic approach to vocal pedagogy. He placed great emphasis on the study of vowels as indispensable for beauty of tone, and insisted that vocalizes should be practised on all vowels and was aware of the importance of the tongue, lower jaw movements and laryngeal positioning in vowel formation:

> The high or low position of the tongue, the lip modifications, the shortening or elongation of the cavity of articulation, and the great resulting variety of vibrations, giving corresponding

shades of vowel tone, require a lower and quieter position of the larynx in singing than in speaking (1884, p. 11).

Although acknowledging a debt to Garcia, Stockhausen does not slavishly reproduce his teaching. He disagrees with the 'fixed' low larynx taught by his master and thought by many to be the basis of Garcia's method: 'It is still more surprising that he [Garcia] does not make his theory of the [fixed] lowered position of the larynx the basis of voice culture and technique in general' (ibid., p. 16–17). Stockhausen quotes from Garcia's *Nouveau traité sommaire*:

> The pupil must commence the note *piano* in *falsetto,* and in the sombre quality. As has been seen, this process fixes the larynx and contracts the pharynx. Afterwards, without varying the position, and consequently the quality, he must pass to the register of the chest, by fixing the larynx more and more, in order to prevent it making the abrupt motion that produces the hiccough at the moment of the separation of the two registers (ibid., p. 17).

As we shall see in a later chapter neither the 'fixed' or 'low' position of the manipulated larynx is correct.

Stockhausen makes much use of the fifteen vowels and twenty-two consonants of the German language, and even in the English translation of his work vowels and consonants are of great importance and used specifically in his many exercises: 'By the study of the elements of speech we not only lay the basis for distinct pronunciation and good quality of tone … ' (ibid., p. 9). Stockhausen's method anticipates the phonetic/phonemic work of D. Ralph Appelman and Berton Coffin in the twentieth century.

Emile Behnke, born in Germany (1836–92), was a London-based teacher of voice production for speakers and singers. He researched alongside, wrote with, and was supported in his conclusions and method by, the laryngologist Lennox Browne and here they pronounce upon the *coup de glotte*:

> The vocal ligaments meet just at the very moment when the air strikes against them; they are, moreover, not pressed together more tightly than is necessary … the attack is clear and decisive, and the tone consequently gets a proper start. The mechanism by which this is done is the 'coup de glotte' or 'shock of the glottis' (1890, pp. 128–9).

Behnke very much dislikes the *tremolo* (vibrato which is too fast and too narrow), which he finds frequently among the French teachers at the Conservatoire de Musique in Paris. He states that:

> students are deliberately taught the wrong method of inspiration; for, as we gather from the 'Methode de Chant du Conservatoire de Musique,' they are told to 'flatten [or draw in] the abdomen' and to 'bulge out the chest' (1880, pp. 20–21).

Here we have a view of breathing technique completely opposed to that of Mandl. Behnke espouses the theory of the stability of the larynx as opposed to the fixed larynx favoured by some of his contemporaries:

> a teacher who insists upon his pupils keeping their voice boxes perfectly still commits a serious mistake, because it is always injurious to do violence to nature … [or] to attempt to prevent movements which have to serve a great purpose (ibid., p. 70).

Enrico Delle Sedie (1822–1907), an Italian and one of the very early Verdi baritones, ended his musical career teaching in Paris. His treatise *L'estetica del canto e dell'arte melodrammatica* was published in Italy in 1885. It is among the first books to make use of the acoustical theories of vowel resonance advanced by Helmholtz, a professor of physiology. Delle Sedie devised a vowel chart which was entitled *Modifications of the French A in the Modulated Voice of Singing.* He was aware that 'the intensity of the voice depends on the vigor with which the vocal cords put sound into vibration' (cited by Coffin, 1989, p. 45). Preferring the word 'sustain' to 'support' for the breathing mechanism, he postulated that 'support' suggests tension or pressure, which may lead to fatigue of the vocal instrument. This use of the word 'support' is, unfortunately, still used freely in twenty-first century studios. That the voice should be produced as naturally as possible was his great concern. Delle Sedie divides the voice into two kinds: the 'articulated' voice that is used for speech and the 'modified' voice that is used for singing. The former requires, but the latter does not necessarily require, articulation. He remained within the tenets of the historic Italianate school and had a great influence on American vocal pedagogy.

Emma Seiler (1821–87), a German singing teacher and writer, studied with Friedrich Wieck and was also a student of Helmholz. Taught to sing in both the Italian and German schools, and advocating the voice as the most natural of instruments, she mastered the rules that she was taught but not the reasons for them, and eventually succumbed to vocal problems. These led her into psycho-acoustic investigations with Helmholtz. Her goal was to become a good teacher, yet, surprisingly, she felt that the best way to teach was by imitation, and so argued that men should teach men and women should teach women. Teaching in Germany, she acquired an admirable reputation as a skilled and careful singing pedagogue. She wrote *The Voice in Singing* (1875), which is grounded in scientific investigation. Like Stockhausen and Delle Sedie, Seiler was especially interested in the formation of vowels, but she also specialized in the registers of the female voice. Her work is cited to this day. However Miller sees her treatise as 'a prototype of forthcoming Germanic pseudoscientific pedagogic literature that attempts in imaginative ways to apply physiology and acoustics to the singing-voice' (1998, p. 308).

Mathilde Marchesi (1821–1913), a German mezzo-soprano, was born in Frankfurt-am-Main and died in London. Her earliest training was in Germany, but her most influential teacher was Garcia II, with whom she studied in Paris, and she applied his methods in her teaching. She preferred to teach groups rather than individuals:

> I am of the opinion that class-tuition in every branch of study is superior to private lessons, and more especially for singing. The pupil learns a great deal by listening, the teacher is enabled to give those with weak voices frequent rests, while pupils who intend devoting themselves to teaching learn how the different kinds of voices have to be managed (1898, pp. 212–13).

Marchesi taught women only, and among many celebrated students were Nellie Melba, Emma Calvé, Emma Eames and Mary Garden. Henry Pleasants describes her as 'the woman who produced more prima donnas than any other teacher in vocal history' (1983, p. 272). However it was not only her teaching ability which resulted in the success of her pupils.[16] She had many influential contacts with such composers as Delibes, Godard, Gounod, Liszt, Massenet, Meyerbeer, Rossini, Rubenstein, Thomas and Saint-Saëns. For Marchesi technique had to be mastered before interpretation: 'It is essential that the mechanism of the voice should be trained to execute all possible rhythmical and musical forms before passing to the aesthetical part of the art of singing' (1970, p. vii). Marjorie Kennedy-Fraser is quoted in her *A Life of Song* (1929) as saying that Marchesi 'made a great point of the attack of the glottis, a dangerous practice possibly and one that the old Italians would have none of' (Walls, 1994, p. 30). However Cornelius Reid sums up in her defence when he writes:

> Both Garcia and Marchesi were highly cultivated and refined musicians, and it is inconceivable to conclude that either of them approved of a rude, energetic approximation of the vocal cords in the form of a tonal explosions (1983, pp. 73–4).

Unfortunately, as with so many carelessly worded statements, *coup de glotte* has been misinterpreted, and this mistake has found its way into the less skilled teachers' studios.

Scientists of today have difficulty in finding fault with the basics of Marchesi's writing. She believed in and taught from the scientific findings of that time. Marchesi recognized three types of breathing: '*Diaphragmatic* or *Abdominal*; Clavicular; Lateral or Intercostal' (1970, p. xi). It can be deduced however that the foundation on which she built her technique was correct abdominal and diaphragmatic breathing. For female voices Marchesi believed that there were three registers: chest, medium and head, and she would not allow her pupils to sing vocalizes with consonants or words until the registers were blended:

> To equalize and blend the *Chest* with the *Medium* register, the pupil must slightly close the two last notes of the former in ascending, and open them in descending. The same instructions that we have given for the change and blending of the *Chest* and *Medium* registers apply also to those of *Medium* and *Head* (ibid., p. xv).

Marchesi said that the vocal resonators rather than the vibrators were responsible for the register transitions: 'no alteration [of the *Vibrators*] can be discovered in its functional activity as a *Vibrating body* that would account for the different nature of the sound in the change of registers' (ibid., p. xiii). Unfortunately, with regard to registration events she recommended a lowered and mainly immoveable jaw. The many books of elementary and progressive vocalizes she produced demonstrate the thoroughness of her teaching. These vocalizes are still used in many studios around the world today. Many of her elementary exercises begin with ascending passages, while current vocal fold function research recommends beginning with descending passages when warming up and, particularly for the young student and the less technically advanced. Doscher suggests that 'Ascending intervals, particularly over the register bridge, often are troublesome. The quality and weight of the higher pitch must be anticipated and prepared for in the lower one' (1994, p. 194). The last word about Marchesi at this point should be given to Pleasants: 'Marchesi's studios, first in Vienna and later in Paris, were the most efficient workshops ever designed for the developing of the human voice' (1983, p. 272).

Giovanni Sbriglia (1832–1916) was a Neopolitan tenor who, after having an international singing career, settled in Paris to teach. Among his famous students were Edward and Jean de Reszke, Pol Plançon and Lillian Nordica. He did not write a book, but Margaret Chapman Byers has left a record of his work in an article, 'Sbriglia's Method of Singing' published in 1942 in *The Etude*, and reproduced by Berton Coffin (1989, p. 98). Although Sbriglia denied having a particular method he abhorred the new pushing method of breathing with the collapsed chest and declared: 'The foundation of my teaching is perfect breath control without tension' (ibid., p. 99). He had belts made for his singers to support the abdomen, 'You must have intestinal fortitude to support your *point d' appui,* or the focal point in your chest' (ibid., p. 99). The reason for the pushing out of the lower abdomen, he proposed, was that as singer/teachers aged there was a natural appearance of a stoop and so they experimented with what they thought was a new 'easier' method of breathing for their aging muscles. This method was, unfortunately, handed down to their pupils and is still adopted today in some studios. Nothing is known of Sbriglia's own training but from the evidence of his teaching it appears that he was originally of the historic Italianate School, but departed from it.

Lilli Lehmann (1848–1929), born in Germany and taught by her mother, believed that technical efficiency was more important than interpretation. In 1902 she published *Meine Gesangskunst* which was translated into English in 1914 as *How to Sing*. It has proved very popular.[17] She draws on a mixture of traditions in her attempt to justify her own technique physiologically and acoustically. Lehmann advised that students should direct the effort of breathing towards the chest 'thereby setting the chest muscles in action. These combined with the elastically stretched diaphragm and abdominal muscles; the abdomen is always brought back to its natural position during singing' (cited by Coffin, 1989, p. 114). She devised a particular diagrammatic scheme for subjective description of tone placement, stipulating a reference point for each sensation of rising pitch, moving the lower notes from the front of the skull over the top of the head to the back of the skull as the notes got higher. Geraldine Farrar and Olive Fremstad were two of her more famous pupils. As well as proficient technique, singers, as in earlier centuries, were expected to have competence in other musical disciplines.

Vocal health was important and many useful tips were given to singers. Female singers were advised not to wear tight corsets which, among other things, restricted the breath; singers were advised to maintain a careful diet, avoiding everything that is indigestible; to drink chocolate and coffee in preference to tea; to avoid new bread and alcohol; to rise early and take a short walk before breakfast. Many singers smoked. Some thought a cigarette prevented the singer from taking cold on going outside after singing in a hot room. Some advice was good, some was bad. There are many tales of the idiosyncratic habits singers cultivated before performance: eating two salted cucumbers; drinking an egg beaten up with a little sugar; sipping champagne; smoking two cigars; taking snuff; eating lamb cutlets and sucking a glycerine lozenge. Many remedies were suggested for weak chests, dry throats, throat clearing, hoarseness and colds. Again, some advice was helpful and some not:

> Gentlemen troubled with a *weak chest* and susceptible to *Colds*, should bathe the chest and throat with Brown Vinegar, and afterwards daub it on with a sponge, letting it dry. Ladies may use White Vinegar. (Dunn, 1893, p. 82).

Recordings made in the early twentieth century by such singers as Adelina Patti (1843–1919), Emma Albani (1847–1930), Nellie Melba (1861–1931), Emma Eames (1865–1952), and Sir Charles Santley (1834–1922) give us some idea of the changes in style and performance practice.[18] In addition to the golden ages of singing mentioned above in the eighteenth century, Pleasants suggests two further 'golden ages': first, the period of Pasta, Malibran, Lablache and Manuel Garcia *père* during the first half of the nineteenth century; and secondly, the more distinguished noted period *circa* 1880 to 1914, for which we have recordings of many of the singers.

During the nineteenth century three features stand out. First, the need to cultivate more powerful voices because of competition with larger orchestras and denser orchestration. Secondly, because of the demands made and the nature of the new style of opera (for example, Wagner's more mature works) and song, the art of improvisation and ornamentation tended to die out.[19] After hearing the embellishment of one of the arias from his opera *Aureliano in Palmira* in 1814 by the castrato Vellutti, in which his own melody had become almost unrecognizable: 'Rossini found himself confronted with insuperable difficulties in trying to identify what Vellutti was supposed to be singing; his own music, in fact, had become completely unrecognizable' (Stendhal, 1970, p. 340). In 1824 Stendhal suggested that Rossini was a great influence in bringing excessive improvisation to an end (ibid., p. 340). For his part, Verdi, from *Ballo in Maschera* (1859) onwards, banned singers from inserting their own cadenzas and ornamentation. Thirdly, there was the rise in the serious study of voice science. However as Margaret Kennedy-Dygas writes:

> Dogmatism, elitism, and a naively complete trust in the new scientific evidence produced a dizzying muddle of publications from the final third of the nineteenth century into the twentieth century. Not surprisingly, many in the singing profession reacted negatively to the scientific study of singing, because it often seemed to confuse more than clarify (2000, p. 24).

All in all, the nineteenth century witnessed an important transition from the historic Italian School, which had been taught in all the major cities in Europe, and was largely based on observation and imitation, to experimentation and more scientifically grounded justifications of pedagogical method. There was a massive increase of pedagogical literature. Most of the 'classical' repertoire which includes lieder, the art song, the *mélodie* and opera, was composed and performed at the latter end of the nineteenth century.

The Twentieth Century

In addition to the new *verismo* operas, a wealth of songs was produced by the Italian composers known as *giovane scuola*: Catalani, Cilea, Francetti, Giordano, Leoncavallo, Mascagni, and Puccini.[20] The historic Italianate School of singing continued to flourish, but alongside it, other tonal ideals were beginning to be embraced in France, Germany, Northern Europe and Britain. These in turn encouraged different vocal styles, which were not unrelated to the growth of nationalism in the several countries. Under this influence the traditional methodology began to be converted into supposedly 'national' styles of singing that in some respects were viewed as opposed to one another. Peculiarities of language began to emerge: French nasality; Germanic hard consonants and the Spanish aspirate. In France, distaste for the florid Italian style and dislike of the castrati began to prevail, and so we have one of the first examples of the emergence of national style. The Germanic states became united; an individual liturgical style developed in the Lutheran tradition; song recitals were established, and the operas of Weber, Marschner and Wagner set out to glorify German culture. In Russia, Glinka, Mussorgsky and Borodin turned to Russian history and literature for their operas. Words were deemed more important than vocal display, and were accorded equal rights with the accompaniment. Even so, Italy continued to have a great influence upon the emerging national pedagogies.

It is important for singing teachers to be aware of the divergences in national vocal pedagogies in order that they can pass soundly based judgments upon them, and defend their own tonal preferences. In the nineteenth century teachers absorbed and mixed aspects of different methods and twentieth century teaching is mainly an extension of the same. As with the previous section I shall sample a few of the main pedagogues who have made, or who are making, distinctive contributions.

With reference to the vocal pedagogical literature of the twentieth century, Jander says:

> Musically this has been a rather barren tradition resulting in such books as E G. White's *Science and Singing* (1900), which may have some interest for the physiologist, but which have served also to bolster the charlatanism to which the singing teacher has at times been prone (1995, p. 346).

William Shakespeare (1849–1931), born in London, was a tenor, one of the non-Italians in the line of the Lampertis. His treatises *The Art of Singing* (1899) and *Plain Words on Singing* (1924) mention the *la lotte vocale* taught by the Lampertis and support the historic Italianate School. Unfortunately some untoward aspects of technique creep into his work, among them, the spreading of the upper back as alleged assistance for breathing: a ploy favoured in many British studios.

Herbert Witherspoon (1873–1935) studied with G.B. Lamperti and was one of the founders of the oldest voice-teacher's associations in the world, The American Academy of Teachers of Singing. His treatise of 1925, *Singing,* is recognized as a 'standard' of modern vocal pedagogy. According to Miller:

> Witherspoon's unique contribution originated in his conviction (1) that the singing voice primarily is a physical instrument that obeys the laws of efficient physical function, and (2) that the singing voice is an acoustic instrument that must be produced naturally in accordance with the laws of vocal acoustics (1998, p. 310).

Again:

> His pedagogy was based on the language of function, yet Witherspoon stressed that singing deals not simply with mechanics ('muscles and organs cannot be locally controlled') and that it is linguistic and musical interpretation that finally control technique (ibid., p. 310).

Witherspoon founded an Institution of Vocal Art in America, which attracted over two hundred students and eight assistants. The students covered all aspects of vocal study including, unusually, vocal pedagogy. He went on to say of *bel canto*:

> Because these magic words are in the Italian tongue does not mean that they apply to something only possessed by Italians ... In fact, I consider American voices, in general, better trained than those of Italy, Germany or France. The Italian, in particular, has very little knowledge of the scientific side; he usually sings by intuition (cited by Brower, 1996, p. 133).

Franzisca Martienssen-Lohmann (1887–1971) was an important figure in German pedagogy, precisely describing in her writings, *Das bewusste Singen* (1923) and *Der Opensänger* (1943), details of breath-management and registration events according to the tradition of the Italian school. She disliked many of the German practices, for example, heavy covering of the voice, too much use of head voice, and the low positioned larynx.

Georg Armin (1871–1963), a German, was noted for the advance of the 'heroic' voice of the German School and its influence on the North American scene. Miller describes Armin's damaging approach:

> His breath-damming *Staumethode,* by which he believed the *Urkaft* (primal strength) of the vocal instrument could be rediscovered, led to several techniques of induced low-trunk breath-management maneuvers, including anal-sphincteral occlusion and the culti-vated grunt (extension of the vocal fold closure phase during phonatory cycles, with sudden release of glottal tension at phrase terminations) (1998, p. 309).

Frederick Husler (1889–1969) was born in the United States, taught mainly in Germany and died in Switzerland. He dedicated his life to the teaching of singing because of his own vocal ineptitude as a teenager. Yvonne Rodd-Marling, a British pupil of Husler, collaborated with him in the production of his book, *Singing: The Physical Nature of the Vocal Organ* (1965, revised 1983). Many teachers in Germany, Britain and Canada follow the Husler method. Husler believes that the teaching of singing has become too complicated and proposes a simpler and more natural way to sing. He bewails the traditional empirical method that was passed on from teacher to pupil. Husler criticizes singing teachers for having lost the ability to listen with a trained ear and regrets that so many singers today now specialize in one of the many fragmented methods of training the singing voice. He explains in the Introduction to his book that 'It deals almost entirely with the *nature* of the singing voice and its organ and only incidentally with the "art of singing"' (1983, p. xvii). This could be a protest against contemporary methods that were heavily scientifi-cally biased. He goes on to say:

> The instrument of *singing* is a natural one, unlike that of speaking which is an obvious superimposition. Speaking (intellectual) is not singing (emotional, affective) and singing in itself is not yet music-making. In speaking and in singing even the simplest kind of music, the voice is engaged in services directed by the intellect (ibid., p. 9).

The chapter on 'placing', referring to resonance balancing, is dangerous and misleading. Sound, as the acoustician will tell us, cannot be placed anywhere. While the authors acknowledge this, they then proceed to ask the singer to place the tone at the edges of the upper or lower front teeth; on the upper edge of the breastbone; at the top of the head and at many more locations. They attempt to justify these manoeuvres physiologically, whereas, the vibrations or sensations felt by one singer or teacher are very unlikely to be felt in the same way by the next singer or teacher.

Jean de Reszke (1850–1925) was a Polish tenor who wished to express his own personal ideas about the art of singing rather than advocate a new method. He made an enormous impact on the art of singing in France. Although having some training in the Italian School as a baritone, he came to disregard the teaching, particularly with regard to posture and its influence on breathing, and later studied with Sbriglia.[21] His aim for his students was relaxed breathing. To this end he favoured a collapsed chest with rounded shoulders. He advised the use of the sigh as a means to release the glottis and the tongue; a raised head position with the head slightly back as though singing to the gallery; and placement of tone in the masque (de Reszke's own terminology 'singing in the masque'), and on the bridge of the nose (which probably induced unwanted nasality). He further advocated the 'singer's grimace' for high notes.

Paris at this time was the opera centre of the world and de Reszke was renowned for his French roles until, unfortunately, he lost his voice. Apart from one or two isolated cases France did not produce famous singers during the twentieth century. This is sometimes attributed by French singing teachers to de Reszke's teaching. The situation, latterly, has begun to improve owing to participation by singers and teachers in international methods of study.

H. Plunket Greene (1865–1936) was another Englishman trained in the Italianate School. He wrote *Interpretation in Song* (1914). His Appendix in the book is devoted mainly to breath management and *legato* and reflects accurately the teachings of the Lampertis:

> His [the singer] chest, being raised, does not press on his lungs, and there being no chest to push out, he fills his lungs instantaneously and automatically without feeling it; not only so, but if the chest is raised and the breathing muscle expanded, rib-expansion – on which good teachers rightly insist – follows of itself automatically, without any special attention. (1914, p. 293).

In Britain, there are at least three tonal ideals still being espoused. Of these one is generally based on the Italianate ideal; the next has traces of German technique, and the third is the very English 'cathedral' tone which has its roots in the British liturgical tradition, with its fondness for the seeming 'purity' of tone as produced by the choral treble voice.[22]

E.G. White (1863–1940) was born in England. In his book *Science and Singing* (1909) he advanced his theory of Sinus Tone Production, namely, that resonance occurs in the sinuses. Most current vocal scientists would repudiate this strongly on the ground that there is very little, if any, resonating space in the sinuses except, possibly, for necessary nasal sounds. White answered his critics in later editions, and finally expanded his theory in *Sinus Tone Production* (1938). His theory when practised is likely to result in the 'cathedral' tone ideal and because of the popularity of this sound E.G. White's ideas are still in use in some studios in Britain and America, even though there is no scientific support for his theories.[23]

E. Herbert-Caesari (1884–1969) was another influential pedagogue on the British scene. He wrote several books which endeavour to blend natural singing with the mechanical, and postulates six interrelated features or trains of thought. He contends that if any one of these is omitted his mental-physical ideal of the singing voice will not be realized. Herbert-Caesari lists three points of vocal technique, which in his reasoning are confirmed by science, and I quote the second:

> (2) VOCAL TECHNIQUE demands a small piece of cord, flexibly firm, for the high notes (the higher the pitch the smaller must be the dimensions of the vocal cord employed).
>   *Acoustic science* demands a small and flexibly firm vibrator for producing high pitches (the higher the pitch the smaller the vibrator) (1936, p.176).

Douglas Stanley (1890–1958) was born in England and qualified as a Doctor of Science, had a damaged voice as a result of British teaching, and left to study voice in America. This resulted in his writing several books, among them: *Your Voice, Its Production and Reproduction* (1933) in which he discusses the scientific details of voice production, and *Your Voice: Applied Science of Vocal Art* (1945) in which he applies his updated scientific findings to vocal pedagogy. He writes:

> All figurative or imaginative language has been avoided … Complete understanding of the scientific principles involved and the proper application of the devices and procedures employed are essential in order that the pupil's voice may be radically improved (1945, p. vii).

William Vennard (1909–71) in his *Singing, the Mechanism and the Technic* (1967) made an important contribution to the art of singing in the middle of the twentieth century. He nails his colours to the mast thus:

> There are those teachers who feel that applying science to an art is quackery, but I believe that our only safeguard against the charlatan is general knowledge of the most accurate information available (1967, p. iii).

Vennard largely follows the historic Italian School, but, unfortunately, strays to the German/Nordic methods of 'yawn/sigh', lower abdominal breathing, vocal registration and vocal tract positions. In his section on breathing he informs us:

> In teaching [breath control] I sometimes make a fist and push it into the student's epigastrium while he attempts a long phrase. The muscular antagonism which he must set up in order to maintain a stiff epigastrium against my pressure often enables him to sing a considerably longer phrase (ibid., p. 34).

Berton Coffin (1910–87) was an American who travelled widely and became an internationally known vocal pedagogue. He is mainly of the historic Italianate School, but deviates in some aspects, for example, his ideas of posture are very much of the French School – he argues for a 'sword-swallowing position' which encourages an elevated larynx and an appearance of singing to the gallery:

> When one observes the taking of a breath as a reflex action, the head usually tilts back, just as before a burst of laughter or just as one begins to speak after a "brilliant idea." Likewise the sound comes out with the head slightly back. This inhaling action 'opens' the throat (1989, pp. 140–41).

Ralph Appelman (1908–93), a renowned singer, wrote *The Science of Vocal Pedagogy* (1967). He attempts to combine vocal pedagogy and scientific principles, but because his language and theory are difficult to render into lay-language, his work may not have had the impact that it deserves.

Richard Miller (1926–) was born in America, was a leading tenor, and is, among very many other things, Professor of Singing and the Director of the Otto B. Schoepfle Vocal Arts Center at Oberlin Conservatory, also an Adjunct Staff member of the ENT Department of the Cleveland Clinic. He has contributed many articles to journals and written several books, many of which are standard textbooks in the field. His eminence as a vocal pedagogue is securely rooted in considerable performance experience, masterly teaching and extensive scientific research. In the opinion of many, Miller is the doyen of American vocal pedagogy. He was trained in the Italianate school. Among his teachers were Luigi Ricci and Mario Basiola, followers of the Lampertis. In the Preface to *The Structure of Singing* he declares that 'Artistry cannot be realized without the technical means for its presentation. Systematic vocal technique and artistic expression are inseparable' (1986, p. xvi). In the opinion of Craig Timberlake:

> Miller's devotion to *Italianità* has resulted in a unique and valuable pedagogy. In his study of other techniques as well – English, French, German, he introduces a multi-lingual vocabulary. In passing it on, he has substantially enlarged the possibilities for the development of a pedagogical *lingua franca* (1995, p. 38).

There are other pioneers and contributors to vocal pedagogy who should not go unmentioned.[24] In addition there are voice scientists, laryngologists, physicists and acousticians who have contributed to learning in physiology, acoustics, vocal function and vocal health and hygiene.

At the present time there are in Britain many disciples of the American pedagogue Jo Estill (1921–), who has pioneered her highly organized system which is orientated to 'feel'. The system is called 'Compulsory Figures' and involves exact controls of parts of the vocal mechanism, each of which has to be distinctly 'felt' and mentally numbered for a quick recall. 'Postural anchoring' is her term for *appoggio*, and she identifies what she describes as six voice qualities: speech, falsetto, cry, twang, opera and belt.

> [Her] innovative system of developing voluntary control of the vocal mechanism through simple, effective exercises known as Compulsory Figures, has placed her at the forefront of voice trainers in the 20th century (Anne-Marie Speed, advertising leaflet, February 2001).

Estill has built up a language for her Voicecraft philosophy using imagery, for example, the '*sob* and *laugh*'; the '*twang*' and '*sirening*'. The benefits of these imaginative coinages are not altogether apparent. It makes for simplicity and precision and facilitates cooperation with those in cognate professions if recourse is had to realistic terminology which is readily understood by all.[25]

There are other speciality studios, for example, the crano-sacral therapy method which focuses upon the realignment of the jaw and overall posture; a school of Voice Movement Therapy which proposes to offer a synthesis of physiology, aesthetics, psychology and education, and trains usually with non-verbal sound; and an animal noise imitation studio as a basis for singing: the list is disturbingly endless.

Michael Scott contends that the successors of nineteenth century pedagogy

> abandoned the attempt to impose the classical virtues on a generation which despised its traditions and had no use for its graces. Instead, embracing the new realism, they busied themselves with giving their pupils sufficient technique, chiefly a matter of power and stamina, to cope with its demands: in Italian opera with the strenuous accents required by 'verismo'; in Wagner with the forceful declamation of 'Sprechgesang'; in French vocal music with a style that preferred literary values. In all of them, the essentially vocal imagination of bel canto was sacrificed (1993, p. 1).

It is now generally accepted that the scientific era of vocal pedagogy began with Garcia II's publications. Monahan suggests that treatises during the first half of the nineteenth century were written by singers or teachers. By the middle of the nineteenth century the number of scientific books on the voice roughly equalled the number of empirical ones, and by the end of the century almost all books published contained some references to vocal anatomy and physiology. By that time several important treatises were written by medical doctors and scientists (1978, p. 226).

Because there are so many methodologies and variants, singing teachers have to make informed intelligent choices. They need to know which method is most likely to encourage vocal freedom and efficiency. Singers must have no doubt about how their voices are going to perform technically. Without a sound technique one is building on sand, and without this sound technique there will be very little artistry in the performance. Let Rupert Bruce Lockhart on breathing, and Elster Kay on mental imagery as used by an unnamed but famous singer/teacher conclude this chapter:

> I once attended in Paris a meeting of the Union des Maîtres-Chanteurs and the subject for the evening discussion was 'Breathing.' In the auditorium were over a hundred professors of singing or speech and on the platform three doctors (throat specialists) and one

physical-culturist. I was taken by one of the most famous musicians and singing professors in Paris. We laughed helplessly all evening. There was almost a free fight. No two people in the whole assembly seemed to agree on a method of breathing. Insults were hurled around and two of the doctors finally turned their chairs back to back and refused to speak to each other. The evening ended with the physical-culturist illustrating an entirely different method from anything that had been exposed by the singing fraternity (Lockhart, cited by Rushmore, 1971, p. 149).

One is required to think of a ladder (two ladders) in one's head, a biscuit mould and a Hoover in one's mouth and a chimney in one's throat ... The upper jaw has to be thought of as a long pointed bird's beak which, during singing, stabs into an apple. And, of course, during singing one 'must relax completely both body and soul.'

The picture conjured up ... by all this metaphorical nonsense is of a strange comatose (and therefore silent) bird supported on the stage by a pair of stepladders, with a large green apple stuck on the end of its enormous beak, while a flow of dust-coated pastry streams into (for Hoovers are instruments of suction) its additional mouth while clouds of black smoke billow out through its ears (Kay, 1963, pp. 85–6).

Notes

1 For a history of singing, before singing pedagogy was first documented in detail in the sixteenth century, see Appendix 1a.

2 Registration terms by now became Italian, for example, *voce naturele* or *voce piena* (natural or full voice) and *voce finta* (false voices or falsetti) (Reid, 2000, p. 32).

3 See further, Appendix 1a.

4 See further, Celletti, Rudolfo (1991), *A History of Bel Canto,* trans. Fuller, Frederick, Oxford: Clarendon; Heriot, Angus (1956), *The Castrati in Opera,* London: Secker and Warburg.

5 See further, Appendix 1b.

6 Compare with the Alexander Technique of the twentieth century.

7 See further, Kay, Elster (1963), *Bel Canto,* London: Dennis Dobson.

8 See further, Appendix 1a.

9 See further, Charles Burney's work of 1789, *A General History of Music, II,* London, Meyer, Frank (ed.), New York: Dover, 1957.

10 To this day the message has passed some 'grunting' singers by. See Chapter 4 below.

11 See further, Mackenzie, Morrell (1890), *The Hygiene of the Vocal Organs,* New York: Macmillan.

12 See further, Reid, Cornelius (1950), *Bel Canto; Principles and Practices,* New York: Coleman Ross.

13 See further, Garcia, Manuel (1841 and 1872), *A Complete Treatise on the Art of Singing: Parts I and II,* trans. and ed. Donald V. Paschke (1975), New York: Da Capo.

14 See further, Chapters 3 and 4 below.

15 See further, Chapters 3 and 4 below.

16 Douglas Stanley has this to say,

Her pupil – Melba – sang beautifully in spite of her teaching, because she did not interfere with this great singer's natural technic ... She did radical harm to virtually every other pupil who studied with her and she developed an absolutely destructive school of 'white,' throaty, falsetto only singing (1945, p. 279).

17   Douglas Stanley writes very scathingly of Lilli Lehmann,

She knew nothing of science and had almost entirely lost her voice when she started to teach. In a book on singing [*How to Sing,* 1914] she propounded theories which can only be designated as preposterous nonsense (1945, p. 279).

18   See further, Scott, Michael (1993), *The Record of Singing, Vol I, to 1914*, London: Duckworth, with the accompanying *The Record of Singing*, EMI Records, I (RLS 724), 1977.

19   It must be said that Wagner greatly appreciated Italianate singing technique and Ernest Newman quotes him as saying:

why cannot we [Germans] openly and freely admit that the Italian is superior to the German in Song, and the Frenchman superior to him in the light and animated treatment of operatic music? ... The Italians are singers by nature. The less richly-endowed German can hope to emulate the Italian only by hard study (1963, p. 188).

20   See further, Kimbell, David (1991), *Italian Opera*, Cambridge: Cambridge University Press.

21   See above, The Nineteenth Century.

22   See Chapter 3 below on vocal abuse.

23   Elster Kay pulls no punches when he says, 'First prize for idiocy goes to the writer who said that vocal tone originated not in the vocal cords but in the sinuses' (1963, p. 83).

24   R.M. Baken, W. Bartholomew, D.M. Bell, M. Bunch, J. Chapman, T. Cleveland, R. Edwin, V.A. Fields, T. Fillebrown, V. Fuchs, W.J. Gould, J.W. Gregg, T. Hixon, V. Lawrence, S. Mabry, M. Mackenzie, M.S. MacKinlay, W. McIver, J. McKinney, M. Meylan, D.C. Miller, D.G. Miller, J. Potter, R. Sataloff, H.K. Schütte, C. Seashore, R. Sherer, T. Shipp, D. Slater, A. Sonninen, J. Sundberg, J. Teachey, I. Titze, W. van den Berg, H. von Leden, K. Westerman and P.S. Wormhoudt.

25   See further, *Vocal Process Ltd* which is the new name for EVTS (UK) – Estill Voice Training Systems. This company has evolved from British singing teachers, who are licensed by Jo Estill to teach her methodology. See also Kayes, Gillyanne (2000) *Singing and the Actor*, London: A&C Black.

Chapter 2

Ethics, Psychology, and Vocal Pedagogy

Having discussed the historical background to the singing teacher's work, I now turn to consider the contribution that ethics and psychology (which, as we shall see, are frequently closely related) make to vocal pedagogy.[1] As already indicated, much of what will be said has applications to other branches of music teaching and, indeed, to the teaching of disciplines other than music. We may, however find that at certain points there are applications of particular relevance to vocal pedagogy.

Ethics

Richard Bonynge declares, with not a little gusto,

> To say that five per cent of teachers are good would be an overstatement. There are a few who know what they're talking about, but there are an awful lot of charlatans (1995, p. 16).

However Bonynge is stronger on diagnosis than prescription, though his use of the term 'charlatan' does highlight the fact that the ethics of vocal pedagogy may not be overlooked. Throughout this work my proposals turn upon the conviction that in an unregulated profession, one way of raising pedagogical standards is to encourage those who employ the services of singing teachers to take great care in selecting those to whom they entrust their voices. That such selecting – and, indeed, the entire teacher/student relationship – has a significant ethical dimension I shall now proceed to show.

The scope of ethics is vast and varied. Very broadly it concerns the moral standards by which people live. In *descriptive* ethics accounts are given of the moral principles and practices of individuals or groups – from the ancient Greeks or Hebrew prophets to the modern entrepreneur or politician. But when we ask 'By what principles *ought* people to live?' we are seeking norms or guidelines; and when we ask 'What is the *analysis* of the ethical pronouncements made by people?' we are entering into the realm of meta (second order) ethics which is the territory of many modern moral philosophers.

Sufficient has been said to show that the normative question, *Ought* I to teach? may not responsibly be shirked.

Business Ethics

In a singing practice there are ethical obligations upon both the teacher and student.[2] The acceptance of a student is a business agreement that necessitates the drawing up of a formal contract, which should be clearly understood.[3] A contract may cover some, or all of the following matters:

1. Number of lessons per annum
2. Payment of fees
3. Holidays
4. Cancellation of lessons
5. Required notice for the termination of lessons
6. Participation in examinations, competitions and public performances
7. The necessity of cooperation between student and teacher for progress to be made.

The teacher has an ethical decision to make in the setting of fees.[4] The response to the amount charged will reveal much. In an unregulated profession like voice teaching fees vary considerably. There are 'pin money' teachers who, as my own remedial work demonstrates, literally do not know what they are doing with the voice; and there are top professional singers who, whether or not they have peda-gogical expertise, expect high fees. The rule of thumb is that fees charged should reflect the training and experience of the teacher and cumulatively they should not only cover living costs, but should allow for ongoing professional development which, in the case of the private teacher, will normally be self-financed. Since the students will benefit from the results, some allowance should be made when setting fees for the hours each day when the teacher is working (practising/rehearsing) but not earning.[5]

There is good reason to suggest that advertising be honest and dignified, clearly describing the services offered.[6] Miller has this to say: 'To present oneself as having had career experiences and professional training not actually encountered is a form of professional robbery' (1996, p. 211). Exaggerated claims concerning, for example, the development of character and personality, should be avoided. Punctuality on the part of both teacher and student is obligatory. A useful idea is to have a notice on the door of the studio that invites the student to knock and enter at the appointed time. It is highly desirable that only a dire emergency should be allowed to interrupt the lesson; the switched-on answering machine is essential during teaching time.

General Pedagogical Ethics

We come now to ethics in relation to pedagogy. The singing teacher's primary moral obligation is not to do harm.[7] It is vital that the teacher is readily able to diagnose the singer's problem(s) and competent in prescribing the proper solutions. It seems to me, based on long experience, that teachers should possess a soundly based singing technique and be aware of the latest vocal research in scientific and medical circles.[8] Teachers are under the obligation to teach self-sufficiency in their pupils; whereas refresher courses with teachers are desirable, students should not be dependent on teachers for every breath they take! While there are general principles upon which to base a sound philosophy of vocal production, nobody has the perfect teaching method. Hence the duty of the teacher to share information and experience with colleagues and professionals in cognate fields. Gone surely are the days of vocal teachers charging each other with stealing their 'secret' vocal techniques.[9]

The underhand recruiting or poaching of other teachers' students must be regarded as unethical. If approached by a prospective transferee, it is not inappropriate to try to discover the reason for transfer either from the student or the current teacher; and it is quite in order to decline to take a student so as not to jeopardize one's professional relationship with that teacher. On the other hand if the student has come to the point that an alternative pedagogical viewpoint might be helpful there are various approaches that might be taken. For example, a consultative relationship with the other teacher/s might be established during voice lessons, or a student could actually be shared for a term or two: a young baritone being taught by a soprano teacher might benefit from studying simultaneously with a baritone teacher for a short time. These ideas would tend to lead to a cooperative, mutual observation and improvement arrangement, rather than the more destructive competition of times past.

Accountability to students and colleagues is ethically of great importance, particularly in an unregulated profession where, traditionally, singing tuition has been highly subjective and even 'mystical'!

The Teacher and the Student

The philosopher Sir W. David Ross used to speak of the clash of *prima facie* obligations.[10] This clash occurs when we are confronted by more than one duty and find it hard to determine which to perform. Many of the singing teacher's ethical puzzles are of this kind. On the one hand we have a duty to encourage students, some of whom may be nervous or self-conscious. On the other hand we have a duty not to pronounce a seriously flawed performance perfect. The way forward is often to focus on something that was right, to praise it, and give *positive* guidance which will improve matters. A good deal of this is at one level common-sense tact; the ethics has to do with our *obligation* to build up, not to destroy, the person who is paying us and for whose training we have assumed *responsibility*. Birgit Nilsson, a Swedish soprano who had a farming background, was told by her famous Scottish tenor teacher at her first Academy lesson, 'It doesn't matter if you have the best voice in the world if you have no brain, because it's really not for a farmer to become a singer' (Hines, 1988, p. 195). She went home in tears. In a similar vein, teachers should not take money under false pretences, praising the ungifted, encouraging unreasonable fantasies, promising the impossible. The ethical response may turn upon the degree of motivation of the student. An ethical question may arise such as whether to discourage a less than talented student or not. Every time a teacher decides whether or not to query or make recommendations concerning a student's vocally adverse life-style he or she is making an ethical decision as well as a pedagogical one. In conservatories teachers are more vulnerable than private teachers and would not be looked upon favourably, for various reasons (including enrolment considerations), if they rejected such students as the one whom the teacher suspects as having vocal nodules, the smoker or the resistant student. In these cases private teachers have much more freedom to make their ethical decisions. Every teacher must weigh the factors involved when deciding whether or not to accept a student.

It is good ethical practice, and it builds up the student's confidence in the teacher, if a proper degree of confidentiality is maintained in teacher/student relations. Students' foibles, difficulties and calamities should never be the subject of gossip among other professionals.

Lessons must give value for money. The student has paid to learn how to sing. Too easily lessons can become counselling sessions of the unburdening-of-the-soul type. Whereas we must always present a sympathetic ear few of us are qualified counsellors. In this connection E.W. Jones surely goes too far in suggesting that teachers 'must consider accepting a responsibility combining that of teacher with rabbi, parent, confessor, confidant, critic, analyst, fellow-artist, and a further list of required roles limited only by their empathy and imagination' (1989, p. 25).

Some teachers, perhaps because they are insecure, unprepared or incompetent, constantly interrupt performances; talk about non-musical things; discuss their own personal problems; tempt the student to go off at tangents; pay no attention to the performance; have students repeat performances unnecessarily; encourage visitors to interrupt; give a long-winded lecture for every mistake; cut lessons short; spend most of the lesson showing off; evangelize or preach to the student about religious, social or political issues when the slightest link to the music is found, all in order to fill up the lesson time.

The teacher, also, has an obligation not to reject those who appear to be lacking in ability, least of all those who go to great lengths to improve their performance. Miller reminds us that 'Some singers bloom early, some singers bloom late' (1996, p. 181).

Students, too, have ethical responsibilities. Some will attempt to waste lesson time in several fashions: interrupting their own singing several times – 'I just can't seem to get going'; taking control of the lesson by determining the order of procedure; requesting demonstrations; asking questions to avoid or delay performing; changing conversation from musical to non-musical topics; talking about personal problems; getting upset or nervous – trembling or crying; arriving late or cancelling or not completing the assignment.[11]

The Teacher and the Parent

The teacher has a moral obligation to invite the participation of parents or guardians of those under eighteen, not least because they are probably footing the bill. An open studio policy will encourage the parent's involvement in the child's progress. It will provide opportunities to observe lessons and to have questions answered. In this way parents will become aware of the kind of support and home practice facilities needed if progress is to be made. Practice arrangements should be discussed.[12]

The Teacher and the Professional Performer

When professional singers come for consultations confidentiality is supremely important. It is unfortunately the case that many singers begin a promising career only to 'fade away' at quite an early age. They may have been under commercial pressure to do too much too soon; they may have over-worked; they may have faulty technique; they may not have had time for those regular check-ups with a competent singing teacher which are vital if the onset of bad habits is to be avoided. The result is that they have vocal problems. When such professionals come it is imperative to observe the confidentiality of the confessional. It would be quite wrong, and it could have disastrous career consequences, to let it be known that this *Tosca* or that *Figaro* is having vocal problems. The ears of the media would be alerted in potentially career-damaging ways. Teachers should go to the length of not arranging such consultations during normal studio hours, so that regular students will never pass a diva on the doorstep.

It is also unethical to use professional singers as 'advertisement fodder' for the teacher unless the singer's written permission has been sought and granted.

The Teacher and other Musical Colleagues

Students who are members of choirs, choral societies, or musical theatre groups can be at the mercy of directors who may not be trained in vocal pedagogy themselves, and who make unrealistic and premature demands upon the voices in their charge. Enter the choir director who insists that a changing-voice adolescent male remain in the tenor section because of shortage of tenors, when his voice is sliding healthily into the baritone range. Then we find the conductor who can destroy musicality, defy the composer's intentions and threaten the reputation of soloists (who should not have to compete) by having the orchestra play at a constant *fortissimo*. Wherever possible in such cases singing teachers have an obligation to intervene discreetly on behalf of their students. Such teachers should not be regarded as interfering busybodies. A precious instrument belonging to someone else has been placed in the singing teacher's charge, and money is being paid to have it properly trained and cared for.

The teacher and other professionals

Let us take the otolaryngologist as an example. It would be ethically unacceptable for a non-medically qualified teacher to diagnose a physical or psychological vocal health problem or even to suggest, for example, that a student has vocal nodules. However the properly trained teacher cannot avoid *suspecting* such problems in some cases, and is ethically obliged not to work with a sick voice. The suggestion should be made that the student seek professional help first and, with the student's written permission, the teacher may have a word with the appropriate general practitioner or otolaryngologist. Here, of course, the well-trained teacher will of necessity be equipped with technical terminology that the physician can understand.

In subsequent chapters I shall consider the ethics of examining, adjudicating, conducting master classes and performance.[13] For the present we must conclude that apart from its inherent desirability, the teacher who proceeds with ethical integrity is, psychologically, creating an atmosphere of trustworthiness that can only benefit the student/teacher, teacher/parent relationship. But this reference to psychology prompts us to turn to the contribution made to vocal pedagogy by that discipline.

General Psychology

Since human beings are complex, most psychologists realize that no one psychological approach can encompass them. The available approaches can, for our purpose here, be classified into broad groups, although, owing to human diversity, aspects of different groups may overlap. Thus, for example, Hayes explains that 'the experience of emotion ... has a physiological dimension, a cognitive dimension, a social dimension, a personality dimension and several more' (2000, p. 13).

Cognitive psychology is concerned with the various modes of knowledge: perception, memory, imagination, conception, judgment, language, representation, and reason. It is closely related to social psychology, in as much as if the circumstances of individuals are unknown then it is unlikely that there will be adequate understanding of why they make certain decisions. This is both an example of overlap of the various approaches and also a useful principle for the voice teacher to grasp in relation to students. Physiological psychology involves the study of the mental and nervous systems. Stress, sleep, dreaming, consciousness and motivation fall within the purview. Psychologists are concerned with the connection to be made between cognitive, social and cultural aspects of human behaviour. Social psychology concerns the interactions of people with each other.[14] Comparative psychology is preoccupied with animals; it endeavours to relate animal behaviour and development to that of human beings and is not directly relevant to this study.[15] Developmental psychology will be dealt with later.[16] Hargreaves and North are keen to point out that:

The rapid growth of research in music psychology has meant that several distinct tributaries of the mainstream are now clearly identifiable, the most prominent of which are those that focus on the cognitive, developmental, and social aspects of musical behaviour. These are of course closely interrelated, and indeed the interdisciplinary boundaries amongst the parent disciplines of music, psychology, education, sociology, anthropology, and cognitive science are in a constant state of change. In one sense 'music psychology' will always be an interdisciplinary area since musical behaviour itself is not functionally coherent (1997, p. 3).

Singing teachers would do well to familiarize themselves with the long-standing tradition of educational psychology, and also with developmental psychology and music psychology. The challenge is creatively and sympathetically to utilize the relevant findings of developmental and music psychology in relation to students at various stages of personal psychological development. Obvious though such a strategy may appear to be, even some well-known teachers continue in the line of William Lovelock who said: 'My own view is that the psychology of teaching is learnt by experience allied to common sense' (1978, p. 12). His own teacher asked, 'What's it all about anyway? Get on and play your Bach!' (ibid., p. 13).

Developmental psychology concerns human development throughout the whole of life, from birth to old age (life-span). Among other things it investigates the development of language, cognition, intelligence, and social understanding. Hargreaves is among those who have argued that developmental psychology can provide a firm foundation for theory and practice in music education and he claims that 'the cognitive-developmental approach of which Piaget's theory is the predominant representative, holds the most immediate promise in this respect' (1986, p. 227).[17] He goes on to say that it is up to the teacher to combine theory and research in the developmental psychology of music into a solid basis for their teaching and curriculum.

There are three main theoretical perspectives within developmental psychology:

1. Cognitive psychology embraces cognitive social psychology and cognitive behavioural therapy. Some cognitive psychologists focus upon the processes of perception, memory, thinking, attention, reasoning, language and some types of learning.[18] However these themes are construed in a variety of ways. According to Hargreaves the main emphasis in cognitive psychology is on the internal rules, procedures and actions that people use in intelligent behaviour (information processing). Piaget's cognitive-developmental theory (*scheme*) complements information processing. Information-processing theory researches the flow of information taken into the mind, the way it is processed, and the resulting output, or behavioural response (Hargreaves, 1986).
2. Cognitive developmental psychology, which is the branch most easily employed in music education, has not been a main interest of many researchers in psychology.[19] It is mostly associated with Piaget's *scheme*, whereby children make use of the 'building blocks' of cognition to understand their environment.

These 'building blocks' change with experience and learning, but are developmental, related to age, and have common stages. Gardner questions the validity of Piaget's work (1973, pp. 73–88). He suggests that the medium of music, being time-based, is different from the concrete 'building blocks' which are applied by Piaget's disciples to, for example, mathematical concepts. Gardner is interested in the development of aesthetic sensitivity, which he understands as irrational and intuitive owing to the nature of the arts. He advances a theory focused on a child's acquisition of *symbols*. He describes the *symbol system* as the pre-school child's way of learning *via* the use of words, drawings, and make-believe. This, Gardner believes, is the main developmental basis for subsequent artistic development.

3. Behavioural psychology is a broad term which includes many different theories and may therefore be considered eclectic. Behavioural psychology in relation to musical development has often been researched in terms of *motivation* or *affect*.[20] The latter refers to the influence upon music learning of any kind of feeling or emotion attached to ideas or idea-complexes.

Against this background of general psychology an attempt will be made to apply the developmental psychology of music, along with general psychology, to vocal pedagogy. I shall set out from some general psychological points applicable to all age groups. I shall then turn to specific age groups, describing the developmental psychology of pre-school children, children aged five to twelve, adolescents and adults. In each case I shall consider the pedagogical responses appropriate to the developmental stage. As announced in the Introduction, other aspects of psychology such as psychology and health, performance anxiety, and emotion in relation to interpretation, will be treated in subsequent chapters.

General Pedagogical Principles

Student/Teacher Relationships

The student must always behave like a student and the teacher must always behave like a teacher. The teacher needs enthusiasm, efficiency, friendliness, good humour, humility, the realization that he or she can never know too much, an open mind and the experience and knowledge to change repertoire and method from time to time as appropriate. In an holistic or inter-disciplinary studio the first question of the lesson, 'How are you today, John/Mary?' (incidentally, the pupil's name should be used frequently throughout the lesson), should be more than a polite formality. An honest answer by the student may establish their physical or emotional state (this is not a question to be posed out of curiosity, or an excuse to indulge in amateur counselling), which may determine a change of content in the originally planned lesson. Should students with a personal crisis be challenged to deal with their programme or do teachers need to modify the lesson? An emotionally distraught person may not feel comfortable singing an emotionally intense song or aria. On the other hand a release of emotion from singing that particular work may be a good thing. Again it could be said that students should be prepared to control any personal crises during the lesson and get on with the job in hand.[21]

I have found that on psychological grounds it is good that lessons end on a positive note. Mackworth-Young offers the following advice, 'Give unconditional positive regard to the pupil, believing and trusting in him and his potential ...' (2000, p. 12). Pupils should always leave the lesson feeling better, more confident and fulfilled. They should have enjoyed the musical experience, and should understand and look forward to what is expected from them in their home practice. As to home practice, I, in common with many other teachers, have made the not very surprising discovery that there is practice and practice. There is the unintelligent kind that is purely repetitive and builds in errors. Younger pupils' practice is often slapdash and hurried. This is often a result of distractions or lack of motivation. Teachers would do well to be aware, not only of the results of inadequate practice but of the reasons for it and should try to help the pupil find the remedy by careful instruction in the lesson. Harris and Crozier give much helpful advice including the suggestion

> that practice takes place four or five times a week, perhaps at a regular time: before or after breakfast, before supper, before or after a favourite television programme (2000, p. 94).

It should be remembered that learning to sing can, for the total non-singer who is keen to sing (sometimes referred to as 'tone-deaf'), be a long, arduous task for both teacher and student. Mitchell begins his study of adult non-singers by saying, 'Poor pitch singers have traditionally been referred to as "tone-deaf"', implying that an aural disability underlies the singing disability and then continues:

> But more recent research (... reviewed by Welch, 1979) has rejected the notion of tone-deafness, suggesting that poor pitch singing is first of all a production problem, and that aural skills may suffer as a result, not a cause, of the inability to use the voice musically (1991, p. 74).

At the initial stage, lessons for the poor pitch singer should be frequent and short. A tremendous amount of concentration is needed by pupil and teacher alike. Much repetitive, constructive, teacher-directed practice will be required of the student between lessons. The rewards of this industry are immense. There is the students' delight and excitement as noticeable improvements are made, and amazement as the treasure chest of vocal literature is opened and ever more of its contents are placed within their reach.[22]

Teachers should reinforce their tuition by recommending recordings and concerts. In order to relate to the student's other world they should keep up to date and not be strangers to TV soap operas, the world of computers, current dress fashion, pop groups and their hits, and football league tables. As mentioned above, teachers should be aware of body language, being especially careful to note the effect on the student's face as a result of advice given or repertoire proposed. Accepting both positive and negative feedback is helpful, making sure that pupils feel that their own comments are useful. There is much to be said for capitalizing on success and being aware of sensitivity; everyone has low self-esteem at some point in their life. Teachers would be well advised to identify students' strengths and weaknesses with a view to offering relevant guidance.

In addition to the requirements mentioned a teacher needs a love of music, musical imagination, a thorough knowledge of the scientific basis of the subject being taught (a point to bear in mind by those who rely excessively upon image-based exhortations in their teaching[23]), sensitivity, patience, perseverance, tact, enthusiasm, administrative skills, good time-keeping and the ability to impart knowledge. The teacher should say, 'Try this,' rather than 'Don't'.[24] Patience is required on the part of the teacher so as to avoid teaching too much too soon. Something simple should be demanded, and the pupil complimented upon performing it successfully. Students' faith in the teacher may be rewarded by increasing students' own faith in themselves. Teachers would do well to be flexible: is a lack of progress genuinely owing to a lack of personal discipline or to something else, such as an unduly self-critical personality, or a lack of patience?

Each learning experience should be creative, stimulating, appropriate and orga-nized. What the teacher knows and takes for granted may be something completely new to the student. Each pupil should be treated as an individual with specific musical objectives, abilities and weak points, for whom the best kind of teaching will in some respects be different from that planned for other pupils. There should be constant checking of progress, of standards achieved, quality control, and an awareness of boredom, frustration, and the degree of personal satisfaction of the pupil.[25] Lessons should be a dialogue between partners. Teachers should foster the ability of pupils to think musically and technically for themselves, eventually becoming independent and developing their own high standards and musical personality. Harris and Crozier comment:

> Perhaps the most demanding and stimulating challenge faced by the teacher is to draw from the pupil that subtle ability to communicate something of their innermost self through the medium of musical performance. Without developing musical 'personality', performances will remain uninspired and the central message of the music will not be communicated (2000, p. 4).

Sensitive questioning like, 'What did you think about your singing?' or 'What would you have done differently?' allows students to get what they want to say out into the open. The teacher should wait for answers. Questioning helps to develop a self-critical, listening approach and encourages students to think for themselves.

The teacher may say, 'If you don't understand something, ask me straight away and I will try to explain more clearly'.

Occasionally there may be danger of the student/teacher relationship breaking down perhaps because of hostility, or its opposite, adulation on the part of the student. Bruscia offers this guidance: 'While both parties are responsible for maintaining the relationship's integrity, the teacher must accept responsibility for spotting trouble signs and for taking steps to correct problems as they arise' (1989, p. 13). This can raise the ethical question of whether or not to relinquish that particular student.[26]

For musical effort to be rewarding, the teacher has to recognize the student's musical achievements and give a good measure of teacher approval.

> When a student has been granted an indication of respect for part of what he or she can accomplish, that student is willing to accept almost any degree of specific criticism. The important part is to start with some positive assessment, no matter how disturbing the student's limitations may be. Thereby a comradeship, a team ship is born (Miller, 1996, p. 7).

There must be a level of trust and effective communication. The teacher would be well advised to discuss with parents any problems which young students are experiencing as soon as they present, so that suitable action may be taken in good time. It is also advantageous to welcome parents to the occasional lesson and to informal concerts when all pupils sing to an audience.

Children learn to speak their first language by imitation and the method is very successful. Demonstration is 'showing how' by example. As we saw in the preceding chapter this has been an accepted way to teach singing through the ages. But imitation alone is never sufficient and can be problematic if a singer attempts to force his or her voice into the mould of another.[27]

Explanations need to be clear. There is a great art in being able to explain clearly. A teacher may be exceptionally well qualified, but this is of no avail if knowledge cannot be imparted to the student. It is wise to avoid disseminating redundant information and assuming knowledge in the student which the student may not have. Explanations should be logically ordered, simple and short. A wise suggestion may be to include a summary of the key points, building on knowledge already possessed by the student, being both persuasive and patient. Both abstract and concrete explanations may be used where appropriate. The latter are more easily digested than the former. Teachers would be well advised to use, appropriate to the age and interests of individual pupils: analogy and comparison; *reductio ad absurdum*; visual representation; and to express themselves unambiguously, always trying to hear what they themselves are saying through the pupil's ears. There is much to be said for always encouraging students to ask if they do not understand; for reinforcing previously learnt material regularly, and for setting challenging but not unreasonable goals. We teach unconsciously by setting a good example, presenting only the best and having high standards. To aid the learning process pupils must be sure of what is required of them, why it is required, and the best way to do it. They must have practice, which is checked and evaluated, and opportunities to review what they have learnt. As teaching is a two-way operation and because, as stated above, students initially only absorb part of the teaching, they have to make their own efforts to correct their own understanding. Learning is a personal hidden mental process over which teachers have no direct control and it is crucial for motivation that the level of work is appropriate. Teachers must be aware that the jargon they use every day may need clear explanation, similarly they must be aware that they probably have a wider vocabulary than their students and, therefore, some words may not be understood. Petty comments: 'teachers may tend to use more complex grammar than their students. Keep your language simple; don't try to impress with over-formal English – it may alienate students instead' (1993, p. 28). In particular, in communicating to the young it is vital to use a more limited vocabulary geared to their experience, while not patronizing them.

Non-teachers sometimes believe that teaching is telling pupils something, and learning happens if pupils remember it. Not so: pupils don't just remember what the teacher has told them, but make up their own personal version of it. Learning is an active process; it is not simply a matter of receiving information. It is very important for students to be encouraged to think over, discuss and process the ideas in order, so that they become their 'own'. One-way of doing this is for students to teach the teacher what they have learnt, using the ideas, skills and knowledge that they have been taught. Skilful questioning is an effective tool, giving instant feedback. Petty states that

> it ensures that the lesson moves at the student's pace; it gives student's practice in expressing their newly learnt ideas and vocabulary; it reveals incorrect ideas and assumptions; it can be motivating in that it demonstrates the success of the knowledge acquired; it allows the teacher to evaluate the learning and it develops high level thinking skills (ibid., p. 149).

Without questioning it would be impossible to develop genuine understanding and it teaches students to think for themselves. It is not only young students who misunderstand, it happens in all age groups. Exam howlers provide a good example: 'A common disease in wheat crops is wheat germ'. The teacher had never told the student that wheat germ is a cereal.

Learning and Memory

Psychologists are still not absolutely sure how we remember or forget.[28] There is short-term memory, which stores information for as little as a few seconds; there is long-term memory, which can store information for a lifetime. However most of what passes through the brain is promptly forgotten. Sometimes short-term memories are passed on to long-term memories. The brain does all this automatically. If students are given too much information, or given it too quickly, they will not have time to process it into their long-term memory. Teachers would be well advised to continually review and impart information frequently. Seashore in 1938 (and still referred to today), had this to say:

> While retentive and serviceable memory is a very great asset to a musical person, it is not at all an essential condition for musical-mindedness. A person may have naturally very poor memory of all kinds and get along well in music, just as an absent-minded philosopher may get along very well in his field. Furthermore, the possibility for the development of memory is so very great that with careful training a person with a very poor memory may improve this many-fold to the point of serviceability (p. 7).

Students cannot be expected to remember every single word said by the teacher, but they can be encouraged to remember key information. Some teachers review the previous week's lesson at the beginning of the new lesson, or the last topic before the new one. This is all excellent practice as mentioned above.

> The learning process in music involves two primary aspects: acquisition and retention of musical information and experience, and the development of musical skills. Both of these are included in the common use of the term 'memory'; thus, we have conscious memory, which is the making available of stored information and experience, and subconscious memory, which is a phase of habit, such as is exhibited in all the various types of musical skills in performance (ibid., p. 149).

Lovelock enunciates three basic principles for learning:

1. All that we learn is ultimately based on memory.
2. All that we learn is cumulative.
3. All that we learn must be based on understanding (1978, p. 19).

Learning can only be done by the pupil; the teacher has to provide the stimulating environment in which learning can take place. The student must take the responsibility for the learning; the teacher does not exist to pack knowledge into the passive or unresponsive student. Since students learn more by doing than by listening only to the teacher, this augurs well for the teaching of singing.[29] They need to be rewarded for their learning and this is where praise and encouragement come in.

Motivation

Good pedagogical practice would suggest that the teacher communicates enjoyment, and assumes success and commitment while not being afraid to challenge the pupil appropriately. It is necessary that the environment be stable, pleasant and non-threatening. Students should be motivated by enjoyment, the desire to succeed and success. Strong motivation advances learning because it increases attention to the job in hand, to mental effort, and to perseverance with difficulties. A good case can be made for praising partial success, for example, there is usually something being done correctly, and one can always praise effort (technically, behavioural psychologists call this 'positive behaviourism'). Criticism should be positive, constructive and sincere. The effect of self-praise and self-criticism is greater than teachers sometimes realize. Self-praise is an important motivator; it is the glow of satisfaction from achievement. Self-criticism can be destructive. Few teachers realize how little they praise.[30]

Motivation is something that causes a person to act. Mackworth-Young contends that the student 'must be able to feel or "see" in his mind's eye the light, bright success beckoning at the end' (2000, p. 37). A good case can be made for teachers to reflect upon the purpose of trying to motivate students.[31] Is it to aim for a perfect performance? Is it to inflate teachers' own egos? Is it to enable students to become more musically efficient and enjoy the act of music making? Excellent teachers are self-motivated and their behaviour acts as a model for their students. Ultimately, it is up to the individual students to make choices as to what actions they should take. If teachers understand their own motivational habits then they can knowledgeably help students motivate themselves. Motivation appears to be a learned behaviour; it is not innate. Self-discipline is necessary to reverse 'lazy', or 'can't be bothered' situations.[32] High achievers are aware of the exhilarating feeling of success and have learned the goal-achieving actions that have led to their achievements. Self-motivators have clearly defined goals and a time frame; they are persistent and do assignments when they might not want to; they are dedicated to self-improvement; open to new learning; emotionally mature; they use failure to their advantage, and they take satisfaction from completed tasks well done. Eventually these habits become ingrained. Specific honest and worthy praise is the teacher's best tool here. Innate student ability does not necessarily make a 'super-star', but effort and perseverance just might.

Learning Plateau

A commonly accepted idea is that when learning a new concept or skill there is an initial response from the student that gains momentum as the student gains confidence. This surge of progress tends to flatten out as a plateau of achievement is reached during which it is often difficult for students to feel that they are making progress. At the plateau stage the student may easily lose interest, motivation and confidence without careful guidance from the teacher. The teacher could use this stage to expand the areas of musical experience in a variety of ways. Once over this stage students will once more make progress at a rate which is obvious to both student and teacher.

Pedagogical Structure

Why do many singing teachers teach as they were taught? As well as teaching in the same way as their previous teacher/s, even the technical work and repertoire may be the same, with no thought being given to the stage of development and needs of the pupil in front of them. Teaching singing is not a hit-or-miss affair. Realistic goals must be established and an efficient, systematic, individualized programme made available to ensure success. A teacher should not teach a series of isolated facts, but rather help students organize information into larger coherent principles or rules. Lessons should be organized around integrated themes, not trivial, unrelated bits of this and that, so called vocal 'wisdom' or 'quick fixes'. A coherent soundly based approach is far more likely to be internalized than isolated, unrelated 'tips'. Concepts are learnt through experiences, they cannot be taught directly, and it is the teacher's place to facilitate these experiences. They are not fixed, but are always in the process of formation at increasing levels of sophistication.

The cognitive domain is the area of learning associated with facts and ideas. It is recommended that teachers structure learning experiences that cause students to comprehend and apply knowledge, to solve musical problems, to create and select varying musical answers or responses, which requires them to use their knowledge in new situations. There is no one right way to teach. The mechanistic teacher ('do this') does not have a better method than the teacher with the aural method ('imitate me'). The best teachers have a variety of strategies for their students. The affective domain is concerned with the development of attitudes and values. Students should be encouraged to make informed choices within the subject area, thereby developing musical values.[33]

Forward planning is important – knowing exactly what is to be taught and what the pupil needs to learn is essential. This is determined in relation to the individual's technical and artistic progress. Materials can be organized for lively home practice periods. It is not denied that the imagination plays an important part in teaching strategy, but even inspiration needs to be rooted in reliable method.

It is necessary for teachers to decide on what they want to achieve, and how best to attain it. The plan can then be carried out and evaluated and the question – Did you achieve your aims? – answered. The answer may reveal that the aims need to be changed. This pedagogical question should be addressed in relation to the several domains of psychology. These are as follows:

1. The cognitive domain (intellectual skills and abilities): knowledge, comprehension, application, analysis, synthesis, and evaluation.
2. The affective domain: attention, interest, awareness, aesthetic appreciation, moral aesthetic and other attitudes, opinions, and feelings or values.
3. The psychomotor domain: motor or physical skills, sense perception, hand and eye coordination.

Against this general background let us now consider the psychological situation of specific age groups.

Specific Age Groups

Pre-school

Singing has a strong biological basis, and can facilitate cognitive abilities.[34] We begin to sing (or should) as soon, or even before, we learn to speak. Unborn babies' hearing develops as early as three months.[35] At three and a half months into pregnancy babies are able to distinguish their mother's voice, and are capable of hearing voices in the outside world. 'Babies learn to recognize their mother tongue in the womb, can distinguish a foreign language within days of being born ...' (Bailey, 2000, p. 2). They not only hear voice, but also feel it. Embryos become accustomed to the vibrations they receive in the womb when their mother sings. This is carried over into infancy and childhood – parents speaking or singing cheek to cheek with their offspring are often easily able to comfort them. The combination of vibration and contact appears to be soothing and reassuring. Midwives worldwide quote examples of the newborn who sing at birth – a very different sound from the usual birth cry, and then they discover that the mothers are opera singers. Tiny babies, lying in their baby seats, have been known to 'sing along' at their mother's singing lessons. As Carl E. Seashore has pointed out,

> ... we find that the basic capacities, the sense of pitch, the sense of time, the sense of loudness, and the sense of timbre are elemental, by which we mean that they are largely inborn and function from early childhood (1938, p. 3).

The strong sense of rhythm with which children are born probably comes from the nine months in the womb spent next to the mother's heartbeat. Shuter-Dyson and Gabriel have produced an interesting table:

Milestones of Musical Development Ages

    0–1   Reacts to sounds.
    1–2   Spontaneous music making.
    2–3   Begins to reproduce phrases of songs heard.
    3–4   Conceives general plan of a melody; absolute pitch may develop if it learns an instrument.
    4–5   Can discriminate register of pitches; can tap back simple rhythms (1981, p. 159).

During the first year of life song babbling is evident.[36] Between three to six months there is a positive response to musical sounds and the baby will often turn its head in pleasure towards the direction of the sound. Conversely, 'Research in Canada shows that six-month-old babies recognize wrong notes. "Play *Twinkle Twinkle Little Star* to them and put in an incongruous note and they are on to it like a shot'" (Fawkes quoting Paul Robertson, 1996, p. 25). Babies experiment in making different sounds as they learn to control their lips, tongue and mouth. Sometimes a sustained sound turns into a musical note. Later they may react with movements, rhythmic or not, to the music. There is often recognizable spontaneous singing as early as six months.[37] The developmental sequence usually proceeds as follows: the child is able to sing melodic-rhythmic patterns of higher and lower notes, but without accuracy of pitch because of the inability of the larynx to coordinate with the mentally envisaged sound. However infants of six months have been able to learn, with training, to match pitches in their range (C4 to A4).[38]

In the second year there is much more physical movement and babies enjoy dancing with other people and by the age of eighteen months they can often co-ordinate rhythmically with the music. Two-year-olds are capable of repeating a single, brief melodic phrase, such as 'Miss Polly had a dolly', and will sing sponta-neously short phrases of their own composition repeatedly, but with varying pitches. The ability to develop complex phrases advances. Some three-year-olds may sing the correct pitch, but that usually comes later. Welch suggests that after infant babbling, where sound is played around with as

> glissandi and groups of musical pitches and phrases in a repetitive fashion … words and fragments of song text … become the focus of attention, followed by certain rhythmic features, and, subsequently, the pitch components (1994, pp. 4–5).

Supplanting this, he continues, is the sequence of: 'words – rhythm – pitch'. This 'becomes further elaborated into: pitch contour – individual phrase stability – overall key stability'. He goes on to say: 'By the age of five to six years, young children's singing may have acquired many of the features of the significant adult models' (ibid., p. 5).[39]

Spontaneous singing of four-year-olds was studied by Veldhuis, who reported that the singing was organized, generally with restricted intervals in pitch, and had clear short melodies. She notes that for stimulus they used objects like musical instruments and environmental sounds, and that their singing was contagious (1984, p. 15–24). L. B. Miller found that preschoolers create songs and imitate rhythms with body movements and, unprompted, will chant and sing-a-long with recorded music (1989, p. 206–224).

Parents, carers and all adults should listen to pre-school children more closely and encourage their singing so that they may benefit both directly musically, and indirectly in respect of other aspects of their development. During pre-school and primary years children show very positive attitudes towards many kinds of music. Therefore this is an ideal time to draw upon their responses and introduce them to a wide variety of music. There is much to be said for active interplay between parent and child: singing at bath time; story time; on the way to the park; in the car; and listening to sounds that occur naturally all around them, encouraging movement to such musical sounds and rhythms as are found in singing games and nursery rhymes. Rhythm is the first thing children grasp when learning a song, and teachers would do well to capitalize on this. Nursery rhymes are useful here, for they benefit children's general education as well as their musical development. They can aid listening, concentration, memory, good speech through careful pronunciation of the words, vocabulary extension, the recognition of rhyming words and rhythmic patterns, awareness of musical phrases and dynamics (the list is endless), and ultimately the awareness of pitch which leads to singing in tune. Care must be taken that the rhymes are sung at pitches appropriate to the age and physical development of the child, beginning with rhymes that contain only a few notes and progressing to those with a wider range. Most three-year-olds can cope with a range somewhere between C4 and G4, the perfect fifth above.

The singing of such rhymes is more productive than passive listening to music, which becomes musical wallpaper. However exposure to music that includes wide varieties of rhythms, timbres, volumes or harmonies that excite the child may be played. Children will be their own critics of what they consider boring and will 'switch off'. There are many pre-school music groups in the United Kingdom and elsewhere some drawing on the traditions of Orff and Kodály. There is much to be said for pre-schoolers having access to percussion instruments such as chime bars, castanets, maracas, marimbas, gongs, bells, drums, cymbals and rattles. The use of these encourages experimentation with and delight in sound and rhythm. At all times singing or chanting along either individually or with others should be encouraged. Spontaneous, improvised chants often develop into impromptu singing games and others, probably, will join in. The important thing is to make available these opportunities for young children in order to nurture their musical invention and development and, it goes without saying, their enjoyment.

Piaget made the following basic assumptions about how children learn:

1. The child does not think like an adult.
2. The child learns by becoming involved with concrete objects.
3. The child learns intrinsically (from within) not extrinsically (from without).
4. The child evolves intellectually through the generative nature of the prior experience and the quality of the current experience.
5. The child learns through the adaptation of new schemas (formation of concepts; categorizing perceived data).
6. The child uses two interdependent activities, assimilation and accommodation, in this adaptive process. Assimilation is the taking in of perceptual data, accommodation is a modification in the way of thinking to accommodate perceived data.
7. The child strives to establish equilibrium when assimilating and accommodating new data (cited by Andress, 1980, p. 133).

Piaget goes on to divide intellectual development into four stages:

Sensorimotor – up to 2 years
Preoperational – 2 to 7 years
Concrete operations – 7 to 11 years
Formal operations – 11 to 15 years (ibid., p. 133).

Childhood Aged Five to Twelve

Our consideration of children aged five to twelve may begin with Hargreaves' lament that there are, 'no coherent psychological theories of the specific developmental processes underlying children's musical perception, cognition or performance' (1986, p. 3). On the other hand there have been several studies of development in rhythmic perception, notably by Zenatti (1976), who found that children aged four to five were able to clap back two to four note rhythms, and that they improved with practice.[40] Other studies have shown consistent development in the rhythmic skills of children aged between six and eleven (Stambak, 1960).[41] Hargreaves goes on to say, 'that by the age of six or seven, children possess many of the fundamental skills required for full-scale musical perception and performance' (1986, p. 83). Gardner is in total agreement and once again implies that Piaget's philosophy of 'concrete operational thought' (ibid., p. 83) is not applicable to the 'artistic process' (Gardner, 1973).[42] He further suggests that:

> a reasonably competent 7-year-old should understand the basic metrical properties of his musical system and the appropriate scales, harmonies, cadences, and groupings, even as he should be able, given some motifs, to combine them into a musical unit that is appropriate to his culture, but is not a complete copy of a work previously known. What is lacking is fluency in motor skills, which will allow accurate performance, experience with the code, tradition and style of that culture, and a range of feeling life (ibid., p. 197).

Following on from this, Hargreaves and Zimmerman (1992) say that psychologists are now moving away from the identification of age related stages – the problem has been in determining the specific ages at which changes take place in cognition – towards a more culture-specific and domain-specific description of human development. Unfortunately this relies on children's verbal ability, which may affect their understanding. Research by Bamberger (1982) and Davidson and Scripp (1988) has used graphic representation by children, for example, in pitch and rhythm variations.

School has an important influence on musical experience; this involves exposure to songs and music and builds on children's pre-school learning. Much of this experience is unstructured and spontaneous as opposed to direct training. Sloboda uses the terms *enculturation* and *training* to make a distinction between the two types of development (1985, p. 213).

Incidentally, how damaging to young children to be told that they cannot sing – a hurt that typically stays lifelong and can cause much distress. Many believe that *all* music is not for them, and alienate themselves from this great source of pleasure and enjoyment. In turn, their own offspring may be deprived. Very often, unfortunately, this sorrow is instigated by singing teachers who ban 'growlers' from the school choir or ask them to mime.[43] This in turn raises the ethical question of auditioning a prospective young schoolchild before registering them for singing lessons. Whereas over-protection of a child is unhealthy, what psychological damage will be done if the child is rejected? As the voice is a reflection of the personality much harm may be done. In this situation teachers would be well advised to assess the enthusiasm for singing shown by the child and provide the opportunity to learn to sing if appropriate.

Most researchers agree that pitch discrimination improves as the child gets older but are not agreed about how, and precisely when, this happens.[44] Singing teachers should be aware of young children's interpretation of such words as 'more' and 'less', 'higher' and 'lower' with regard to pitch discrimination. For example, a pair of tones are played melodically and the question is: 'Does the second sound move up or down?' Similarly the use and concept of the words 'same' or 'different' can influence the child's decision. Understanding of these words varies between the child and adult. The musical competence of the child should not be in question.

Pitch discrimination can be improved by training, see above, the 'tone-deaf' singer. Welch suggests that poor pitch discrimination is the result of poor pitch control in singing (1979, pp. 50–58). Children need to be taught to listen with concentration, similarly, adults need their listening skills to be honed. Teaching any age group to listen is hard work; it takes time, patience and imagination on the part of the teacher. Learning to listen carefully is essential for motivation and development to take place. Various fun listening games – listening with eyes closed to the noises of the immediate environment, listening to different musical instruments, the list is endless – can be devised to aid this learning skill. Frequent practice is necessary. Because of the need for lots of constant reinforcement in order for children to progress in a lively and interested way many teachers have found it helpful to present the same material in many different imaginative guises – quite a challenge. The enthusiasm of the young child must be constantly monitored and ways devised to maintain it.

Coming now to the acquisition of tonality, scholars are agreed that children conserve familiar tonal melodies more readily than unfamiliar atonal music. This seems rather an obvious proposition, but much is made of the fact that they are absorbing the melodic contour of tunes rather than assimilation by pitch/interval relationship. Bartlett and Dowling suggest from their experiments that transpositions to different keys of a familiar melody, 'Twinkle, twinkle little star', were easily recognized. However when an incorrect interval was played in the same tune it went unrecognized.[45] This varied with the age of the child. Five-year-olds were able to recognize transpositions in a far key but not a near key transposition. They were unable to recognize the interval change in the melody. Eight-year-olds were much more able to distinguish between both near and far key transpositions and interval change. Hargreaves sums up by saying: 'The acquisition of tonality is thus comparable with language acquisition, in that the general capacity to master a language is a maturational one that is independent of exposure to and training in the particular language acquired' (1986, p. 92).

Harmonic skills appear to develop in the same way as melody acquisition but more slowly, in some cases not reaching their peak until the age of seventeen. Experiments have been made in recognizing melodies in counterpoint, and being aware of the difference between consonance and dissonance subjectively perceived. Here terms such as 'beautiful', 'pleasant', would be used for consonance. P.A.D. Gardner and Pickford propose that the context of the chord sounded can make a difference in the perception of whether or not it is consonant or dissonant (1944, pp. 274–5). It is interesting to note that some children do not like the sound of certain intervals, as played on the piano, and this changes with age. For example, according to one study there was no preference for discords over concords until the age of nine, whereas at eleven children preferred concords and disliked discords.[46] Many other studies have been made of these preferences.[47]

It goes without saying that children with a musically stimulating home respond better than those without. Such an environment includes parental singing and instrumental interaction with their children, the availability of recorded music, and parental attitude towards all aspects of music. It is interesting to note that in a study by Davidson, Howe, Moore, and Sloboda it was found that the most successful children in music were those whose parents played a full role in lessons and practice, and that the children without this support tended to be the ones who lost motivation, became bored and gave up their instrument.[48] Unfortunately, conclusions could be drawn from the relationship between social class and musical development. Researchers are often middle class and the test materials used are often intellectual classical music. This raises the question of possibly overlooked variables, and hence the question of the validity of the research findings.

Problems may arise because of peer pressure; this often happens with the boy singer, or the boy singer who is the only male member of the school choir. The teacher needs to be aware of this and support the pupil where possible.

Children learn through play and through positive social reaction with others.[49] Music is a part of this and children find this an ongoing component of their individual and social place in everyday life. For this reason it is well for the teacher to think of the child as he or she is now, and not to think only of the singer he or she may become. Flusser has drawn upon the Polish paediatrician, Korczac Janusz in order to underline this point:

> first, [Korczac] affirms that the child is not to be considered as a 'future-state being' but as a 'present-state being'. Second, he maintains that in order to enter into a true pedagogical relationship with the child, we have to hold affection for him ... Maintaining that the child is a 'present-state being' starkly contrasts with a wide range of educational theories, strategy sequences or behavioural studies that aim to help children 'progress'

from their present state towards the realization of a project that we have decided for them. Maintaining that the child is a 'present-state being' modifies the assertive pedagogic approach, because it alters the relationship of *authority* between the child and the educator in that the educator is no longer sole *author* of the pedagogic project (2000, pp. 43–4).

Adolescence

Adolescence has traditionally been considered a more difficult developmental period than childhood. It is a period of change, not only physical, sexual, psychological, and cognitive, but social. Youngsters have reached the stage in cognitive development known as the formal operations stage, in which they can reason about hypothetical problems and explore alternative possibilities in a systematic search for solutions. Some become preoccupied with self, think others are thinking about them all the time, and may become self-conscious. Others sail smoothly through adolescence. It is important to give them a sense of purpose, stimulating their 'realistic' ambitions, and encouraging self-confidence.[50] It is very often a period when because of examination pressures at school they feel that they must terminate their singing lessons. Again, the teacher's support and encouragement are necessary, and imaginative ways should be sought to deal with the situation. Termination of lessons must be discussed thoughtfully, perhaps suggesting a lightening of the workload at revision and school examination times in order to avoid complete withdrawal from singing.

The physiological aspect of the changing voice of both boys and girls will be dealt with in the following chapter. All the training and habits of earlier years can suddenly get out of kilter. Both teacher and young person should be well prepared for this; possible embarrassment can then be avoided. If this change is anticipated, the temporarily 'awkward' area of the vocal range is unlikely to go out of control and technical vocal work can continue in a limited way, working carefully with the pitch and range available. The motivational approach for the adolescent boy can be something like: 'You are about to be given a new voice, deeper, richer, stronger, maybe more beautiful. A whole new repertoire of songs will be available.' Incidentally some boys deeply regret the loss of their treble/alto voice. Recordings of the progress of the voice are interesting for them to hear, and physiological explanations, videos, and diagrams of the changing of the vocal mechanism are sure winners. Very often, under an appearance of bravado or assumed indifference the adolescent of both sexes really wants to sing well. Teachers must also look to themselves, and it is interesting to note here research referred to by Harris and Crozier:

a significant number of adults were asked what ... appealed least in their teachers throughout their whole adolescence.

Characteristics least appreciated by pupils:

sarcasm
severity
absence of laughter
indifference (2000, pp. 13–14).

Boredom is considered to be a common state for many adolescents, but it can arise at any age. However children and young people are not slow to articulate their feelings when bored: 'Bor-*ing*, it's bor-*ing*.' This is sometimes expressed indignantly and with gusto: 'Been there, done that.' Monotony in the singing lesson is frequently a cause; doing the same things over and over again becomes dull, the routine of practice can become tedious. If students do not see purpose in what they are doing work becomes wearisome. Lack of challenge can make students feel as though their progress is standing still. Teachers must try to find what is responsible for the boredom and what may help the student to develop interests in order to find learning stimulating. Unfortunately, what adolescents find interesting and stimulating depends on what they have been exposed to as well as their present development needs, and we are back, among other things, to parental responsibility for influencing and extending children's experiences. Very often pop music is preferred to Beethoven. We are now coming into the realm of aesthetics.[51]

Some tried and tested methods to regain interest are: providing variety in learning; relating where possible to pupils' interests; being intentionally unpredictable; using unusual teaching methods and content; asking questions which go beyond the usual rote memory and require reasoning ability and creative thought; providing consistent feedback; creating lessons that have a finished product to aim for; encouraging student choice in the learning situation; fostering success in learning; using as much encouragement and praise as possible within the constraints of integrity. It must be remembered that the teenager, like the adult, may bring musical sensitivity and experience to the pedagogical situation that can be utilized by the teacher.

Adults

Methods of teaching adults are similar to those of teaching younger age groups, but there will be differences. Adult learners are usually highly motivated – no one is making them have lessons and they are usually paying for themselves. Some have clear ideas about what they wish to achieve, others are apprehensive as to whether their voice is good enough to warrant lessons, or even whether they have any talent at all for singing. Some feel vulnerable. Others wonder if they are too old, and some wish, on retirement from differing careers, to return to their childhood love of music. Others are reminded of how they learnt skills as a child and were in awe of the teacher, and are very dependent on approval. Adults need respect, praise and encouragement in the same way as – perhaps even more than – the young person. Some are quick to say that they understand rather than admit that they are unclear on a teaching point. Others may want to go into great detail on specific points and hesitate to take the teaching at face value as a child might. Mackworth-Young goes as far as suggesting that the adult student may 'Probably prefer to direct their own lessons in consultation with the teacher (they know what they want to learn and what they want to achieve)' (2000, p. 100). Teachers should consciously aim to foster an equal relationship based on mutual interaction and respect. It takes a lot of courage to attend the first lesson. Well-taught singing lessons should benefit any voice and nobody is too old to learn to sing well. Involvement in music can help adults stay more alert at any age, including the later years, and can increase the quality of life.

An interesting question is, 'Does lack of pitch response in adults affect their aesthetic judgement?' There has been, to my knowledge, no research done on this so far. 'Tone-dumb' (an alternative description to 'tone-deaf') adults have a problem of listening to themselves singing and not recognizing that they are out of tune. Whereas Welch focuses on this problem of listening to oneself (1985, pp. 3–18), others emphasize the role of perceptual learning independent of what the singer hears. But it still remains unclear how the singers who are competent to listen and enjoy music cannot hear when they themselves are out of tune.

As suggested earlier, teachers have to be adaptable in their teaching methods when dealing with different age groups. For example, the teacher will more easily be able to encourage the improvement of physical posture in the pupil who starts early enough. However, an adult may well have developed long-standing physical habits that are difficult to correct.[52] One must not necessarily assume that because a singing voice has never been used it will be fresher and last longer than a voice that has been used since childhood. Muscles and tissue age whether used or not. Longevity of the singing voice is rather more dependent upon efficiency and regularity of use.[53]

According to some schools of thought, by the age of thirty, one is too old to begin to learn to sing. In my experience, however, training voices in their sixties and seventies has been successful. The voice should, if carefully used, be able to maintain most of its power and clarity until advanced old age. Psychologically the chief object is to overcome the feeling that they are 'past it'. Isobel Baillie was singing publicly until a month or so before her death in her mid-eighties.

Returning to the plight of the non-singer, designated 'tone-deaf': when singing lessons begin, patience is necessary. The rate of progress varies from individual to individual. Non-singing children will normally learn more quickly than adults, for they are often less inhibited than their adult counterparts and have younger muscles. The teaching situation needs to be one in which encouragement and praise are given generously in order to build the student's confidence, particularly when dealing with the adult pupil. Teachers must be extremely sensitive to these budding vocalists. The voice is inextricably interwoven with the personality, and all students require training that is as skilful as it is compassionate.

In this chapter it has been argued that psychology, often mingled with ethical considerations, makes a significant general contribution to vocal pedagogy and, more particularly, that singing teachers can only benefit from a strong foundation in the developmental psychology of music, albeit this multi-faceted discipline is relatively young. Cognitive, social, behavioural and affective psychologies cannot be applied in isolation from each other in music education. Since people learn in different ways provision made in teaching styles must be appropriate to individuals at whatever stage they are in their development. The responsibility of the teacher lies in the selection of the methods necessary for the progress of the student of whatever age or ability. Much more of this developmental psychology and diagnosis would be welcome in the teacher training situation and more links between theory and practice are desirable.

From the epigram 'teachers are born not made' comes the reasoning of teachers who think that knowledge of psychology is unnecessary. No doubt there are teachers who appear to have taught successfully without having studied psychology, but there are many more who have been handicapped by a lack of psychological knowledge. Even the successful teachers would have gained from the information – their failures are seldom mentioned. Tampering with what is not well understood could result in psychological damage. Hollien says:

> ... the voice teacher must be a reasonably good practicing psychologist with both technical knowledge about personality and insightful perspectives relative to the elements that underlie specific behavior. Indeed, it is not enough to be well meaning in this regard as behavior modification is not always a positive and maturing force; it can be dangerous if mishandled. Thus, the voice teacher must have specific training in applied psychology; it is also helpful to be intuitive and insightful about personality, learning, and deviant behavior (1993, pp. 197–8).

And Harris and Crozier say:

> Perhaps the most demanding and stimulating challenge faced by the teacher is to draw from the pupil that subtle ability to communicate something of their innermost self through the medium of musical performance. Without developing musical 'personality', performances will remain uninspired and the central message of the music will not be communicated (2000, p. 4).

Of course, inspiring performances also depend upon a firm technical foundation. Into the establishment of such a foundation we must now enquire.

Notes

1 It would not be difficult to show that ethical-cum-psychological considerations come into play before ever a student signs up for singing lessons. For some indications of how this can occur in the context of a voice studio see Appendix 2.

2 From the ever-increasing number of books and articles on business ethics (many of which concentrate on the corporate world), the following may be selected as containing chapters relevant to issues in professional ethics: De George, Richard T. (1999),

Business Ethics, Upper Saddle River, NJ: Prentice Hall; Chryssides, George D. and John H. Kaler (2001), *An Introduction to Business Ethics*, London: Thomson Learning.

3   See further, Watt, Laurence (1996), 'The law of contract', in Ford, Trevor (ed.), *The Musician's Handbook*, London: Rhinegold Publishing.

4   See further, Ford, Trevor (1996), 'Income tax and national insurance', in Ford, Trevor (ed.), *The Musician's Handbook*, London: Rhinegold Publishing.

5   See further, Polunin, Tanya (1996), 'The independent teacher', in Ford, Trevor (ed.), *The Musician's Handbook*, London, Rhinegold Publishing.

6   See further, Diggle, Keith (1996), 'Marketing yourself', in Ford, Trevor (ed.), *The Musician's Handbook*, London: Rhinegold Publishing.

7   See further, Introduction above.

8   Throughout this study, where I give advice in this way, it arises from my experience.

9   See further, Miller, Richard (1996), *On the Art of Singing*, New York: Oxford University Press.

10   See further, Ross, W.D. (1930), *The Right and the Good,* Oxford: Clarendon Press, pp. 18–36.

11   See further, Harris, Paul and Richard Crozier (2000), *The Music Teacher's Companion*, London: ABRSM.

12   See further, Davidson, Jane W., Michael J.A. Howe, Derek G. Moore, and John A. Sloboda (1996), 'The role of parental influences in the development of musical performance', *British Journal of Developmental Psychology*, **14** (4), November, 399–412.

13   See further, Chapter 5 below; Read, Donald (1997), 'A pronouncement: ethics revisited', *Journal of Singing, **53*** (4), March/April, 27–30.

14   See further, Spender, Natasha, and Rosamund Shuter-Dyson (1980), 'Psychology of music', in Sadie, Stanley (ed.), *The New Grove Dictionary of Music*, 20 vols, London: Macmillan, Vol. XV, 388–427; Thurman, Leon and Graham Welch (2000), *bodymind & voice: foundations of voice education*, 3 vols, revised edn, Collegeville, Minnesota and Iowa City; London: The Voice Care Network, National Center for Voice and Speech, Fairview Voice Center, Centre for Advanced Studies in Music Education, Vol I.

15   See further, Hayes, Nicky (2000), *Foundations of Psychology*, London: Thomson Learning, p. 701.

16   See further, Hargreaves, David J. (1999), *The Developmental Psychology of Music*, Cambridge: Cambridge University Press; Swanwick, Keith (1999), *Teaching Music Musically*, London and New York: Routledge Falmer; Radocy, R.E., and J.D. Boyle (1969), *Psychological Foundations of Musical Behavior*, Springfield, IL: C.C. Thomas.

17   See further, Zimmerman, Marilyn Pflederer (1970), 'Percept and concept: implications of Piaget', *Music Educators Journal, **56*** (6), February, 49–50, 147–8; Hargeaves, David (1996), 'The developmental psychology of music', in Spruce, Gary (ed.), *Teaching Music*, London: Routledge.

18   See further, Günter, Horst (1992), 'Mental concepts in singing: a psychological approach, Part I', *The NATS Journal*, **48** (5), May/June, 4–8, 46.

19   See further, Deutsch, Diana (1982), (ed.), *The Psychology of Music*, New York: Academic Press; Sloboda, John A. (1985), *The Musical Mind: The Cognitive Psychology of Music*, Oxford: Oxford University Press.

20   See further, Greer, R.D. (1981), 'An operant approach to motivation and affect: ten years of research in music learning', paper presented at the National Symposium for the Application of Learning Theory to Music Education, Ann Arbor, MI, Reston, VA: MENC.

21 See further, Mackworth-Young, Lucinda (2000), *Tuning In*, Swaffham, Norfolk: MMM Publications.

22 See further, Goetze, Mary (1989), 'A comparison of the pitch accuracy of group and individual singing in young children', *Bulletin of the Council for Research in Music Education*, **99**, Winter, 57–73; Rutkowski, Joanne (1999), 'The nature of children's singing voices: characteristics and assessment', *Canadian Music Educator*, **40** (3), Spring, 43–7.

23 See further, Chapter 4 below.

24 See further, Vennard, William (1997/8), 'The psychology of the pupil-teacher relationship', *American Music Teacher*, **47** (3), December/January, 24–7.

25 See further, Evans, Colin (2000), 'Keeping track of progress', *Music Teacher*, May, 22–3.

26 See further, Bruscia, Kenneth (1989), 'Building effective student-teacher relationships in the private music studio', *American Music Teacher*, **39** (2), 12–15, 56, October/ November, 12–15, 56.

27 See further, Chapter 4 below.

28 See further, Chapter 5 below on the memorization of songs.

29 See further, Kemp, Anthony (1990), 'Kinaesthesia in music and its implications for developments in microtechnology', *British Journal of Music Education*, **7** (3), 223–9; Petty, Geoffrey (1993), *Teaching Today*, Cheltenham: Stanley Thornes.

30 See further, Anderson, Margaret (1996), 'A study of motivation and how it relates to student achievement', *Canadian Music Educator*, **38** (1), Fall, 29–31.

31 See further, Miriani, Dorothy (1992), 'Motivation and personality types', *American Music Teacher*, **41** (6), June/July, 18–21, 56.

32 See further, Wlodkowski, Raymond J. and Judith H. Jaynes (1992), 'Overcoming boredom and indifference', *American Music Teacher*, **41** (6), June/July, 12–17, 56.

33 See further, Chapter 5 below.

34 See further, Swanwick, Keith (1988), *Music, Mind, and Education*, London: Routledge, pp. 52–87; Fox, Donna Brink (2000) 'Music and the baby's brain', *Music Educators Journal*, **87** (2), September, 23–7, 50.

35 See further, Amtmann, Inger-Marie (1997), 'Music for the unborn child', *International Journal of Music Education*, **29**, 66–72; Morgan, Rhian (2002), 'Young ears', *Music Teacher*, October, 38–9.

36 See further, Titze, Ingo R. (2001), 'Should vocal training follow vocal development in childhood?' *Journal of Singing*, **58** (2), November/December, 161–2.

37 See further, Moog, H. (1976), *The Musical Experience of the Pre-School Child*, trans. C. Clarke, London: Schott; Ries, N.L. (1987), An analysis of the characteristics of infant-child singing expressions: replication report', *Canadian Journal of Research in Music Education*, **29**, 5–20.

38 USA Standards Association (middle C = C4) will be used throughout this text rather than Helmholtz (middle C = C1). See further, Dowling, W. Jay (1982), 'Melodic information processing and its development', in *The Psychology of Music*, Deutsch, Diana (ed.), New York: New York Academic Press, pp. 413–29.

39 See further, Morphew, Richard (1997), 'Let the children sing', *Singing*, **32,** Summer, 28–32.

40 See further, Zenatti, A. (1976), 'Jugement esthétique et perceptive de l'enfant, entre 4 à 10 ans, dans des épreuves rhythmiques', *Année Psychologique*, **76**, 185–90.

41 See further, Stambak, M. (1960), 'Trois épreuves de rythme', in Zazzo, R. (ed.) *Manuel pour l'examen psychologique de l'enfant*, Paris: Delachaux and Niestlé.

42   See further, Warrener, John J. (1985), 'Applying learning theory to musical devel-
     opment', *Music Educators Journal*, **72** (3), 22–7; Andress, Barbara (1980), *Music
     Experiences in Early Childhood*, New York: Holt, Rinehart and Winston; Mussen, Paul
     Henry, John Janeway Conger, Jerome Kagan, Aletha Carol Huston (1990), *Child
     Development and Personality*, New York: Harper Collins.

43   See further, Welch, Graham F. (1985), 'A schema theory of how children learn to sing in
     tune', *Psychology of Music,* **13** (1), 3–18. Jones, Merilyn (1979), 'Using a vertical-
     keyboard instrument with an uncertain singer', *Journal of Research in Music Education*,
     17 (3), Fall, 173–84. Rutkowski, Joanne (1999), 'The nature of children's singing
     voices: characteristics and assessment', *Canadian Music Educator*, **40** (3), Spring.

44   See further, Shuter-Dyson, Rosamund, and Clive Gabriel (1981), *The Psychology of
     Musical Ability*, London: Methuen; Yarbrough, Cornelia; Judy Bowers, and Wilma
     Benson (1992), 'The effect of vibrato on the pitch-matching accuracy of certain and
     uncertain singers', *Journal of Research in Music Education*, **40** (1), 30–38.

45   See further, Bartlett, J.C., and W. Jay Dowling (1980), 'The recognition of transposed
     melodies: a key-distance effect in developmental perspective', *Journal of Experimental
     Psychology: Human Perception and Performance*, **6** (3), 501–15.

46   See further, Valentine, C.W. (1962), *The Experimental Psychology of Beauty*, London:
     Methuen.

47   See further, Bridges, V.A. (1965), 'An exploratory study of the harmonic discrimination
     ability of children in kindergarten through grade three in two selected schools', unpub-
     lished PhD thesis, Ohio State University; Sloboda J.A. (1985), *The Musical Mind: The
     Cognitive Psychology of Music*, Oxford: Oxford University Press.

48   See further, Davidson, Jane W., Michael J.A. Howe, Derek G. Moore, and John A.
     Sloboda (1996), 'The role of parental influences in the development of musical perfor-
     mance', *British Journal of Developmental Psychology,* **14** (4), pp. 399–412.

49   See further, Wood, David (1988), *How Children Think and Learn*, Oxford: Blackwell.

50   See further, Osborne, Corrynne (2001), 'Encouraging confidence and self-esteem in
     young singers', *Singing*, **40**, Summer, 21–2; Cooksey John M., Graham F. Welch
     (1998), 'Adolescence, singing development and national curricula design', *British
     Journal of Music Education*, **15** (1), 99–119.

51   See further, Chapter 5 below.

52   See further, Thurman, Leon and Graham Welch (2000), *bodymind & voice: foundations
     of voice education*, 3 vols, revised edn, Collegeville, Minnesota; Iowa City and London:
     The Voice Care Network, National Center for Voice and Speech, Fairview Voice Center,
     Centre for Advanced Studies in Music Education, Vol. III.

53   See further, Chapter 3 below.

Chapter 3

Science and Vocal Pedagogy

'Why should a successful singing teacher bother about the functioning of the voice?' asks Johan Sundberg (1988, p. 11). He goes on to suggest that a reliable terminology has been developed by teachers over the centuries which achieves the correct results, therefore, what does science have to offer the singing teacher? He answers, 'My view is that science does not have very much to offer ...' (1988, p. 11). He does, however, agree that some teachers may be curious about the scientific aspect of vocalization, and that others may want to discover a common terminology that will help them to relate with other singing teachers and with other professionals, for example, otolaryngologists. I have already hinted that I question the 'reliability' of some of the language used by singing teachers, and I shall have more to say about this shortly.

In the Never-never-land of optimal vocal health many speech language therapists, in their professional meetings, are desperately asking: 'Where are the singing teachers who are fully equipped to continue our work with singers who have sick and inefficiently functioning voices? Few of us are trained to develop the singing voice of the ultimate vocal athlete'.

Thomas Hemsley states that he is trying to redress the balance between the advent of the 'how' of vocal science against the traditional 'why' and 'what' (feelings, intuition, and imagination) (1998, Foreword). Of course, any competent singing teacher with a firmly grounded scientifically based pedagogy is the very last person to decry imagination. Artistry and imagination thrive in concert with a voice which functions efficiently and healthily. However Hemsley, who rightly opposes the substitution by singing teachers of 'half-digested scientific jargon for true understanding' (ibid., p. 9), nevertheless himself offers questionable advice, as when he recommends singing with the jaw 'opened as for chewing, approximately one thumb's width' (ibid., p. 86). In fact this rule leads to vocal abuse by creating tension in larynx and pharynx.

Many singing teachers avoid anatomy and physiology. Even the pioneering British laryngologist Norman Punt (1979) sympathizes with H. Plunket Greene who recommends avoidance of the 'anatomical jargon man' because knowledge of anatomy and physiology will only 'worry him into senseless solicitude about organs whose movements are mainly automatic' (1914, p. 6). I would disagree: the movement of organs should be automatic, but owing to bad habits or ill-informed teaching, they frequently are not functioning either freely or healthily. Accordingly, the singing teacher needs to know what is going on if *positive* corrective action is to be taken. Ralph Appelman says:

> Vocal pedagogy cannot survive as an independent educational entity if the physiological and physical facts, which compromise its core, remain subjects of sciolism (superficial knowledge). Researchers must constantly interpret these scientific facts so that they might become realistic pedagogical tools that may be employed by future teachers of voice (1967, p. 5).

Some voice teachers complain that scientists assume that all voice teachers understand the principles of physics and mathematics relevant to current scientific thinking. They very often do not, and have been heard to ask, at voice conferences, if the scientist presenting the paper can explain so that they understand, since most of what is said sounds like a foreign language. On the other hand, some teachers feel too embarrassed to seek aid of this kind. However, it must be said, in fairness to medical and acoustic scientists, that an introductory programme is often arranged at the beginning of a conference for those who feel insecure in their knowledge of anatomy and physiology. Many scientists will take time to listen to what teachers have to say, but others dismiss them as not qualified to comment. When one hears a singing teacher discussing the 'larnyx' (sic) with a medical person one can understand why scientists come to that conclusion. Similarly scientists often find it very difficult to understand the subjective descriptions of technique, with their weird and wonderful language, in which some teachers indulge. Small wonder that physicians who have no singing experience have dismissed their singer patient's vocal problem as insignificant.

Miller writes:

> There is a body of information that ought to be drawn on by anyone who claims to teach anything to anybody. No one can know it all, but we must be willing to modify what we do know as information expands. Demythologizing the language of vocal pedagogy is part of that process (cited in Sataloff, 1997, p. 734).

Some teachers even have a fear that science will take over, defensively declaring that science has no place in art. They may even be so arrogant as to say that they know all there is to know about the singing voice already. The truth is however that science can confirm what the teacher sees and hears. For example, some students have difficulty in hearing what is happening as they sing and may not understand the teacher's instruction so visual reproduction such as spectrographs, pictures of muscles and models of the larynx may help to accelerate their understanding

From experience I find it vital to know something about the 'how' and 'why' of vocal function. How else can the teacher objectively discriminate between what is, and what is not, functioning healthily and efficiently in the singing voice?

Anatomy and Physiology

It is important that voice teachers understand the physical and physiological bases of the singing instrument and the repercussions from lack of knowledge and incorrect application. Hollien agrees that: 'there is no doubt that the voice teacher has to learn a lot of things [about] a lot of areas' (1993, p. 200).[1]

Posture

'Posture determines the alignment and balance of the body, and good bodily alignment is the beginning of efficient breathing and fundamental to healthy singing' (Bunch, 1995, p. 24). It is rare to see someone with proper physical poise. Young children, adolescents, and adults for that matter, tend to acquiesce into the slouching habits of the general population. Singing teachers have to point out these bad habits and encourage their correction. This task of changing habits, possibly acquired over many years, is formidable. As F.M. Alexander has stated: '... my teaching experience has taught me that when a wrong habitual use has been culti-vated in a purpose, its influence in the early stages of the lessons is practically irre-sistible' (1941, p. 35). The aim of Alexander Technique is to promote better posture, freedom of movement, and easy breathing by a process of awareness and self-mastery. In attempting to help students deal with wrong habitual use singing teachers would do well to remember their studies in psychology.[2] Wrong habitual use is not only found in postural problems, but in many aspects of singing. Good posture can improve health, self-image and performance. Alexander also says

> ... that the most valuable knowledge we can possess is that of the use and functioning of the self, and of the means whereby the human individual may progressively raise the standard of his health and general well-being (ibid., p. 20).

By good posture is meant the achievement of balance and poise. Everyday tasks such as standing, walking and sitting can then be performed without unnecessary effort or obvious increase in muscular activity.[3] In 1737 Nivelon[4], looking back to the precepts of the dancing master De Lauze who in 1623 stressed great importance on the position of the head for elegance in deportment, wrote:

> The Head being the principle part of the human Figure, must be first considered, because it entirely governs all the Rest ... [the back] straight and light, [assists the] motion of the Hips [they in turn affect the knees and feet] ... a Person whose Head is rightly placed, is capable of Standing, Walking, Dancing, or performing any genteel Exercise in a graceful, easy and becoming Manner' (1737, n.p.n).

Among other things, when the head is correctly poised and balanced on the top of the spine, the extrinsic and intrinsic muscles of the larynx are released and the breathing mechanism functions more freely.

Good posture is not a static or fixed position, rather it is an active stillness or a physically quiet attitude. A feeling of lightness and ease of movement and an 'up' uplifted feeling is present when there is balance and poise. The energy level is high and we are ready for action. In poor posture, although it may feel comfortable (the security of habit), there is an imbalance of muscular activity which may, for example, result in back problems. The feeling is one of heaviness and is, in fact, a pulling down.[5]

The body is correctly aligned when a plumb line suspended at the side of a person falls from the top of the head through the centre of the ear, the middle of the point of the shoulder, the highest point on the hipbone, the knees, and just in front of the ankle.[6] Some technical problems of the singer may disappear when the body is efficiently aligned and used well. Axial alignment of the body enables singers to coordinate muscular activity, particularly of the torso, to assist in managing the breath for singing.

A singer must be able to move freely. Performances may require singers to bend, dance, twist, crawl, sit, lie down or stand quietly without movement while singing throughout most of the vocal range. Tension in any part of the body should not be apparent. Veins, arteries and muscles of the neck should not protrude in an alarming way. Shoulders should not rise and fall when breathing. Energy, vitality and dynamic presence are essential. The objective is to balance being relaxed against being alert and ready for action. Total relaxation would put the singer in a prone position and no sound would emerge.

As we saw in Chapter 1, Manuel Garcia II advocated the noble posture. His father suggested this in the early nineteenth century and it was maintained by the members of the Lamperti school. It is vital to establish and maintain this posture for *appoggio* technique. Garcia asked the student to place the hands in a crossed position, palms outward, at the lower back at the bottom of the rib cage (the Garcia position). This brings the pectorals into a proper relationship with the clavicle, sternum and rib cage. The muscles of the lower abdominal wall are then free to move outward on inhalation. It is a practice technique only; how it feels and looks should be monitored until the noble posture becomes habitual.[7]

The following suggestions have been shown to improve a singer's posture, and are here phrased as if to a student:

1. Consider training in Alexander Technique (a re-education of body use), the ideal way to improve posture. It is necessary to be taught by a qualified teacher.
2. Observe yourself in various situations. As you walk by shop windows, discover whether or not you are walking tall or looking slouched, whether you appear to be leaning forward or backward. How do you sit down, and how do you rise from sitting?
3. Make use of mirrors, arranged so that there are full-length side, front and back views. Watch as you talk or sing to the mirror. What happens as you begin? Do you look poised, balanced, and full of energy and joy? Does your reflection suggest presence and charisma? Or, does your head pull down, tilt to one side, pull back? Do you raise your chin or thrust it forward? Do you frown or raise your eyebrows? Does your chest collapse? Do you breathe noisily? Do your shoulders rise and fall? Is your abdomen tight? Are your knees released? Is your weight on one leg only? Would you pay money to watch this person sing?

4. Master the traditional noble posture of the historic international school of singing.[8]
5. Understand that singing is a joyous, exhilarating activity. Paradoxically, it is joyous to communicate even sombre emotions effectively. Let this joy manifest itself inwardly and outwardly. The feeling of lightness resulting from good posture encourages this joyous energetic approach; it is in combination with poise, balance, and enthusiasm. Endeavour to cultivate the 'smiling with the eyes' of Alexander Technique. This releases facial tension which, in turn, releases tension inside the mouth and pharynx. As the muscles release, the soft palate rises, the tongue relaxes and many other positive features are brought into play. How does one 'smile' with the eyes?
   (a) Ideally, by cultivating a sense of 'feeling good' and the sense of lightness mentioned previously.
   (b) But we all have 'off-days' so sometimes we have to pretend.
       (i) Imagine that someone has just given you an enormous amount of money. 'Ah!!' you may say, and the face and eyes light up.
       (ii) Imagine yourself in a pleasant situation that you enjoy being in – it may be relaxing on a sunny beach or in a country meadow – there are endless examples.
   (c) Traditionally, the same effect was achieved by asking students to imagine that they were inhaling the scent of a beautiful, fragrant rose.

An inane grin on the face is not demanded, although some singers do take energy and joy to extremes, resulting in flashing eyes, raised eyebrows, facial contortions of every description, and grotesque mouth openings. These extremes result in muscular tension and distorted sound, not to mention possible embarrassment or hilarity among members of the audience. And, of course, performers may have to sing serious and sad music, but the positive, 'uplifted' feeling has still to be present to allow for dynamic, vibrant, energized sound.

The Energizer or Breathing Mechanism

Bearing in mind that the whole body is involved in singing, we can say that the vocal organ is made up of three main parts: the energizer, the vibrators and the resonators. The energizer consists of the breathing mechanism; the vibrators are the vocal folds; the resonators are the cavities of the vocal tract.

It is almost certainly the case that breathing is one of the most controversial subjects in vocal pedagogy. The following quotations will illustrate some of the diversity of opinion on the subject, and will pave the way for a view of the matter which seems most fully to accord with human anatomy and physiology. Of the five quotations, the first two are perfectly acceptable, while the last three leave much to be desired.

First, the distinguished voice teacher Giovanni Battista Lamperti summed matters up when he said: 'The moment you have energy of breath sufficient for the phrase, re-adjustable for all details and all pitches in the phrase, yet continuous from start to finish, you can sing' (cited by Brown, 1931, p. 64). Secondly, in Luisa Tetrazzini's opinion:

> A singer must be able to rely on his breath, just as he relies upon the solidity of the ground beneath his feet.
> A shaky, uncontrolled breath is like a rickety foundation on which nothing can be built, and until that foundation has been strengthened the would-be singer need expect no satisfactory results (Caruso and Tetrazzini, 1909, p. 11).

Thirdly, Caruso said:

> To take a full breath properly, the chest must be raised at the same moment the abdomen sinks in … The diaphragm is really like a pair of bellows and serves exactly the same purpose (ibid., p. 53).

Fourthly, Pavarotti's contribution to the breathing debate describes the sensation he feels when taking a breath:

> The sensation is very simple. I don't know how you are going to describe this … but you take a breath and stay in the position as when you are in the bathroom … and you keep this position until the phrase is finished. You'll have to explain this, perhaps … with other words … You must push, like a woman in labor, giving birth … it is the same thing. When you push like that, the diaphragm comes up (Hines, 1988, p. 220).

Fifthly, as late as 1996 the singing teacher/pioneer in voice therapy, Oren Brown advocated the expression 'pinching a penny between the buttocks' (1996, p. 22) in order to firm up the lower abdominal area to create a 'firm foundation for the breathing action which takes place above it' (ibid., p. 22). With these examples in mind, let us now approach breathing in what we take to be the most appropriate way.

Because we all do it we are apt to take breathing for granted. But there is breathing to sustain life; breathing for speech; and breathing for a variety of other activities, including singing:

1. Normal quiet breathing without phonation (vocal sound) consists of an inhalatory and expiratory breath cycle of about four seconds; approximately one second for inhalation and three seconds for exhalation.
2. In speech, the breath cycle may frequently need to be lengthened. Inhalation and exhalation will be determined by linguistics, and may be irregular.
3. Breathing for singing is more sophisticated. Sung phrases are often long, and at high pitch levels. It is necessary to make adjustments to the normal breathing cycle over and above those needed for speech. In singing the expiratory phase is prolonged.

Hence specialist training is necessary. A major part of voice teaching concerns the coordination of breath and laryngeal action. Not all teachers of singing agree on how this should be attempted. Some methods of breath management oppose each other, while others ignore the teaching of breath management completely, or place it very low down on the agenda. For example: 'I do not think that breathing is as important as we have been led to believe in traditional singing training' (Kayes, 2000, p. 1). This is very different from Lamperti's view (see above). And Kayes contradicts herself later: 'For good singing, you need airflow (without breath you cannot get vibrations) … In addition you will need a support system for your airflow' (ibid., p. 5). What is the poor student to believe? Perhaps this quotation discovered by Freed may lighten the gloom: 'Abdominal breathing better called "abominable,"' or, 'Lungs are empty sacks into which the air drops like a weight; fill bottom first' (2000, p. 9).

The basic functioning of the breathing apparatus should be understood.[9] The description that follows results from contemporary scientific study and seems to be accepted as the norm. For normal living we inhale and exhale to move oxygen into the lungs and remove carbon dioxide from them.[10]

Most of the important structures of the respiratory apparatus are housed in the trunk or torso. The torso is divided into two cavities (upper and lower) by a dome-shaped partition called the diaphragm. The diaphragm is attached posteriorly to the spine, and anteriorly to the lower borders of the ribs and the lowermost cartilage of the sternum. The upper cavity, the thorax or chest, contains the pulmonary system (heart, respiratory airways and lungs). The lower cavity, which is the abdomen, contains much of the digestive system. Both the thorax and abdomen participate in respiratory function.[11]

The thorax is like a barrel-shaped cage made up of bone and cartilage. At the back of the torso is the vertebral column or backbone consisting of thirty-four irregularly shaped vertebrae. The top seven vertebrae are the cervical (neck), the next lower twelve are the thoracic (chest) vertebrae, and the remaining three lower groups of five, the lumbar, sacral and coccygeal (abdominal). Attached to the thoracic vertebrae are the ribs: twelve flat arch-shaped bones on each side of the body. At the front most of the ribs attach by cartilage to a long flat bone, the sternum (breastbone). Usually the two lowest ribs (floating) are not attached at the front.

At the top of the barrel-shaped cage is the pectoral girdle (shoulder girdle), the front of this being formed by the two clavicles (collar bones). The clavicles run from the upper sternum to the scapulae (shoulder blades) at the back of the thorax and complete the thoracic skeleton.

The vertical walls and spaces between the ribs are made up of muscular and non-muscular tissue. These muscular tissues are especially important in respiratory function, as is the diaphragm, a sheet of muscle which doubles as the convex floor of the thorax and the concave roof of the abdomen.

At the back of the abdominal cavity is the lower portion of the vertebral column with two large irregular shaped coxal bones (hip bones) at the base, which form the pelvic girdle (bony pelvis). The muscles of the abdominal wall are large and powerful and, together with the muscles of the thorax, are important in respiration.[12]

The main features of the pulmonary system are the respiratory tract (airways) and the lungs (organs of respiration). The respiratory tract consists of the cavities of the nose, mouth and throat (upper airways), the larynx functioning as an airway valve. The lower airways are the passages below the larynx.

Immediately below the larynx, in the thoracic cavity, is the trachea (windpipe). The lower end of the trachea divides into two smaller tubes, the left and right bronchi. Each of these bronchi divides many times culminating in very tiny alveolar air sacs where oxygen and carbon dioxide are exchanged during the respiratory process.

The lungs, in which the bronchi and alveoli are housed, are cone-shaped, spongy textured and encased in thin pleural membranes. Both lungs rest on the upper surface of the diaphragm, extend upwards, one on each side, and almost fill the thoracic cavity. The thorax and lungs normally operate together as a unit.[13]

In normal breathing the air is inhaled through the nose or mouth and goes on its journey passing through the larynx and into the trachea. It enters the lungs via the various bronchi. To allow this to happen the rib cage expands laterally (the bucket handle movement) and with an anterior-posterior expansion (the pump handle movement) and the diaphragm contracts and descends, flattening and pulling the elastic lung tissue with it. This increases the dimension of the rib cage resulting in negative pressure in the lungs; therefore the air is let in. The abdomen protrudes to escape the downward pressure of the diaphragm. On exhalation the air flows out of the lungs, into the trachea, passing through the larynx and out through the mouth or nose as the diaphragm ascends and the abdomen muscles contract thus encouraging this upward return.[14] As has been already pointed out, good posture is essential to allow this function to occur efficiently.

It is important to understand that air does not have to be pulled into the lungs; air flows from regions of higher pressure to regions of lower pressure. Breathing is a cyclical activity (inspiration, expiration, inspiration). On inspiration the size of the thorax is enlarged thus decreasing air pressure in the lungs and the air flows in. Conversely, on expiration air flows out of the lungs when the air pressure inside the lungs is greater than atmospheric pressure. This is accomplished at different times by both muscular and non-muscular forces. There is no need for complicated breathing techniques that are based on conscious, even noisy efforts to fill the lungs – the air simply arrives there. As Ingo Titze puts it:

> The voice is *powered* by the air stream moving upwards from the lungs. It brushes past the vocal folds, flaps of tissue that vibrate to produce the pressure waves that our ears pick up as sound (1994, p. 38).

In singing long phrases exhalation has to be delayed by controlling the airflow. This demands coordination of the muscles of the torso. The normal cyclical activity is disturbed when exhalation is delayed. The management of this interruption to enable controlled airflow in singing is defined as *la lotta vocale* (the vocal contest). The upward movement of the diaphragm and the inward movement of the rib cage are delayed during *la lotta vocale*.[15] *Appoggio* technique is a classical approach to breath management; a particular method of managing the breath in which the act of inspiration resists the act of expiration.[16] Sung phonation (sound) can be lengthened by ten to sixteen seconds, followed by silent breath renewal.

In the breath cycle the muscles of the torso, the external intercostal muscles and the intercartilaginous intercostal muscles raise the ribs and the interosseus internal intercostals depress the ribs. Their effective actions depend upon good posture that gives balance and poise, and which also encourages a relatively high sternum (traditionally the noble posture – see Chapter 1). The postural function of the sternum, which has the first two ribs attached to its upper portion, determines the extent of costal (rib cage) expansion and diaphragmatic movement. If the sternum is lowered during the breathing cycle the muscle relationships are different and function less efficiently – hence the usefulness of the study of Alexander Technique, particularly here with regard to posture.

The abdominal muscles of the lower torso, although not organs of respiration, play an important part. Together with the postural muscles of the upper torso, they delay the inward collapse of the ribcage and ascent of the diaphragm, thereby preventing loss of air.

Some Pitfalls to Avoid

In the light of experience derived from observation in a variety of voice studios, and from attendance at numerous vocal workshops and masterclasses, I am able to caution against inadequate instruction in the matter of breath management. This takes various forms, as follows:

1. Incorrect information about physiological functioning which may include:
    (a) Demands made on the musculature, which are impossible to accomplish, such as 'fill the diaphragm with air'.
    (b) 'Raise the diaphragm for high notes, lower the diaphragm for low notes.'
    (c) The instruction, 'breathe from the diaphragm'.
    The examples in (a) to (c) above all incorrectly assume that the diaphragm can be controlled locally; however it must be said in defence of the old adage, that muscles which control the action of the diaphragm can be trained, but directly controlling airflow with the diaphragm is not possible.
    (d) Inaccurate location of the diaphragm, for example, the 'spare tyre' method in which teachers instruct students to lie on the floor with telephone directories balanced on the abdomen, pushing the books up with abdominal muscles in an attempt to strengthen the diaphragm.

(e) The instruction, 'breathe like a baby' – we no longer inhabit babies' bodies.

(f) The statement that because breathing for singing is natural breathing, training in breath management in unnecessary.

(g) The ambiguous statement that breathing for singing is the *same* as breathing for speech – the mechanism is the same, but the use to which it is put differs significantly.

2. Breathing techniques which are based on:

(a) Noisy or conscious efforts to fill the lungs with air – breath is not pulled into the lungs, it arrives there silently.

(b) The 'pear-shape-up' approach or the 'up-and-in' approach, which encourage a too high rib cage and a 'pumping of air' from the abdomen.

(c) The 'pear-shape-down' approach or the 'down-and-out' approach, where pressure is shared between the lower abdomen, buttocks and colon.

(d) Upper chest breathing with a consequent rising of the shoulders and tension in the laryngeal area.

(e) Lower back breathing, which encourages a rounding of the shoulders and collapse of the rib cage.

(f) Extreme relaxation – singing is an athletic activity, singers should not be under-energized, and a balance between excitement and relaxation should be sought.

3. The assumption that all bodies are the same:

(a) Some singers have short rib cages with a greater distance between the lowest ribs and the top of the hipbone, while others have long rib cages and less space between the ribs and hipbone. These dissimilarities in body shape account for the visually different degrees of muscular expansion as between one singer and the next.

(b) Some singers whose posture appears to be slouched may be standing as well as they can given their physical characteristics, while others may give the appearance of standing well but, in fact, have a lowered sternum. Appearances can be deceptive.

4. Subjective imagery that, apart from its use in stimulating the imagination for purposes of interpretation, usually obscures more than it reveals where technique is concerned.

The singing teacher's most important task is systematically to teach freedom and efficiency of function in the singing voice, which can then be put to artistic use. In this connection the achievement of good breath management in order to ensure that the vibrating larynx and airflow are in harmony is crucial to cultivated, stylish performance.

The Vibrators

The vocal folds generate the sound as they oscillate by breaking up the airflow from the lungs into a sequence of air pulsations which is actually a buzz-like noise and which contains a full set of harmonic partials. The ever-changing resonating qualities of the throat and mouth influence the accentuation or suppression of the air vibrations. Similarly, the changes in pitch produced by the vocal folds are altered by the changes in tension of the laryngeal musculature. As we shall see, sophisticated coordination of the intrinsic and extrinsic musculature of the pharynx, larynx and breathing mechanism is essential for excellent phonation.

The larynx is located at the front of the neck, above the trachea and below the hyoid bone.[17] The fingers can be placed at the mid-line of the neck where there is a prominence with a notch. This is the thyroid notch and denotes approximately the anterior attachment of the vocal folds. Above the thyroid notch is the hyoid bone, which as well as having some laryngeal muscles attached supports the root of the tongue and is commonly called the 'tongue bone' (*zungenbein*) in the English and German school of singing. It is sometimes said that the larynx is suspended from the hyoid bone (Zemlin, 1988, p. 101).[18] The larynx has a cartilaginous framework made up of muscles and joints and lined with mucous membranes. Its main function is to act as a valve to protect the lungs from inhaling foreign bodies as in choking; it enables us to cough and aids in defecation and childbirth.

The larynx develops most of its anatomical characteristics by the third month of foetal life. At birth the thyroid cartilage and hyoid bone are attached to each other. The laryngeal skeleton then separates. The slow process of ossification then begins. By two years of age the hyoid bone starts to ossify. During the early twenties the cricoid and thyroid cartilages ossify and in the late thirties the arytenoid cartilages ossify. Most of the entire laryngeal skeleton is ossified by the age of sixty-five. At birth the larynx is high in the neck; it begins to descend as life progresses. As the larynx descends vocal tract length relationships change and average pitch tends to become lower. Vocal fold length in the infant is 6–8 mm. It increases to 9–13 mm in the female adult and to 15–20 mm in the adult male.

The larynx contains the vibrators (vocal folds) that are situated at the top of the trachea. Of the cartilaginous framework the most important is the thyroid cartilage that houses the vocal folds. The vocal folds are situated at the top of the trachea Paget (in Guthrie *et al.*, 1938, p. 447) compared their appearance with that of bugler's lips, which remains an apt description (updated to trumpeter's lips). They consist of long, smoothly rounded muscle tissue that may be lengthened, shortened, tensed or relaxed, adducted or abducted.[19] The vocal folds are joined together anteriorly by the cricoid cartilage and surrounded by it. The cricoid cartilage is wider and thicker posterolaterally, in appearance like a signet ring, and it rocks and tilts on top of the thyroid cartilage. Posteriorly the vocal folds are connected to a pair of cartilages (the arytenoids, supported by the cricoid cartilage) that are activated by muscles which allow these ends of the folds to move together and apart. The space (glottis) between the folds when abducted, as in inspiration, is roughly triangular with the apex at the front. On expiration without phonation the glottis is narrow.

During phonation the edges of the vocal folds are brought together, the air pressure causes them to vibrate, not only completely but in sections, and we have sound. The cricothyroid muscle lengthens, stretches and tenses the folds, thus changing pitch. The pressure beneath the vocal folds (sub-glottal pressure) must be higher than that in the glottis (supra-glottal pressure) to allow phonation. Then an event occurs which has been compared by some, though not all, scientists with the Bernoulli effect. It can be likened to the action in an hourglass. When the slowly moving sand reaches the restriction in the middle of the hourglass it speeds up through the narrow restriction resulting in a lowering of pressure. In the vocal mechanism this narrowing point is the glottis. When air moves from the lungs and is forced through this smaller space, the lowered pressure has a suction effect. The vocal folds are adducted in this suction. A chain of actions, such as coordinated muscle activity, follows which assists in the maintaining of vocal fold vibration. On closure of the vocal folds sub-glottal air pressure causes the abduction of the folds and so the cycle continues.[20]

The puff of pressurized air released through the mouth is one complete vocal vibration cycle. The frequency of these puffs (the number emitted per second) determines the frequency of the sound. For example, 440 puffs of air will sound the pitch A4. The sound becomes amplified by the pharyngeal and oral cavity.

The pharynx, as resonator, consists of an irregularly shaped flexible tube, closed at one end, the beginning opening being the nose and mouth. There is some controversy as to whether the nasal cavities resonate or not. The nature of their physical structure with their complex folds suggests there is little space for resonation to take place. Of great importance for the singer are the mucous membranes which line the whole vocal tract and act as lubricants to encourage easy flowing movement in the moveable parts of the tract, particularly the vocal folds.[21]

Vocal Science

I shall not deal with acoustical science in general, but only with that discipline as it applies specifically to the training of the singing voice.[22]

The vocal tract acts as a flexible resonator that converts the sound generated by the vocal folds. It is shaped acoustically according to vocal tract configuration promoted by the articulators: tongue, lips, mouth, jaw, velum and pharynx.

Some sounds with particular frequencies pass through the vocal tract resonator more easily resulting in high amplitude. These resonances are called formants and the resonance frequencies, which are peaks that determine the shape of the acoustic spectrum (spectral envelope) of a vowel, are called formant frequencies. Tones, which have frequencies in between these formant frequencies, have less amplitude.

Formants are extremely important in the production of vocal sound. They determine the quality of vowels and make a major contribution to the individual timbre of the voice. There are four or five important formants in the vocal tract. The two lowest formants govern most of the vocal colour and the third, fourth, and fifth are more indicative of individual voice timbre.

The length of the vocal tract affects all formant frequencies. In the adult male the formant frequencies occur at 500, 1500, 2500 ... Hz. In a child they are apparent at about 40 per cent higher and in the adult female about 15 per cent higher.

How is it that we can hear a singer above an orchestra? The answer lies in another aspect of formant frequency that usually appears in resonant singing regardless of the vowel. Vennard called this phenomenon the '2800 factor' (1967, p. 128). He went on to suggest that this ringing quality of the sound results when the resonators are in tune with the vibrators. In practice this technique is sometimes described as tracking the laryngeally produced vowel by the resonator tube (see Chapter 4 below).

> It is now well established that a sound that strikes the listening ear as aesthetically pleasing (in 'classical' singing) is the result of verifiable acoustic and physiologic conditions. Precisely, it is the relationships, adjusted for vowel definition, among the fundamental frequency and the first, second, and third (and at times the fourth and fifth) formants that determine the listener's perception of resonance and the singer's proprioceptive response to the sounds he is making. It is the acoustic energy ... exhibited in the 2500–3300 Hz region regardless of the vowel being defined, that sets the resonant singing voice apart from normal speech. This relationship among the levels of acoustic energy (formants) determines the unique beauty of the singing instrument. It explains the traditional "resonance" of the professional singing voice (Miller, 1993, p. 74).

It is my contention, justified from my experience in schools, voice studios, workshops and master classes, that there are many methods of training singers to achieve this resonance which are hazardous. The method of many teachers seems to be 'hit and miss', especially in the case of those whose pedagogical armoury is replete with subjective imagery. More will be said of this in the next chapter. The case for at least basic scientific knowledge of the singing voice is unanswerable. Titze offers here:

> Quantifying the characteristics of an ideal voice should become possible in the sound studio of the future, with fibreoptic viewing systems that can peer deep into the working larynx, synthesizers that can mimic voices and sound frequency analyzers that can pinpoint their make-up. Such technology will help dispel some of the mystery and metaphysics that has plagued singers – and their teachers – for so many years (1995, p. 42).

The Use of Scientific Instrumentation in Singing Studios and Voice Clinics

Although throughout history singing teachers have relied on external observation and skilful listening, which in many cases have produced excellent results, judgements about the singing voice have have been subjective. The teacher has had to rely on memory to assess a student's progress. As we have already seen in this study there has been much controversy over teaching methods and what constitutes beautiful sound production, what is 'good' and what is 'bad'. Instrumentation which can be used for objective assessment of the voice is now available. Much of it can be used in the singing teacher's studio and it certainly should be made available to teachers in conservatories. Teachers and students can then accurately assess vocal performance and progress and be made aware of technical singing difficulties as yet undiscovered. Of course such technology will never substitute for the excellent voice teacher. Even if teachers are not able to use the instrumentation regularly, they should at least be aware of it. Some of this technology can be used only by a medical practitioner but, even here in the case of certain students it may highlight a problem not resolved by the traditional method of teaching.

Many teachers have available audio equipment for recording their students – the better the quality, the more accurate the reproduction of the sound. Other useful equipment may include: a spectrum analyzer; a computerized speech/singing programme; systems that measure airflow and air pressure; a nasometer; an electroglottograph (EGG); oscilloscope, a sound level meter; and a spirometer. Some of these will be elaborated upon below. Cassette recorders can be modified reasonably simply to provide Aural Real-Time feedback, in which singers are able to hear their voices as they sing.[23] For instant visual feedback more and more teachers are adding to the homely mirror, the video recorder, which both teacher and student can view together, linking the visual with the aural in the playback and thereby analyzing the performance as a whole.

Phonatory Ability

Maximum phonation time can be measured easily in the studio with a stopwatch, the student vocalizing on a vowel in medium range. Physiological frequency range of phonation (lowest and highest pitches), musical frequency range of phonation (lowest and highest musically acceptable notes), and limits of vocal registers can be measured by recording with a good quality tape recorder, and then formally and spectrally analyzed by a computer programme. This allows singing students to link ear with eye analysis. If a computer is unavailable in the studio then the recording can be sent elsewhere for analysis. Ingo Titze is enthusiastic about analytical technology:

> Vocologists are encouraged to become familiar with a sound spectrograph. It is an important tool for analysis that can be used not only for research but also for instantaneous biofeedback in vocal training and therapy (1994, p. 165).

Acoustic Analysis

The ear is still the best acoustic analyzer, but since it cannot quantify, accurate explanations are extremely difficult without the visual aid of a spectrograph. The spectrograph is probably the most used machine in voice analysis. It will measure, among other things: onset and release of sound, resonance balancing (the historic *chiaroscura* timbre), vowel tracking, vowel modification, presence or absence of *legato*, vocal stability, vibrato, accuracy of pitch, and formants (particularly the singer's formant).[24] Spectral analysis allows singers to 'see' the voice as well as to 'feel' and 'hear' it. It goes without saying that a series of spectrograms will be a positive aid for the teacher in monitoring the singer's progress. Computer programmes are now available so that this recording can be undertaken in the teacher's studio. Singers are then able to work on their technique alongside the teacher, with the aid of the programme.[25] The spectrograph provides immediate feedback, valuable because the voice can be heard, acoustically analyzed and singers can watch themselves singing at the same time. It is extremely useful for young potentially professional singers in particular to have constant feedback in order to refine their singing and, some would say, expedite their technical progress. Of course, the teacher and student will require the necessary competence in setting up the programme, working with it, and reading it. Working with one's own voice can be helpful when first learning how to use the spectrogram.

The Vowel Chart and Nasometer

The Vowel Chart measures the resonance in the singing voice which can then be compared with the spoken voice. The nasometer measures the amount of nasality in the singing tone. This is particularly useful when rehearsing French texts.

The Electroglottograph (EGG)

The electroglottograph monitors the efficiency of the closure of the vocal folds by passing a high frequency electric current between electrodes fastened externally at laryngeal level. It is not invasive or painful.

Psychoacoustic Evaluation

Psychoacoustic evaluation, which describes how we perceive sound and acoustics, could be of help in adjudication where so many different subjective opinions, taste, personalities and biases are prevalent.[26] This might possibly lead to improvement in the assessment of the singer. Sataloff has this to say:

> Many researchers have tried to quantify and standardize psychoacoustic evaluation of the voice. Unfortunately, even definitions of such basic terms as hoarseness and breathiness are still controversial. Standardization of psychoacoustic evaluation protocols and inter-pretation does not exist ... Nevertheless, recognizing that the human ear and brain are still our best tools, we try to optimize the validity and usefulness of our psychoacoustic obser-vations (1997, p. 238).

Laryngeal Examination

Laryngeal examination, undertaken by a medical doctor can be made in various ways too numerous to list in full. There is indirect laryngoscopy where the mirror or laryngeal telescope is used, stroboscopic examination, rigid endoscopy, the use of an operating microscope plus camera, magnifying laryngeal mirrors, and more sophisticated systems of fibreoptic strobovideolaryngoscopy. Video equipment provides a permanent record, useful for reassessment and discussions with other professionals, not least, the singer and teacher. When the tapes are played back, the doctor, student and teacher are able to watch the position of the palate, pharynx, tongue base, vocal folds and other parts of the larynx as the singer speaks and sings. Sometimes singers will instinctively adjust the vocal mechanism healthily as they are made aware of a functional problem. In some colleges in North America it is mandatory for beginning students to have this examination before their course of singing study begins so that it can be compared with future examinations, in order to discover whether problems have been solved or new ones created. This is also important in cases of litigation made against the teacher by the student. It is also extremely interesting to watch whatever the situation. All of these measures can be useful to singing teachers, particularly if they are attempting to deal with a problem of technique that may be the result of a specific physical problem.

Aerodynamic Measures

Aerodynamic tests reveal lung capacity. Small lung capacity may suggest that aerobic exercise is necessary. Worsening of lung capacity during singing may indicate asthma and, following medical evaluation, remedial technical measures should then be taken in singing lessons to prevent voice abuse. Airflow rate testing across the vocal folds will show the extent of glottal efficiency, for example, if the singer has an excessive breathy or pressed phonation. Airflow can also be measured by a spirometer, a pneumotachograph, or a respitrace. The respitrace tracks a singer's inhalation, exhalation and breath management. It shows the movement of the abdominal and chest walls during inhalation and exhalation. Thus the machine is invaluable in appraising breathing techniques. A qualified physician will undertake these tests.

Laryngeal Electromyography (EMG)

This process is also administered by a medical practitioner as it is an invasive technique. Laryngeal electromyography (continuous recording of the electrical activity of a muscle by means of electrodes inserted into the muscle fibres displayed on an oscilloscope) is sometimes used for diagnosis of complex laryngeal disorders.

Studio Application

As stated above, scientific analysis is not a substitute for the competent voice teacher, but is an extra tool of which the teacher may take advantage. All of the instruments working together provide extra insight to the information usually acquired in the teacher's studio. It is quite amazing how the eye reveals details not heard. As shall be enlarged upon in the next chapter, singers learn in three ways: by hearing, seeing and feeling. Singers hear and listen to their teachers and feel the sensations of correct technique, but to see internal detail of their instrument they need to use scientific apparatus. When the day comes for peer review and standardization of the profession, as in other related professions, more than personal opinion is going to be needed when attempting to quantify beautiful, healthy singing. Objective voice analysis may be helpful here, and much appreciated by those confident in their own singing and teaching ability. Hence the great need for teachers to absorb this material and make use of it when and wherever possible.

Vocal Health and Hygiene

General Health Care

On the basis of scientific knowledge acquired the competent singing teacher will be able to offer vocal health guidance to students along the following lines.[27]

In the first place it may be of help to state the obvious, namely, that the singer's instrument is not on all fours with any other musical instrument. Singers' instruments are personally unique; they are with them wherever they are. Unlike an orchestral instrument they cannot be packed safely away at the end of the day, or before a holiday. Orchestral instrumentalists can repair, exchange, and upgrade their instruments. Not so the singer. Voices can never be exchanged or upgraded, hence the need for specific care. They have to function in heat or cold, come rain or shine, with toothache or a bad back, after arguments and quarrels, during career pressures – the list is endless. Singers, and all who deal specifically with voices need constructive information about vocal function, health and hygiene.

As noted earlier, good posture is of fundamental importance, for posture imbalance sets up tensions. Singers would do well to ask themselves whether they have any of these bad habits: pulling the head back and down; pulling the back in; locking the knees; incorrect weight balance (standing with weight on one leg only); leaning forward, backward; throwing the head back while speaking or singing; tightening the abdominal muscles; wearing half-specs which encourage a looking up and over, thus altering head and neck configuration?

Exercise for flexibility and mobility is important for long-term health, benefiting the muscles for breathing, reducing areas of tension, encouraging vocal longevity and helping to counteract some of the effects of ageing on the skeletal framework.

Physical activities for the singer that produce flexibility and suppleness are excellent, and preferable to those that encourage the development of specific muscles as in weight-lifting and isometrics.[28] Effective and efficient use of the singing voice is possible into old age provided that supple rib-cage movement can be maintained to aid respiration, that there is good head and neck alignment, and that one sings regularly – at least in the daily practice of warm-up exercises. Regular, purposeful, brisk walking is excellent exercise (did you ever meet a happy jogger?). Mooching around shopping centres and malls does not count! Walking improves breathing, strengthens muscle and bone, improves stamina and is a low impact form of aerobics. Swimming is also very good for improving respiration, is completely impact free and therefore may be more suitable for the older or osteo-poritic person. It is advisable to check with a medical practitioner before beginning an intensive exercise programme.

As well as exercise, adequate, regular rest is essential. Every opportunity should be taken of ensuring sufficient, undisturbed sleep at night (eight hours) and refreshing siestas during the day. Use nose-breathing when at rest. A healthy person should not require sleeping pills. Tiredness resulting from over-full days and long rehearsals is vocally damaging – if the body is tired then the voice is tired.

An ideal weight with a regular, adequate balanced diet should be maintained. There is a vast quantity of published advice available. An excess of dairy products, chips, fried food, chocolate, hot and spicy foods, tomatoes, peanuts, concentrated fruit juices, excessively hot or cold food or drink should be avoided. It should be remembered that dairy products and chocolate induce thicker mucous; spicy food aggravates the mucous membranes of the larynx; tomatoes and 100 per cent fruit juices are too acid; peanuts may precipitate a tickling cough. It is well to avoid eating late at night, particularly if one has a tendency to gastric reflux – the condition in which gastric stomach acid is regurgitated during lying down and sleep, and coats the laryngeal mucosa causing a burning irritation. Food should be eaten and chewed slowly. If, for whatever reason, a singer decides to abstain from particular foods it is essential that sufficient vitamins and minerals be obtained from other sources. Good oral and dental hygiene is important too.

Sufficient hydration should be monitored by: drinking 1.5–2.0 litres of water every day, cutting down on caffeine-loaded tea, coffee and colas, sipping little and often. Water should be drunk whenever food is eaten, and be available at all times. Sufficient fluid intake ensures adequate internal irrigation. Fluid intake is not delivered directly to the vocal folds but rather the internal irrigation system is given a larger reservoir of fluids to deal with.

It is imperative that singers learn how to handle stress. Stress may be physical or psychological or a combination of both. It may result in, among other things: vocal problems, sleeplessness, depression, anxiety or panic attacks. There may be personal or family stress, financial or employment difficulties and/or physical illness. Emotional stress may create excess muscle tensions that may eventually encourage voice disorders. Measures should be taken to relieve worries and problems. It is well to find time each day, no matter how brief, to relax, maybe through different activities or hobbies. The singer/teacher must be objective and set realistic goals, learning to say 'No' and develop coping strategies for overload situations. There are many ways to help deal with stress: physical exercise, meditation, or prayer; training in stress management; relaxation methods, Alexander Technique, Feldencrais method, Autogenics, yoga and self-hypnosis, remembering that these skills must be learnt from a competent teacher.

Smoking is taboo. Cigarettes, cigar and pipe smoking dry the vocal tract. The tars and irritants in smoke often cause redness and oedema (swelling) of the mucosal linings of the air passages. Both smoke and heat from cigarettes are dangerous. The puff from a cigarette that comes in at the lips has, it is said, been measured as being above 100 degrees Celsius (above the boiling point of water), therefore burning is inevitable. Smoking can cause shortness of breath, coughing, throat-clearing, lowering of voice pitch and decrease in voice loudness, and as universal medical research shows has repercussions in many other directions. Secondary smoke also claims victims.

The dangers of recreational drugs such as cocaine, marijuana and heroin, in their various forms and strengths, are legion and will not be dealt with here. Suffice it to say, they should be avoided at all costs.

Alcohol can be damaging to the vocal tract; red wine and spirits are the biggest culprits. How excessive alcohol intake has to be before it affects perception and coordination may be a moot point, but where fine-tuning of the vocal mechanism in performance is vital, the pre-performance drink is better omitted. Certainly alcohol affects mucous production, and may result in a husky or low-pitched voice. A combination of alcohol, cigarette smoke (including that of other people) and animated conversation carried on above loud background noise, for example at a pre- or post-performance party, spells vocal suicide.

Environmental Hazards

How are we to deal with what are in the main, uncontrollable environmental conditions? Indeed, what are those conditions?

In the atmosphere we find excessive pollution and dehydrating agents: pollens, dusts, moulds, pets, plants, chalk, felt-tip pen fumes, carpets, household dust, mites and their droppings, stage and backstage dust – dusty curtains, backstage canvasses, and dirty dressing rooms. Outside dust is blown into the home or office from passing cars, subways, busy streets, construction projects, power mowers and leaf blowers. There is smoke: from fireplaces and barbeques and cigarettes (as stated above secondary smoke is hazardous); fog; sprays – hair, perfume, cleaning, and paint – to mention just a few; air-conditioning; vehicle exhaust fumes; industrial emissions; paint fumes from home decorating; chlorine and some solvent-based glues. We find a hot, dry atmosphere caused by central heating and/or air-conditioning in geographical regions where the relative humidity is low, and in air-travel where the relative humidity is even lower, about 5–10 per cent (a healthy humidity level is around 30–50 per cent).

What can be done about all this? We can dampen down dusty areas where possible. The various inhaled fumes mentioned above cause the mucous membranes, particularly of the nose and throat, to become dry or inflamed, so we should drink lots of non-caffeine or non-alcoholic drinks – approximately 2.0 litres each day – urine should be almost the colour of tap water. The eminent American otolaryngologist and promoter of inter-disciplinary education among physicians and voice teachers, Van L. Lawrence, had a favourite maxim, 'The catch phrase is, of course, "pee pale." … Add to that catch phrase another one from Dr Leon Thurman in Minneapolis: "sing wet" and you should be right on' (1991, p. 154). It is advisable to minimize talking in aircraft, to hydrate well before and during flights, and to avoid iced drinks, alcohol, and salted nuts (salt dehydrates). A moist environment in hotel rooms can be achieved by running hot water in the shower. In the home or work environment, since central heating and air-conditioning dries out mucous membranes, the air should be humidified, if possible, by placing bowls of water by radiators, and well-watered houseplants may be introduced. Adequate ventilation is important. Large-scale statistical research shows no appreciable difference in the number of colds caught by those who sleep with windows open as opposed to those who sleep with them closed. Medical opinion is more inclined to suggest that better hygiene would reduce the number of colds, as colds are said to be contagious. Steam inhalers are useful but must be kept meticulously clean to avoid dangers of infection.

All around us is background noise: office equipment, factory machinery, aircraft (the average in-flight noise level is approximately 90–95 decibels – a very noisy environment, in which we have to raise our voices to be understood), buses, railway carriage noise, restaurants, stadiums, telephones, noisy classrooms and public places. We tend to compete with this noise by raising pitch, shouting and yelling. We often speak for long periods in such noisy conditions as are found, for example, in classroom activities, swimming pools, pubs, clubs, discos, parties, television, or when listening to a Walkman at a volume usually too high for us to speak at a comfortable level (loss of hearing will not be commented on in this book). This all leads to vocal strain.

What can we do under these conditions? The following guidelines might be offered to a student.

Try to remove or reduce unnecessary noise when and wherever possible. Recognize the relationship between healthy singing and the appropriate use of the speaking voice – it is often the speaking voice that causes the problem for singers. Use controlled, precise delivery when you speak. Face people or come closer to them – people often lip-read when they listen. Use volume and clarity to match the distance between you and the listener. Try to bring individuals or groups to you, or move closer to them and learn vocal projection techniques rather than calling out. Avoid prolonged talking out of doors – for example yelling at a football match. Find non-vocal ways, to train/discipline pets and children. Don't fight noise and acoustics, use visual hand signals if teaching large numbers of students – stamp foot, pound piano, gesture, raise hand, clap, ring a bell, whistle, blow a horn. Wait until students, audience, or singers are quiet and attentive before speaking or singing.

Choirs are among the noisiest of environments. Enthusiastic choral directors often get singers to sing much more loudly than they would sing in their own living rooms at home. Young professional leaders of sections often feel that it is part of their responsibility to lead the section by singing louder than the section itself. At the other end of the spectrum some choral directors, in an effort to have all the voices blending, demand under-energized sound which, too, can be vocally damaging. Sataloff advises that you should

> sing as if you were giving a voice lesson to the person standing on either side of you, and as if there is a microphone immediately in front of you that is recording your choral singing for your voice teacher (hearsay).

The choral sound will improve too.

We tend to speak or sing more loudly in the presence of background noise. This is the so-called 'Lombard Effect'. When singing in choirs, singers often cannot hear their own voice and therefore sing louder. On such occasions the memory of our singing teacher's disapproving look may act as a dissuasive. It is not necessary to be able to hear your own voice above that of your neighbour when singing in the choir. At parties we shout. Under these circumstances we are rarely aware of good vocal technique. After an evening of performing, when tired, such abuse can wreak havoc on a voice. Singers, who perform regularly, tend to be more aware of post-performance voice conservation than others. However all singers should protect their voice at all times, 'as if the greatest opportunity were to come unexpectedly tomorrow' (Sataloff, hearsay).

If singers are constantly aware of their atmospheric, auditory and vocal environments, it will eventually become second nature to take precautionary protective measures. Their reward will be the minimizing or avoidance of many actual or potential vocal problems.

Ailments, Medications, and Early Warning Signs

Singers have a tendency when under pressure of performance or feeling under the weather to turn to medication for assistance.[29] For most other careers and professions, the use of medication does not pose the same problems as it does for the singer. Singing involves the use of the whole body, which must be in tip-top condition both physically and mentally. Drugs act by enhancing, inhibiting, or imitating a normal function. Virtually all medications can cause many unwanted effects in the body, particularly the larynx. Taking a drug for one specific purpose does not mean that its activity will be restricted to that purpose only. Medications are dispersed throughout the whole body and can have surprising effects. For example, if certain antihistamines are taken to dry up a runny cold, some individuals may find that although they have some relief from the cold, they also have blurred vision or a dry mouth and throat and feel sleepy – conditions which singers can well do without. Vocal problems are sometimes found to be extremely puzzling and to this end vocal pharmacology, with particular reference to singers and singing students, has been introduced as a discipline at Drew University in the United States.[30]

Problems with the voice may be organic or functional; although very many are caused by hyperfunction and/or abuse. Here follows a list of the most common pathologies: Laryngitis – a reddening and oedema of the larynx; Reineke's oedema – oedema in Reinike's space of the larynx; vocal fold polyps; contact ulcers; tumours, and recurrent laryngeal nerve paralysis. Accidents and disease apart, functional disorders are nearly always generated by vocal abuse.

1. *Common infections*   Among these are upper respiratory tract infection without laryngitis and laryngitis without serious damage.

The main concern for the singer is to dry up the nasal drainage. As mentioned earlier in the chapter singers may get relief from antihistamines but the vocal folds must be kept moist in order to function easily. Singers also frequently use decongestants. These shrink the swollen mucous membranes of the vocal tract which may have lowered the pitch of the voice and/or made it sound hoarse or breathy, and may offer some advantage when used appropriately and in conjunction with periods of vocal rest. However, decongestants are related chemically to adrenaline and, therefore, can produce increased heart rate and blood pressure, possibly a slight tremor in the voice, hyper-irritability, and insomnia.

Throat lozenges and sprays have their dangers too. These, as with other OTC (over the counter) drugs are designed to alleviate symptoms and not effect cures, and may promote a false sense of security, by masking the pain and irritation and causing the singer to think that less damage is being done to the vocal tract than actually is. The singer may then continue to perform when vocal rest might be more appropriate. OTC drugs may also produce 'rebound' phenomena – the return of the original problem with more ferocity. Lozenges can be used to encourage secretions in the mouth, but the sugar content coats the teeth, causing caries, and the vocal folds become covered with thick, sticky goo, hardly conducive to singing. Other ingredients such as menthol, eucalyptus, camphor, and peppermint may give an immediate feeling of 'cooling', but can cause excessive thick mucous production later.

Local anaesthetics included in some products to numb pain may also mask vocal damage as the singer sings. Antibiotics commonly used to treat bacterial infection are often wantonly prescribed. The side effects, which may affect the voice, include: allergies, dryness, metallic taste in the mouth, and secondary yeast infection.

Expectorants increase secretions, and are usually taken to 'soften' a cough by providing a surface bathing of the respiratory linings. Gargling has yet to be proved to be effective. Cough suppressant mixtures often include agents that have a secondary drying effect on the vocal tract secretions, especially those mixtures containing codeine; they may also contain antihistamines. Aspirin is best avoided because it may cause a slight haemorrhage of small blood vessels on vocal folds suffering from excessive use or abuse, which can be devastating for the singer. Instead, pain relievers of the paracetamol family are preferable.

Some singers regularly take large amount of vitamin C (ascorbic acid) in an endeavour to fight off colds and 'flu, and this too may have, among other side-effects in different parts of the body, a dehydrating effect on the vocal folds. Steroid medication for singers is controversial. It may well work for a short-term emergency, reducing inflammation in acute inflammatory laryngitis, but because side effects, in the main, are uncommon, there is a tendency for singers to overuse the treatment. If used for any length of time there is a danger of change in voice quality, pitch and function.

The following are among the suggestions that might be made to a student with a common infection:

Avoid throat clearing where possible – the folds are brought together violently, with the risk of damage. Instead sip water, swallow silently or 'huff' a voiceless, silent cough. Use steam inhalation to thin mucous. The steam delivers moisture and warmth to the vocal folds and is often beneficial. However the temptation to add menthol or similar to the water should be avoided as it may be an irritant to the inflamed pharynx, larynx and nasal passages. Sing mucous off the vocal folds by singing arpeggios, *glissandi*, rapid onsets, or trills. Try a 'sniff-swallow' – a sudden exaggerated sniff followed by swallowing. Reduce where possible irritants in the environment. Avoid hurried eating, or the inhalation of foreign material, which may cause coughing (powdered sugar and nuts are notoriously bad). Conserve the voice, avoid unnecessary talk and drink plenty of water in order to keep the vocal tract, and the body as a whole, well hydrated. Some mucolytic agents work well to increase or thin upper respiratory secretions including 'post-nasal drip'.

If a cough lingers then medical advice should be sought. Laryngitis very often requires voice rest – relative, but not always absolute silence (medical opinion varies). Cleveland suggests that 'Voice rest can be appropriate for assistance in diagnosis and treatment of several voice problems' (2000, p. 65). Absolute rest is better, usually for no longer than two weeks. For those who find it easier not to speak at all, rather than speaking infrequently and softly – have a notepad and pencil handy to write down important messages rather than speak. Whispering should be avoided. The mechanism of the vocal folds is used differently in whispering, which may be a more traumatic vocal activity than speaking softly.

In addition there are infections in the lower respiratory tract and elsewhere. Pulmonary infections are disruptive to the voice and demand professional medical attention. Infections such as gastro-enteritis may affect the voice by, in the first instance, interfering with the control of the breathing mechanism. Anti-spasmodic agents are well known for their ability to reduce pain and spasms, particularly those of the gastro-intestinal tract, but there is a likelihood of dehydration of the vocal folds as a side effect.

Finally there is pharyngitis. This produces a sore throat and is usually associated with tonsillitis. Pharyngitis

> is a common complaint with a very diverse differential diagnosis. Despite the many benign and easily treatable causes, it can be a sign of underlying disease that, if missed, can have serious consequences … (Abaza and Sataloff, 1999, p. 37.)

2. *Allergies of various types excluding asthma*   These common conditions do not bypass the singing population. They require specialist medical help and will not be discussed here.

3. *Gastro-oesophageal laryngitis*   Gastro-oesophageal (reflux laryngitis) may have, amongst its symptoms, bad breath, a bitter taste in the mouth, hoarseness, frequent coughing or throat-clearing on wakening in the morning, and vocal warm-up time may be prolonged. There may be the feeling of a lump in the throat, recurring tracheitis or tracheo bronchitis, and heartburn (there is currently debate about heartburn being a symptom). Any or all of these symptoms may be present. Reflux is common among singers and is aggravated by stress and eating late at night after performance. Acid reflux can affect the vocal folds, particularly on lying down at bedtime. It may be useful to elevate the head of the bed, maybe on bricks (having high pillows is not effective because of movement of the pillows during sleep). It is beneficial to avoid eating for three or four hours before going to bed. For persistent reflux appropriate medicines or antacids should be prescribed.

4. *Body injuries*   Injuries such as whiplash, head trauma, nasal fractures, chest and abdominal injuries or injuries to the lower or upper extremities may affect the voice by, among other things, disturbance of postural alignment, altering the efficiency of the abdominal muscles needed for breath control, and introducing tension. Pain will distract the singer. As aspirin is relatively inexpensive it is very popular with singers for reducing pain and inflammation, but as mentioned previously it is also an anti-coagulant and should be discarded in favour of the paracetamol family, even though the latter may not have the same anti-inflammatory effect.

5. *Surgery*   Laryngeal surgery may be performed endoscopically or externally. Microsurgery of the voice suggests delicate vocal fold surgery. Most vocal surgery can be accomplished endoscopically, which is less traumatic for the patient. Should general anaesthesia be required then the anaesthesist must be chosen carefully. Careful and skilful intubation, using the smallest possible tube, is most important to avoid damage to the vocal folds. Laryngologists suggest that singers should write

'SINGER' on adhesive tape and stick it upside down on their forehead by way of alerting the anaesthetist. The advisability of voice rest following surgery is sometimes disputed, but Sataloff advises:

> Although some vocal fold contact will occur inevitably because of swallowing and coughing, more (avoidable) contact occurs during speech. ... Consequently, the author recommends voice rest routinely after surgery, unless the vibratory margin mucosa has been left in tact (1997, p. 641).

Following surgery on other parts of the body it is anecdotally advised that quite a number of the physical exercise 'sit-ups' should be achieved before singing is resumed. Opinions differ about this.

6. *Psychological and psychiatric problems*　Stress, which may be physical or psychological, or both, invades most professions. There are special implications for the singer – not least, stage fright. Beta-blockers prescribed for pre-performance anxiety, it is reported, lessen the anxiety and increase saliva production which help combat the upper respiratory dryness associated with fear.[31] Normally prescribed for those with heart problems, beta-blockers may have voice-related side effects such as throat spasms or sudden loss of voice. Tranquillizers may relax the laryngeal muscles and result in, among other things, off-key singing. They certainly take the 'edge' off performance. If in distress it is important to seek professional help.[32]

7. *Not-to-be-ignored warning signs*　These include increased effort necessary in order to sing; the voice tires easily; pushing is necessary in order to 'get the sound out'; singing piano is difficult; straining to reach high notes; difficulty in singing *legato* from one pitch to another; the voice 'breaks' or 'creaks at the bottom of the range or 'squeaks' at the top; an inability to prolong notes and sustain phrases; loss of tone 'focus'; difficulty in beginning notes smoothly; sudden stops in the voice; sudden unexpected excursions of pitch upwards; changes in pitch or volume; deepening of the voice; inability to raise the voice; reduction in pitch or range; changes in the body; pain in the laryngeal area; dryness in the mouth; irritation, burning or scratchiness in the throat; a 'lump in the throat' feeling; increased need to clear the throat; sore throat during or after singing or talking; tiring of the breathing mechanism; changes in voice quality; hoarseness; increased breathiness; a 'quivery' quality to the sound; uncontrollable or irregular vibrato.

If vocal problems persist longer than three weeks it is important to make contact with a medical practitioner.[33]

'Don't take medicine without consulting your doctor' is timely advice and should be adhered to wherever possible. The wrong medicine, or even the right medicine taken incorrectly, can be disastrous for singers and may even make an illness worse. Some OTC medications can be more powerful than a doctor's prescription. It is important to stress that medications should not be used to mask symptoms that are the result of vocal misuse or abuse. In considering the use of medications the phar-macological properties of the drug should be given attention, as well as the nature of the condition itself and the circumstances of the singer. It goes without saying that it is important to check dates of expiration, to keep medicines in their properly labelled containers, never to share medications with a friend or colleague, and always to complete the prescribed courses of treatment.[34]

Having shown in general terms how historical, psychological, ethical and scien-tific considerations impinge upon vocal pedagogy we are now in a position to discuss the questions of vocal technique, performance and evaluation.

Notes

1   See further, Zemlin, Willard R. (1988), *Speech and Hearing Science*, Englewood Cliffs, NJ: Prentice Hall.
2   See further, Chapter 2 above.
3   See further, Alcantara, Pedro de (1997), *Indirect Procedures: A Musician's Guide to the Alexander Technique*, Oxford: Clarendon Press.
4   Nivelon, F. (1737), *The Rudiments of Genteel Behaviour*, London, cited by Joan Wildblood (1965), *The Polite World*, Oxford: Oxford University Press.
5   See further, Bosanquet, R. Caroline (1987), 'The Alexander principle and its importance to music education', *British Journal of Music Education* **4** (3), 229–42; Rosenthal, Eleanor (1989), 'The Alexander Technique: what it is and how it works', *American Music Teacher*, **39** (2), October/November, 24–7, 57, and Boyd, James (2001), 'Embracing Alexander', *Communicating Voice*, **1** (3), Errata, n.p.n.
6   See Appendix 4, Illustration 1.
7   See further, Macdonald, Glynn (1995), 'Alexander Technique and the singing voice', *Performing Arts Medicine News*, **3** (2), Summer, 26–8.
8   See further, Chapter 1 above and Chapter 4 below.
9   Anatomical and physiological information has been gleaned from various sources including: Perkins, William H., and Raymond D. Kent (1968), *Functional Anatomy of Speech, Language and Hearing*, Austin: Pro-Ed; Minifie, Fred D., Thomas J. Hixon, and Frederick Williams (1973) (eds), *Normal Aspects of Speech, Hearing, and Language*, Englewood Cliffs, NJ: Prentice-Hall; Brodnitz, Friedrich S. (1988), *Keep Your Voice Healthy*, Boston: College-Hill; Zemlin, Willard R. (1988), *Speech and Hearing Science*, Englewood Cliffs, NJ: Prentice Hall; Sataloff, Robert T. (ed.), (1997), *Professional Voice: The Science and Art of Clinical Care*, San Diego: Singular.
10   See further, Sundberg, Johan (2001), 'Consistency of inhalatory breathing patterns in professional operatic singers', *Journal of Voice*, **4** (3), September, 373–83.
11   See Appendix 4, Illustration 2.
12   See Appendix 4, Illustrations 3 and 4.
13   See Appendix 4, Illustration 5.
14   See Appendix 4, Illustrations 6 and 7.
15   See further, Chapter 1 above and Chapter 4 below.
16   For information about *appoggio* technique, see Chapter 4 below.
17   See Appendix 4, Illustration 8.
18   See Appendix 4, Illustration 9.

19   See Appendix 4, Illustration 10.

20   See Appendix 4, Illustration 11.

21   See Appendix 4, Illustration 8. See further the section on vocal health and hygiene, below.

22   See further, Borden, Gloria J., and Katherine S. Harris (1984), *Speech Science Primer*, Baltimore: Williams & Wilkins; Benade, Arthur H. (1990), *Fundamentals of Musical Acoustics,* 2nd rev. edn, New York: Dover; Sundberg, Johann (1991), *The Science of Musical Sounds*, San Diego: Academic Press; Kent, Ray D., and Charles Read (1992), *The Acoustic Analysis of Speech*, San Diego: Singular; Fujimura, Osamu and Minoru Hirano (1995), *Vocal Fold Physiology*, San Diego: Singular; Howard, David M. and James Angus (1996), *Acoustics and Psychoacoustics*, Oxford: Focal Press; Nair, Garyth (1999), *Voice – Tradition and Technology*, San Diego: Singular; Campbell, Murray, and Clive Greated (1987), *The Musician's Guide to Acoustics*, Oxford: Oxford University Press.

23   See further, Nair, Garyth (1999), *Voice – Tradition and Technology*, San Diego: Singular, pp. 66–7.

24   See further, Chapter 4 below.

25   David M. Howard presents an excellent collection of voice analysis programmes on the Internet in his 'Survey of Internet – free and shareware tools for voice analysis', support for paper presented at the 4th Pan European Voice Conference, Stockholm University, 23–26 August 2001, http: //www-users.york.ac.uk/~dmh8/dmh_pevocIV.htm

26   See further, Chapter 5 below.

27   See further, Brodnitz, Friedrich, S. (1988), *Keep Your Voice Healthy*, Boston: College-Hill; Morrison, Murray, and Linda Rammage (1994), *The Management of Voice Disorders*, London: Chapman and Hall; Boone, Daniel (1997), *Is Your Voice Telling on You?* London: Whurr; Sataloff, Robert T. (1997) (ed.), *Professional Voice: The Science and Art of Clinical Care*, San Diego: Singular; Davies, D. Garfield and Anthony F. Jahn (1999), *Care of the Professional Voice*, Oxford: Butterworth-Heinemann; Allen, Rose L. (2000), 'The effects of preventive vocal hygiene education on the vocal hygiene habits and perceptual vocal characteristics of training singers', *Journal of Voice*, **14** (1), March, 58–71.

28   Pilates is becoming very popular with musicians. It designed to encourage 'suppleness, natural grace, and skill that will be unmistakably reflected in the way you walk, in the way you play, and in the way you work', said by Joseph Pilates and quoted by Barkway, Ann (2002), 'Music and Movement', *Classical Music*, 16 February, 15. See further, Robinson, Lynne, and Gordon Thompson (1997), *Body Control: The Pilates Way*, London: Pan Books; Ackland, Lesley (1997), *15-Minute Pilates*, London: Thorsons (HarperCollins).

29   See further, Lovetri, Jeanette (2000), '"Alternative medical therapy" use among singers: prevalence and implications for the medical care of the singer', *Journal of Voice*, **14** (3), September, 398–409.

30   See further, Nair, Garyth (1999), 'Vocal pharmacology: introducing the subject at Drew University', *Journal of Singing*, **55** (3), January/February, 55–63.

31   See further, Chapter 5 below.

32   See further, for specialist books, Butcher, Peter; Annie Elias, and Ruth Raven (1993), *Psychogenic Voice Disorders and Cognitive Behaviour Therapy*, London: Whurr; Morrison, Murray, and Linda Rammage (1994), *The Management of Voice Disorders*, London: Chapman and Hall; Rosen, Deborah Caputo and Robert Thayer Sataloff

(1997), *Psychology of Voice Disorders*, San Diego; Singular. For more general information see vocal health books in the Bibliography.

33 See further, Heman-Ackah, Yolanda D. (2002), 'Who takes care of voice problems? A guide to voice care providers', *Journal of Singing*, **59** (1), November/December, 139–46.

34 See further, Stemple, Joseph C. (2001), *Voice Therapy: Clinical Studies*, San Diego: Singular.

Chapter 4

Voices, Tonal Ideals, Classification, and Technique

Before discussing particular aspects of technique we shall do well to consider voices as such, tonal ideals and voice classification. While my primary focus is on the eighteen-to-sixty-year-old voice, vocal pedagogues may properly be expected to have an understanding of childrens' and seniors' voices. Accordingly, we may usefully set out from a few remarks on these.

Voices

Children's Voices

Currently studies are being made of how girls' and boys' voices differ.[1] As reported by Alison Utley, David Howard, in connection with girls singing in cathedral choirs, is researching the difference between the voices of girls and boys. He says, 'We are not asking whether the sound produced by girls is better or worse, but we are trying to find whether people can tell the difference' (*The Times Higher Education Supplement*, 15 December 2000, p. 48). An experiment using two hundred listeners revealed that over 50 per cent could tell the difference. Welch states, 'vocal physiology is pretty much identical in children (between the ages) of seven and ten' (cited by Haunch, 1999, p. 18). This discrepancy implies that more detailed study needs to be made.

There are different points of view as to when children should begin to be taught to sing. Mary Garden has this to say:

> The girl has no business to sing while she is yet a child – and she is that until she is sixteen or over ... The voice will keep, and it will be sweeter and fresher if it is not overused in childhood (Garden, 1920, p. 64).

Alma Gluck agrees with her:

> ... my vocal training did not begin until I was twenty ... It seems to me that it is a very great mistake for any girl to begin the serious study of singing before that age, as the feminine voice, in most instances, is hardly settled until then (ibid., p. 67).

And so does Nellie Melba:

> ... the vocal training may be safely postponed until the singer is seventeen or eighteen
> years of age. The voice in childhood is a very delicate organ despite the wear and tear
> which children give it by unnecessary howling and screaming (ibid., p. 90).

But Rosa Raiso tells us that she 'began to have singing lessons when I was eight years old' (ibid., p. 99). Ernestine Schumann-Heink speaks about the young male singer: 'I do not believe that he should start until he is past twenty or even twenty-two ... the period of mutation in both sexes is a much slower process than most teachers realize' (ibid., p. 104).

Many who advocate delaying singing lessons suggest other instrumental training, for example, learning to play the piano, plus a good general and music education. But is it appropriate, or even possible, to silence the child who cannot help singing all day long? Surely, they would be better served to be taught to cultivate healthy singing habits in preparation for later years. But, unfortunately, singing teachers sometimes attempt to teach children skills by the use of imagery. On the one hand, 'Using a model of the diaphragm and lungs is one of the many interesting ways to teach low breathing' (Merrill, 2002, p. 38) – a good attempt at basic anatomy – but, on the other hand he says:

> Light and heavy voices can be contrasted by throwing an imaginary feather in the air and
> singing 'light voice' with teeth apart as it falls, and then picking up something heavy and
> singing 'heavy voice' (ibid., p. 38).

Children in the twenty-first century deserve better. If they can absorb the musical terminology, for example, pitch, rhythm, dynamics and phrasing, demanded of them by the same author in a later paragraph, then why not the terminology of singing technique? Later still the same author says, 'Learning to sing should not be a mystery' (ibid., p. 39), thereby contradicting his recourse to imagery.

There is also a great wealth of literature, particularly belonging to children's own cultural heritage to which an early introduction is highly desirable. Of course, talented child singers should not be exploited or pushed to attempt technique or repertoire inappropriate for their physical and psychological development.[2] We must forego the temptation to assume that the immature vocal organs of the child are the same as those of the mature adult but smaller. Many bad habits picked up in childhood are carried over into adulthood. It is a sad fact that sometimes as a result of inadequate teaching, children, no less than adults, develop vocal nodules. Children can abuse their voices by talking too much, too loudly, and by screaming in the playground.

The Adolescent Voice

1. *Boys*   Adolescent voice change cannot be forecast accurately, neither when it will happen, nor how the voice will be affected, nor how long it will be before the

voice settles into maturity. At puberty the male larynx grows bigger and the range of the voice drops by approximately one octave. The vocal folds grow by 4–11 mm, maybe as much as 60 per cent. The boy's larynx becomes about 20 per cent larger than a girl's larynx.

We are now back into the realm of psychology. Adolescent boy singers sometimes become stigmatized, first for singing at all, secondly for having an as yet unchanged voice. This may result in their developing a negative attitude towards singing. For the unchanged male voice a manly identity has to be created. If they are still singing treble it is psychologically appropriate in choirs to stand them next to boys, rather than girl trebles, so as not to appear so obviously a male treble. Eshelman stated:

> Adolescent boys are placed in an unusual predicament. If they sing in their unchanged voice, they may face ridicule from their peers, particularly if there is not a strong representation of male voices in their school choir. Older adolescents are not convinced that singing a soprano or alto part is legitimate. Further, if they try to sing in a changed voice, they cannot physically match the pitches and are subjected to a totally unsatisfying and perhaps damaging experience (1992, p. 25).

It is important that adolescent students should have the voice change explained to them by their singing teachers. They are generally very interested and enjoy the weekly 'testing' of where their voice has 'got to'. It must be fun and not embarrassing for the student.

Many teachers think it wise to keep boys singing through the voice change in a constructive and supportive environment in order to help them develop confidence in their changed voices and self-image and to encourage them to sing after the change. Other teachers advocate non-singing until the voice 'settles'; or singing quietly or mouthing the words in choir. Looking back in history we find that Manuel Garcia II suggested that the voice should be rested during the change. The opposite view was taken by the eminent otolaryngologist Morrell MacKenzie who said that the change was a natural development and the voice should be exercised. Cooksey claims that from Garcia's belief came the 'voice break' theory (1993, p. 16). He then concludes that if boys were encouraged to sing during this transition then more would continue to sing as adults (ibid., p. 37).[3]

Some boys are said to feel emotion akin to bereavement when their pre-adolescent voice disappears. It does not always follow that from an excellent treble or alto voice a voice of professional quality will appear. Nor can a baritone voice be definitely predicted from a treble, or a tenor voice from an alto, although this pattern frequently occurs: it is said that Caruso and Pavarotti sang alto as a boy, and Terfel treble.

Choice of repertoire is an important consideration in the teaching of the changing voice. Songs must have ranges that boys can sing comfortably and with few awkward intervals or leaps – new voices will not yet have much flexibility. Since such music is not easy to find, the teacher needs to be inventive and imaginative.

It is often disheartening for the conservatoire male voice major when he listens to his female counterpart's voice facility, and wide-ranging repertoire. We must bear in mind that the eighteen-year-old male is singing with a three to four year old voice, whereas, because of minimal change, his female peer has been singing with her voice for a lifetime.

2. *Girls*   At puberty the girl's voice may lower in range by about a third. The vocal folds grow by 1.5–4 mm, or as much as 34 per cent, becoming longer and thicker. There may be an adjustment time, although it is generally much less obvious than in her male counterpart. During this adjustment period there may be disinclination on the girl's part to sing higher pitches. However sometimes reluctance is demonstrated because the young singer feels timid or uncertain about herself. By the age of fifteen or sixteen, girls have a preference of range in which to sing (see below, vocal classi-fication). The danger is that the choice of range may be cultural rather than physical – it goes without saying how great is the influence of the 'pop' scene on many teenagers.

Many young girls have breathy sound, which can sometimes be corrected by concentrated work on onset and release. Others have a breathy sound because of a posterior glottal chink, which does not always close, even with good technique, and may still be present in maturity. We shall resume these technical points shortly.

Maturing and Ageing Voice

Between the ages of twenty and sixty the voice is relatively stable, given good health, diet and exercise. Basic vocal activity can be maintained well into the seventies, physiologic age rather than chronological age determines this. The male voice sometimes rises during old age, perhaps because of diminishing testosterone levels. The female voice sometimes becomes lower due to diminishing oestrogen levels at the menopause, although this is often rectified by the administration of hormone replacement therapy. Of course both sexes may suffer from atrophy (wasting away of cells), dystrophy (malfunctioning of cells) and oedema (excessive accumulation of liquids in the tissue) plus ossification and in some cases arthritis.[4]

Typical of the ageing voice is breathiness, loss of range, change in vibrato rate, development of *tremolo*, loss of breath control, vocal fatigue, pitch inaccuracies and other undesirable features. From the age of forty there are body changes that may affect the singing voice. There may be a decrease of blood supply to the larynx, resulting in a stiffening of the vocal folds, and the lungs may lose elasticity. Muscular strength may decline and coordination and reflexes may slow down. Many, but not all, of these conditions can be avoided, delayed, or reversed by regular training.

Tonal Ideals

National Schools of Singing

As we have seen earlier in the historical survey, in Western classical singing the main schools are Italian, German, French and English. They each have a distinctive tonal ideal, which is reflected in the pedagogy of these schools. Some would say there is also a distinctive Eastern European and a Scandinavian school. For purposes of illustration, only the four schools originally mentioned will be used. These schools of singing with their various traditions have been exported from their countries of origin to other countries, not necessarily of the same culture, both singly and in combination with each other. For example, a combination of German and English technique may be found in Japanese singers. The question arises, are these tonal examples based on aesthetic intentions or are they a result of the differing pedagogies? However that may be, if the voice is functioning efficiently and healthily then national schools of singing become redundant. Miller states: 'Vocal efficiency may best be described as producing the most favorable phonatory results with the proper levels of energy' (1997, p. xiii). This can be supported by the information from science now available and readily useable by teachers from all the national schools. This is not to say that all singers sound the same; voices are as individual as personalities:

> In those cases where physical function must be violated in order to produce a tone in keeping with a particular national aesthetic ideal, the singer may wish to re-examine the sound produced and look for some more efficient method of production. Without some knowledge of existing techniques a singer is hardly in a position to assume that the peculiar technique encountered by mere chance or physical location is unquestionably the superior one (ibid., p. xxxvii).

There will, of course, always remain cultural, linguistic, temperamental, and aesthetic differences in *interpretation* of the literature.

If some Europeans have jealously guarded their national tonal ideals, Miller has said of his homeland:

> There is no American national school of singing because teachers trained in each of the national vocal traditions have continued to go their diverse ways; within American pedagogy there is less unity of approach than in any of the major countries of Western Europe (1977, p. 201).

This quotation may be enlarged upon in two ways. First we see that originally classical singers in America came from Europe. During World War II the lack of availability of European singers encouraged the cultivation of singers trained at home. Unfortunately, on his arrival at the Metropolitan Opera House, New York in 1951, Rudolf Bing encouraged European singers back again to the detriment of the

American singers. Later, many American singers were lured over the Atlantic, particularly to the German opera houses. The Americans, with a multi-historical training background from the national schools, and great versatility throughout the literature, today flourish all over the world and dominate the international scene. They are heavily criticized for a generality in their interpretation, but praised for well-trained technique. Secondly, because 'the world has grown smaller' and people travel widely there is a tendency for a basic core technique to develop, which is derived from a mix of the national schools plus the maintenance of distinctive nationality. It may therefore become increasingly difficult to justify the judgement, which the Italian Caruso passed upon the French:

> The "bleat" or goat voice, a particular fault of French singers, proceeds from the habit of forcing the voice, which, when it is of small volume, cannot stand the consequent fatigue of the larynx (1909, p. 58).

In our quest for healthy and efficient vocal technique we may set out from James McKinney's claim that among the characteristics of good vocal sound are those that are:

1. freely produced
2. pleasant to listen to
3. loud enough to be heard easily
4. rich, ringing, and resonant
5. [where] energy flows smoothly from note to note
6. consistently produced
7. vibrant, dynamic, and alive
8. flexibly expressive (1994, p. 77)

He goes on to say, 'Beautiful sounds start in the mind of the singer. If you cannot think a beautiful sound, it is an accident if you make one' (ibid., p. 77). Freed researching into imagery in early twentieth-century American vocal pedagogy advises: 'Make a picture of a beautiful tone, then produce it now' (2000, p. 9).

We may consider the aspects of voice quality emanating from physical character-istics in all humans, for example, the complex vibrating of the vocal folds, and the flexible vocal tract which gives the particular intensities of the various harmonic overtones. Although each singer may share the same basic vocal fold function and fundamental frequency, the nature of human uniqueness determines the individual voice quality. Hence the theory that when the voice is functioning healthily and effi-ciently the result is the individual singer's own, inimitable, most beautiful sound, which will be pleasing to all honest ears which are not demanding their own tonal ideal. In general we have the same physiology and therefore can basically, be trained in the same way, but the resulting sound will be different to the discrimi-nating ear. Of course, the shape of the vocal tract can be changed at will, thus varying the resonance characteristics, even though the distinctive quality of the individual's voice is maintained. Some teachers would say that this is done when, among other things, vowels are changed, colouration of text takes place, and the vocal tract is manipulated to produce special effects.

Can a tonal concept be altered? Here we are back to psychology and the learning process. Singers are very often heavily influenced by hearing beautiful vocal sounds from accomplished singers and they can be tempted to imitate those particular sounds. Why is one tonal concept preferable to another? Does the cultural environment have an influence? How are changes to be made? Miller stresses: '*Timbre does not need to be created to meet some preconceived notion; it needs to be freed*' (1999, p. 28).

It is the singing teacher's responsibility to recognize which of the sounds produced by the student are of free timbre and which are not. Following diagnosis of the faults comes the prescription of beneficial solutions. Persistence on the part of the student to overcome old habits and replace them with new ones will be essential. The singer has to be convinced that the freely produced sound is superior to the one rejected. This is where clear, structured teaching and confidence in the well-equipped teacher is vital. On the part of the singer awareness of the three elements of hearing, feeling and seeing the differences in the freely produced tonal quality from the previous undesirable sound should be apparent.

Singers are sometimes reluctant to make fundamental changes in tonal concepts. The quality of sound that the student is making may have become part of their personality. A critical evaluation of that sound may be felt as an intrusion into personal privacy, the more so if singers have been acclaimed for their singing. There may be fear of losing that prestige. Hence, once again, the teacher's need to understand the psychology involved in proposing changes in what is, strictly, *personal* behaviour. Perhaps an isolation of the particularly good sounds should be made, rather than a complete clean sweep attempted. The singer can then focus on these good sounds determining and understanding how they are better than other sounds, and gradually build the new tonal concept from there. The criticism should be specific; a justification of the judgement should be offered; and the singer should be given factual, linguistically precise, technical suggestions designed to improve matters.

Vocal Classification

Voice Categories

Traditionally, the main categories of the singing voice in Western culture are, for men: bass (low), and tenor (high); for women: contralto/alto (low), and soprano (high). Although statistics are unavailable, most voices appear to have medium ranges, and this is reflected in much of the literature of folk song. Ideally, therefore, general classification should include the medium range voices of the baritone (male) and mezzo-soprano (female). In trained male voices baritones abound, and the tenor is more of a rarity; whereas female trained voices include many more sopranos than altos. The unusual voices are the extremes, bass, tenor, contralto and high soprano.

A well-trained voice with professional potential will generally have a performing range of two octaves, although many singers will exhibit wider ranges. Published material on the 'normal' ranges of the various categories of voice is not altogether helpful, and is frequently unsubstantiated. Professional voices rarely correspond to such suggestions; their range is, very often, much more extensive. It is not unusual for both lyric and dramatic tenors to have several pitches below C3. The tenor Caruso's much publicized feat of singing the bass aria, *Vecchia zimarra, senti* (*La bohème* Puccini), when at one performance the bass's voice gave out, does not impress many professional tenors. Some females can sing the range of both mezzo-soprano and coloratura voices, the latter being traditionally a high voice with exceptional agility; some baritones can sing the range of tenors.

Within the main categories there are many subdivisions. These divisions often overlap, and may vary from country to country. Thus, for example, there exists in the German theatre the *Fach* system. *Fach* refers to a particular category of voice. The male voice may be characterized as *Bass-Bariton; tiefer Bass; Bass-buffo,* or *komischer Bass; hoher Bass; Spielbariton; Heldenbariton; hoher Bariton; Kavalierbariton; Heldentenor; lyrischer Tenor; Spieltenor,* and *hoher Tenor.* Female voices include *Soubrette; hoher Sopran* or *Koloratur Sopran; lyrischer Sopran; dramatischer Sopran; dramatischer Alt,* and *komischer Alt.*

Very often the nature of the character to be portrayed determines the category of voice necessary. For example: the *tiefer Bass* may sing Sarastro in Mozart's *Die Zauberflöte*; the *Spielbariton*, Don Giovanni (*Don Giovanni*, Mozart); and the *lyrischer Tenor*, Max in Weber's *Der Frieshütz.* A *Soubrette* may sing Susanna (*Le Nozze di Figaro,* Mozart); and a *lyrischer Sopran* may play Richard Strauss's Arabella (*Arabella).* France and Italy have similar designations, while English speakers use a compilation from German, French and Italian sources.

But there is more to determining *Fach* than labelling voice types. We must also consider the density of orchestral scoring underlying some operatic roles. A composer may write in such a way that *sostenuto* (sustaining the melodic line) is difficult for certain categories of voice; the *tessitura* (that part of the musical range in which most of the pitches of the melody 'lie') may be unsuitable for some vocal types. For example, the Verdi character Rigoletto is scored for the baritone range, but the upper part of the voice is continuously exploited, making the part uncomfortable for some baritones. Roles that demand agility skills are not always appropriate to certain voices. Some would argue that singers ought to have the technical ability to surmount such obstacles, but a vastly unsympathetic conductor can play havoc with a singer's best intentions. And we must remember that many roles were written with a particular singer of the day in the composer's mind.

At this point mention must be made of the countertenor or male alto. Some teachers would say that these are two different categories. However I suggest that the countertenor is usually a baritone who has made the artistic and aesthetic decision to sing in the male falsetto register. It could be said that 'falsetto' here means an artificial method of voice production using only partial vocal fold vibration.[5] A counter tenor is not a singer with a rare type of vocal instrument, nor is he an imitator of the seventeenth and eighteenth century castrato sound.

How should we try to categorize the individual voice? Most singing teachers appreciate that students need to sing songs as well as practise technical exercises. There is a (probably apocryphal) tale concerning Nicola Porpora, an eighteenth century singing teacher. He is said to have taught the castrato, Cafferelli, to sing by using just one sheet of vocal exercises for six years.[6] However, to make the singing of songs possible (and despite the dangers) even beginning students need to have their voices loosely classified. To this end, it is advisable to begin vocalizing in the middle area of the vocal range, very gradually extending the range of the lower and higher pitches until the voice begins, in some cases as it develops, to classify itself under the care of the teacher. Songs can then be assigned which are appropriate to the range of the beginner. Vennard says:

> I never feel any urgency about classifying a beginning student. So many premature diagnoses have been proved wrong, and it can be harmful to the student and embarrassing to the teacher to keep striving for an ill-chosen goal. It is best to begin in the middle part of the voice and work upward and downward until the voice classifies itself (1967, p. 78).

Range is not the only factor in categorization. The timbre, quality and size of the voice need to be considered. We can be more precise if we determine the pitch at which the voice registers change. Here we step on a hornet's nest, for there are diverse viewpoints about the registers in the singing voice. Some say there are no registers at all; some advocate seven registers and others adopt a middle of the way opinion (Miller, 1997, pp. 122–4). The untrained voice has an easily perceived change in timbre at certain points in the ascending scale. The laryngeal muscles change position and there are corresponding changes in the resonator system above and possibly below the larynx. Together, these happenings determine the register phenomena.[7] The aim of the trained singer is to blend these events into a unified scale.

Even the choice of words for registers may present problems. Some schools of thought use such words as 'break', 'lift' and 'change of gears' which, psychologically, suggest division between registers rather than a totally unified range.[8] In the male voice the first change (registration event) is considered as the *primo passaggio* (first passage); the second as the *secondo passaggio*. In the female voice the terms generally used are the lower *passaggio* and upper *passaggio*. The *zona di passaggio* (passage zone) lies between. The term *passaggio* is part of the international vocabulary of vocal pedagogy.

There are individual variations in the various vocal instruments but, on the whole, changes in register are fairly predictable. In the male voices of a given *Fach* the main registration events will tend to occur on the same pitches, thus, the approximate register events for some male categories are as follows:

	primo passaggio	*secondo passaggio*
lyric tenor	D (4)	G (4)
lyric baritone	B (3)	E (4)
deep bass	Ab (3) (G (3))	D (4) (C (4))

The speaking voice comprises more than one octave and untrained singers are usually comfortable singing in this range. However, adolescent males and untrained male singers find that at a certain point in the rising scale tension becomes apparent, and they involuntarily raise the chin and the larynx. The corresponding pitch is the *primo passaggio*. Pitches may be sung beyond this point but the larynx is raised and strained in order for this to happen.

The quality of tone changes and becomes more noticeable as the scale ascends and the untrained voice will either stop completely or suddenly move into falsetto. This 'stop' usually happens at pitches about the interval of a fourth above the originally felt need to raise the larynx and this point is the *secondo passaggio*. As we have seen, the area in between the *primo passaggio* and the *secondo passaggio* is called the *zona di passaggio*.

There are similar occurrences in the female voice, but they do not directly correspond. Structurally female voices have differences from male voices. As well as the visual external difference in size of the larynx, the change experienced in puberty by the adolescent male differs from that of the female adolescent. Of course there are individual variations in some voices; not all instruments are the same. However on the whole these registration pivotal points are fairly predictable. The following are the approximate register events for some female categories:

	lower *passaggio*	upper *passaggio*
soprano	Eb (4)	F# (5)
mezzo-soprano	E(4) (F(4))	E (5) (F5))
contralto	G (4) (Ab (4))	D (5)

There is no need for urgency in formally classifying a singing voice. Mistakes are easily made which can be embarrassing to the teacher and harmful to the student. The voice may change and call for reclassification. Vocal maturity, the appropriate chronological age, and professional potential do not always appear simultaneously. At all stages complete and adequate preparation is necessary. As technical ability and security develop, and as physical maturity occurs, accurate vocal categorization should emerge. Goethe said, '*Die Natur weiss allein, was sie will*' (Nature alone knows what she wants).

I end this section with another preposterous quotation found by Freed and used at the beginning of the twentieth-century, 'Voice has one register, the Facial Register' (2000, p. 9).

The Dangers of Incorrect Vocal Classification

Shining, resplendent and excited, armed with a generous scholarship and travel grant to study in Europe with a noted singing teacher, a young professional baritone from the other side of the world attends his first lesson. He sings, he mentions various vocal problems that he is having and, to his great surprise, advice from his new teacher, confirmed by a colleague, suggests that the enthusiastic baritone is really a tenor.

What happens next? This singer was making a name for himself in the professional world as a baritone and so he has to start all over again. The scholarship and travel grant was awarded for baritone prowess and now, here he is a tenor, so the funding may be withdrawn. Retraining, which entails learning new repertoire and new roles may take at least two years – who will pay his tuition fees? How will our new tenor maintain himself in a foreign country? This situation is not uncommon. Many professional careers, both male and female, have been disrupted by incorrect vocal classification. My training and experience suggests that the following points are relevant when attempting to classify voices:

1. Chronological age is not a reliable guide as voices mature at a different rate.
2. It is advisable to refrain from classification according to pitch range. Some females are able to sing the pitches of both mezzo-soprano and coloratura. The range of the voice is not the primary factor in determining vocal category. It is more useful to consider the quality and the *tessitura* (the area in the voice which sounds and performs the best and is most comfortable). There is a danger here in the word 'comfortable'. For example, there are many altos – particularly in choirs – who are 'comfortably' singing, but who are really sopranos. As stated above, there are very few altos and many sopranos.
3. Classification by timbre has dangers. Timbre may be disguised in individual voices because of such compensatory methods in vocal technique as over-energized or 'pressurized' sound.
4. Sometimes a genuine change in vocal category occurs in mid-career as the voice matures and vocal technique becomes more secure, particularly in the area of resonance balancing ('voice placement'). For example, a mezzo voice may become a dramatic soprano; a baritone may become a dramatic tenor. It will then be necessary to review the singer's *passaggi* to ensure that the change is legitimate.
5. The imitation of a mature voice on recordings, or even of the teacher's singing voice has its dangers. A fifteen year old girl endeavouring to learn *Arie Antiche*

may sing along with a recording of Cecilia Bartoli, imitating, either innocently or with intent, in order to cultivate Bartoli's sound. At the opposite end of the scale, how many fifty-eight year old Susanna's do we want to see or hear?

6. Female voices often mature earlier than their male counterparts although, of course, there are exceptions. It has to be remembered that an eighteen-year-old male who underwent voice change at fifteen is singing with a three year old voice. He may sometimes become frustrated and discouraged, particularly by the apparent vocal maturity and technical ability of his female peers.

7. The young soprano with a big voice, potential *lyrico spinto*, is likely to mature more slowly than her *soubrette* or *coloratura* colleague. Her instrument tends to be more unwieldy and may not so readily access the upper ranges. She may, unfortunately, be classified as mezzo-soprano and not be encouraged to extend and develop her range upwards.

8. Young mezzo-sopranos should not be required to darken their voices in order to sound more mezzo-like (the chances are that they are sopranos anyway).

9. Both trained and untrained mezzos may be found who dislike their natural, designated vocal category, and thus mistakenly imitate the soprano and even sing her repertoire.

10. There are so few true contraltos and it can be dangerous for the teacher to encourage the student to become one by allowing her to sing only in the lower half of her available range.

11. A male of twenty-one should not sound like a sixteen year old youth; a young female adult should not sound like a girl of fourteen. 'Undersinging' (the voice without energy) should be discouraged. It can cause almost as much harm as 'oversinging' where the voice is pressurized to sound mature.

12. Many young singers sing-along with pop recordings. These usually have a very limited range, which utilizes mainly the lower middle voice. This often results in that part of the voice becoming over-developed. Difficulties ensue when the classical repertoire is attempted and smooth entry into the upper voice is crucial.

13. Some voices have been inhibited in their true development because the teacher was not able to explain how to apply energy without pushing or straining.

14. It is vital that teachers avoid encouraging the development of a voice exclusively to their own taste. For example, some teachers have dislike for the tenor voice. In this instance it is far better that the teacher discreetly refuses to teach the tenor student rather than trying to train him into the baritone range.

15. Although voices are housed in physiques that to some extent dictate categorization, physical appearance can be misleading. Big voices may emanate from small bodies; not all tenors and sopranos are short-necked; not all basses are tall and gangling; nor are all mezzos and dramatic sopranos generously built. Tenor vocal folds may be housed in a baritone-sized larynx and vice versa.

16. There is danger in singing inappropriate repertoire. Most of the literature, particularly songs, does not need *Fach* categorization, but there are exceptions

that the singer/teacher needs to be aware of. The young soubrette, for example, should not be asked to sing Schubert's *Die junge Nonne* and, certainly, most young singers should not be battling away through operatic arias.

17. Choral directors sometimes demand young, changing-voice males to remain in the tenor section of the choir on the plea of being short of that voice, even though the young male is clearly ready to sing baritone.

18. Choir members very often classify themselves into a too 'comfortable', albeit vocally unhealthy, lower to medium range. Medium voiced males may not have explored their upper range – they may be tenors. Similarly many female 'altos' have not learnt to negotiate the upper *passaggio*; consequently, their upper range is undeveloped.

19. It is important to beware the cultural attitudes and national tonal preferences, which sometimes aid in determining vocal categories. For example, the straight-tone of the English choral tradition; the heavy 'covering' (darkening of the sound by the modification to rounded vowels in order to assist in negotiating a smooth register transition) of the German school.

Ultimately, vocal maturity and soundly based secure technical ability will determine accurate vocal classification and this cannot and should not be hurried. Joan Sutherland began as a mezzo and then became a coloratura soprano (it has been suggested that she imitated her mother's mezzo voice and learnt her mother's repertoire as a child). Marilyn Horne was at first a lyric soprano and then became a mezzo. Leonard Warren experimented with his voice as a tenor and became a dramatic baritone.

Technique

In the light of the foregoing discussion I now turn to questions of technique, noting how these require familiarity on the part of the teacher with those psychological, anatomical, physiological and acoustical insights with which the preceding chapters have been concerned.

In this section the general approach may be said to reflect the tradition of vocal pedagogy by which I have been most greatly influenced, namely, that flowing down from William Vennard, Richard Miller, and Donald Bell. So much is it the case that the vocal pedagogue is an apprentice of his or her teachers that through constant repetition on certain technical issues they speak a very similar language. In view of this it should be noted that actual quotations from my mentors are scrupulously specified and referenced.

Caruso stated '... there are as many methods as there are singers, and any particular method, even if accurately set forth, might be useless to the person who tried it' (Caruso, 1909, p. 51). Yeatman Griffith says, 'A student, rightly taught, should know the cause for everything he does, how he does thus and so why he does it' (cited by Brower, 1920, p. 72).

Impulse

The brain knows the sound it wants to make and sends neural impulses through the central nervous system. The desire to phonate is passed by two branches of the vagus nerve to the larynx. Much research has yet to be done to discover exactly what happens.

The Coordinated Onset and Release of Sound

We may discuss this point in the relation to Bernoulli's Principle, as defined by Titze: 'If the energy in a confined fluid stream is constant, an increase in particle velocity must be accompanied by a decrease in pressure against the wall' (1994, p. 331).

The Bernoulli effect has often been applied to phonation:

> Assume that the vocal folds are nearly approximated at the instant the air stream is released by the forces of exhalation. The air stream will have a constant velocity until it reaches the glottal constriction. Velocity will increase, however, as the air passes through the glottal chink. *The result is a negative pressure between the medial edges of the vocal folds, and they will literally be sucked toward one another* (Zemlin, 1988, p. 146).

Ladefoged draws an analogy with bellows (1962, p. 248), Vennard compares the action to an atomizer (1967, p. 40), and Colin Watson believes that it is an over-simplification to associate vocal fold closure as a direct result of Bernoulli effect:

> Closure results from approximation of the vocal folds by rotation of the arytenoids. Thereafter the vibratory locus of the epithelium and fold body brings the folds together and the nature of this interaction is largely defined by the shape and pressure of this closure. The Bernoulli effect does play a part in dictating how the epithelium behaves but the prevalent view of the Bernoulli effect somehow sucking the folds together as the main motive force is wrong (1989, p. 24).

Many singers are puzzled how best to begin and end a sound efficiently and healthily. The matter is technical but not mysterious. Coordinated onset and release of sound simply means the efficient, balanced, beginning and ending of sound. We need to refer again to historical tradition, acoustics, anatomy and physiology and all becomes clear. The way in which the singer, at whatever level of achievement, begins the initial sound determines the rest of the phrase. Similarly, the way the sound is ended influences the beginning of the next phrase. Coordinated onset and release is one of the very first aspects of technique to be learnt and belongs with the teaching of breath management. Practice of onset and release should be part of the daily routine of the singer/student.

As we saw in the previous chapter, at the top of the trachea, inside the larynx, are the vocal folds. In combination with the intrinsic muscles of the larynx the vocal folds act as a valve. The primary use of this mechanism is to stop the movement of breath. In this way food is prevented from entering the lungs. The closure also occurs, for example, in defecation, in the labour of childbirth, and in lifting heavy weights. A secondary or superimposed function is the making of purposeful noise by animals, and the further development of this by humans into an art form – hence we sing.

Balanced onset and release is the result of laryngeal muscle balance and elasticity. This is achieved when the breathing muscles and the muscles of the valve are synchronized. Freedom in the singing voice follows. Uncoordinated onset and release results in either hyper (excessive) or hypo (deficient) function of the musculature.

Wyke suggests that EMG (electromyographic) studies of the intrinsic muscles of the larynx show that they actively but briefly assume positions and degrees of tension necessary for the production of sound; and that expiratory airflow begins and subglottic air pressure starts to rise before actual sound emerges (1974, p. 296). Therefore, attention can be directly or indirectly focused on the position the vocal folds assume before the onset of sound.

There are three types of onset: the hard attack, the soft onset, and the balanced onset.

1. The hard attack is sometimes known as glottal attack, stroke of the glottis, *coup de glotte, colpo di glottide,* and *Glottisschlag.*[9] In glottal attack the glottis closes firmly before sound begins and breath pressure is applied. There is much more early and even violent action by the vocal muscles than in the other two forms of onset. This has been revealed by EMG (electromyography). As sound begins the excess air pressure below the vocal folds explodes suddenly and a catch can be heard in the voice. The technical term is 'glottal plosive' and it sounds rather like the weight lifter's grunt, or a light cough. From our studies in the previous chapter we can see that this hard attack is vocally abusive. The International Phonetic Alphabet (IPA) symbol is [?]. To experience this onset, the spoken sequence 'Uh, Uh, Uh, Uh, Uh' can be repeated slowly as a phrase, lingering over the glottal plosive [?]. The moment when the glottis is released to produce sound can be sensed. This exercise should not be practised.

2. In the soft onset the flow of breath (expired air) is consciously felt by the singer immediately before the sound begins. This, therefore, is an aspirated onset, a breathy beginning, heard as a soft blowing sound (IPA symbol [h], and breath is wasted. Very often the singer will compensate for poor quality sound by tensing the breathing mechanism and laryngeal musculature in order to improve the sound, but this is unhealthy voice production. In the breathy onset, laryngoscopy reveals an open triangle at the posterior section of the vocal folds.[10] The folds begin to vibrate a fraction of a second after the aspirated noise, until the full tone is heard (Luchsinger and Arnold, 1965, p. 85). If the spoken sequence 'Ha, Ha, Ha, Ha, Ha' is repeated several times, slowly as a phrase, lingering over the initial aspirated [h] of each syllable, one can feel or sense the breath passing over the vocal folds first with the sound following.

As can be seen, the hard attack and the soft onset are opposing methods of initiating sound and neither encourage healthy, efficient vocal function. They are best described simply as the 'grunt' and the 'whisper'.

3. The balanced onset occurs when the singer avoids both the pressurized grunt and the whisper, and achieves a balance between the two. This balanced onset is midway between the hard attack and the soft onset. Miller states, referring to Wyke, that '"Prephonatory tuning" of the instrument takes place and this "tuning" occurs with great rapidity throughout the changing utterances of spoken or sung phonation' (1986, p. 4). 'This *prephonatory tuning* of the laryngeal musculature ... is the principal voluntary contribution to the control of the larynx during speech and singing' (Wyke, 1974, p. 297). It goes without saying that this process also involves the breathing and resonating mechanisms. The spoken sequence 'Ah, Ah, Ah, Ah, Ah' may be repeated several times slowly as a phrase, imagining a brief [h] before each syllable but not letting it be heard. There should not be a feeling as of breathing out (although, of course, airflow begins), or that the breath is moving before the sound begins. This can be compared with a laugh. There is a generous flow of air between the 'ha-ha-ha's' of the laugh but the vowels themselves are loud and clear. If precisely performed, balanced onset will improve easily with practice. There will be an awareness of the moment of onset, but the onset is not the same as the glottal plosive of the hard attack. No breathiness should be heard. The tone will begin immediately, clearly and precisely and any jarring or vocal abuse will be avoided. The ear monitors the whole process. The balanced onset should be imagined or heard inwardly before the action begins, as, also, should the whole phrase.

The balanced onset can next be rehearsed in musical exercises, for example, in two bars of 4/4 time, singing four consecutive crotchets, followed by a final semibreve. Each crotchet should be sung with vibrant tone; each crotchet should end with a clean release. There will be a momentary silence between each release and the onset of the next sound. Strict rhythm is essential and the final note must be given its full rhythmic value. A release (breath replenishment) should happen after each note, with expansion taking place in the abdominal area. This breath will feel so slight that the feeling will be one of hardly breathing at all. These exercises should be sung within a comfortable medium range, in a number of different keys, gradually extending the range.

Onset and release exercises encourage balanced and disciplined breathing. The release is effectively the new breath. The nature of the release determines the next onset, which must be executed rhythmically within the phrase, terminating at an exact point. An efficient onset may end badly, although generally, a clean onset results in a clean release (as with the 'ha-ha-ha' laugh above). If the release is hard a grunt will occur; if soft, breathiness will be heard. In the balanced onset-release vocal quality will be consistent from beginning to end. The same exercises as for onset may be used. In all of this we are at the very beginning of technique. Over a period of time exercises may be presented which are even more progressive and demanding. The coordinated onset and release will result in freedom in sustained singing and agility.[11]

Breath Management

> Techniques of breath co-ordination should be uniform among singers ... Learning to manage airflow and subglottic pressure demands a subtle co-ordination of aerodynamic myoelastic factors (airflow and muscle response) that is the foundation of cultivated singing (Miller, 1993, p. 15).

But Titze has this to say about the different theories of breathing technique:

> Theories about breath support are difficult to test because interactions between groups of muscles in the thoracic and abdominal regions are complex. Furthermore, what is efficient for one individual may be less efficient for another (1994, p. 74).[12]

Placido Domingo talks unhelpfully about 'support' when discussing breath management:

> When I started to support, in order for me to remember, I used to have a very tight elastic belt ... which I still use. And also to sing against the piano ... I push the piano away ... So my feeling is that when I am singing, I should be able to push anything that is against me ... I don't use the elastic belt very much today, because I know what I am doing (cited by Hines, 1988, p. 104).

Such 'pushing' only serves to increase unnecessary tension. Sherrill Milnes gets it right when he says:

> When we breathe in, the diaphragm, which is a curved muscle here [he indicated the bottom of the rib cage], as it starts to flatten, pulls the lungs down. That creates a partial vacuum and in goes air. As the diaphragm goes down it tends to displace organs and other things in a manner, which makes expansion all the way round ... *not* just in the front or the sides, but also in the back (ibid., p. 174).

It must be made clear that the diaphragm does not 'support' the tone. Vennard is adamant in pointing out: 'Phonation, for singing, at least, is **ex**piratory, and the diaphragm is an **in**spiratory muscle'. He goes on to say:

> In controlled exhalation, as in singing, the inspiratory muscles resist the abdominals, causing the act to be much slower and more steady ... a well-developed diaphragm is essential to breath control, but it **steadies**, rather than **supports** the tone. In order to sustain the singing sound the breathing muscles have to maintain their inspiratory position for as long as it is comfortable, thus delaying the expiratory section of the breath cycle. This co-ordination or balance of the muscles of the torso is called *la lotta vocale* (the vocal

contest, or struggle) after the nineteenth-century Italianate school. During *la lotte vocale* the upward movement of the diaphragm and the inward movement of the rib cage is slowed down. (Gurnee, nd., p. 12).[13]

The most efficient way to achieve *la lotte vocale* is the application of *appoggio* technique (again from the Italian school).[14] *Appoggio* is derived from *appoggiare*, meaning to lean against/support/sustain/rely upon. The term is not used exclusively in connection with breath management. It covers actions which involve counterbalancing other muscles and organs both at respiratory and laryngeal levels. Both Miller (1986, p. 23) and Davis (1998, p. 10) support the *appoggio* technique. However Davis has tried to simplify the terminology of breathing technique. He writes:

> Diaphragmatic-intercostal breath management is a system of breathing for singing that employs the following parallel activities during inspiration:
>
> 1. Downward movement of the diaphragm and the resulting displacement of the viscera
> 2. Raising of the sternum and increasing the circumference of the thorax
>
> During exhalation the parallel activities include:
>
> 1. Tensing the muscles of the abdomen (which pushes the viscera up against the diaphragm) while –
> 2. Attempting to hold the position of the raised sternum and enlarged thorax (ibid., p. 15).

Davis goes on to say that although it appears simple, it is not. The physiology of breath management is complicated, and added to that are the tensions and bad habits which singers develop.

In *appoggio* the singer is learning to establish and maintain a vital balance among muscles of the abdomen and upper torso. This is in order to delay the emission of breath for sustained phrases and encourages silent breath renewal for following phrases. Visually, on inspiration expansion takes place in the lateral and anterior abdominal wall just below the rib cage, and in the lower dorsal region. On expiration the reverse occurs. Time and practice improves the extent of expansion and the coordination and development of musculature in these areas. Good posture is the priority in *appoggio*, and voice teachers need to be able to apply their anatomical and physiological knowledge in such a way as to encourage this. This is especially necessary as some teachers with little physiological justification may encourage strenuous and dangerous muscular abdominal activity. And, of course, in many studios subjective imagery is still heard, which usually obscures more than it reveals where technique is concerned. There are also the different methods of breathing in the different schools of singing, for example, the German school advocates belly breathing; the French school promotes high chest breathing. The *appoggio* technique has been adopted by many American singers, and in Britain there is a mixture of all three European schools. The following three suggestions work harmlessly with the body rather than against it.

First, Alexander Technique, as discussed in Chapter 3, encourages the ideal posture for singing.

Secondly, a supine position on the back with the head raised by books (sufficient neither to raise or lower the chin – the teacher is needed to assist) can make one more aware of the correct alignment of head, neck and torso and of the stillness of the upper chest during normal breathing. When lying down there will, on inhalation, be a slight, mainly lateral, outward movement of the abdominal wall. Only at the end of each breath cycle will any inward movement be felt. One hand may be placed flat, palm down, between the naval and sternum, while the other hand rests on the side of the torso between the lowest (tenth) rib and the pelvis. Breathing should be normal and silent – notice that there will be some outward and inward movement between the lowest ribs and the pelvis, but less in the area between naval and sternum. On standing up slowly, an endeavour should be made to achieve a similar feeling of body alignment. With the hands in the same position as when lying down, the muscular movement of the breathing mechanism should feel similar and the upper chest should remain still. Although the influence of gravity will prevent the feelings experienced, supine or upright, from being completely identical, the exercise is a useful teaching aid.

Thirdly, as we have seen in the history chapter, in the noble posture of the historic Italianate school the sternum is elevated and the rib cage thus easily expanded.[15] The abdominal muscles are then free to retain their counteracting relationships (*la lotte vocale*) without being tense. We must now explain how this may be achieved. The feet should first be placed approximately hip-width apart, with the weight distributed evenly between the balls of the feet and the heels, the knees released (the study of physiology reveals that when the knees are tense and pushed back, the pelvis tilts forward and true bodily alignment is disturbed) and the arms raised above the head, by the ears, while breathing silently and deeply. The arms are then lowered back down to the sides of the body and the relatively high sternum gained is maintained. The sternum should not be so high that it cannot go any higher. It is very easy to overcompensate in an effort to achieve and maintain the noble position with a resulting compression of the lower area of the lungs in the back. The shoulders should be released (I avoid the word 'relax' in the interests of the poise, balance and energy needed to sing healthily and well) and the chin neither elevated nor lowered. In the Garcia position, advocated by Manuel Garcia II to maintain optimal posture for singing, singers cross their hands behind their backs, with palms outward, at the bottom of the rib cage.

When good posture is securely established, a daily, disciplined systematic regimen of exercises to establish good breath coordination should begin. Breathing for singing will be mainly through the mouth. The way to train the musculature to remain almost in the position of inhalation for extended periods of time is by prac- tising short, vibrant, staccato pitches in a medium range with silent breath replen- ishment following each note. The muscles are thus trained to avoid the habitual contraction of exhalation as in normal breathing. With the sternum remaining elevated, the diaphragm descends further and ascends less rapidly and minimal breath is lost during each staccato sound. In the words of the historic Italianate school's important maxim, handed down from teacher to teacher, 'The release is the new breath' – the rebound from the staccato release results in silent and effortless inhalation. For most purposes in singing the listener should not hear the singer breathing – respiratory conditions apart, a noisy breather has poor technique.

We must not forget the use of silent breathing exercises; there are many to be found in the literature. A fine example, easily available, is the exercise traditionally ascribed to Nicola Porpora (1686–1768) who taught it to his pupil Carlo Farinelli (1705–1768). Farinelli was renowned for his 'silent' breathing while singing, and his great skill in sustaining inordinately long phrases.

Although some of the instrument is invisible, much information about it may be gleaned by both singers and teachers *via* wall mirrors or video cameras. Overall posture, the position of the chest and rib cage, and the movement of the antero-lateral abdominal musculature during the breath cycle can readily be seen. It is also helpful to look at side views. The teacher can also learn much by standing behind singing students and observing their posture. Use may also be made of relevant scientific information and equipment described in Chapter three above.[16]

Miller has well said that:

> The foundation of singing is concerned with the ability to manage the breath so that airflow precisely matches the needs of the vibrating larynx in its response to articulatory demands (1996, p. 57).

Unfortunately, even in 1999 we still find imagery such as the following:

> Sing like you are an ice cream sundae with hot fudge dripping down the sides ... Pretend your diaphragm is an ice rink in front of your body, and every time you begin to sing, a little angel comes down from heaven and lands on the rink, twirling as fast as she can – make your voice sound like that (cited by Dunn, Robert E., 1999, p. 24).

Vibrato

Vibrato is from the Latin verb *vibrare* (to vibrate). With respect to various other instruments it has also been called, *tremelo*, *Bebung*, *flattement*, and close shake. Vibrato was introduced for expressive purposes in vocal, string and wind performance. The traditional definition of vibrato is that of Seashore:

> A good vibrato is a pulsation of pitch, usually accompanied by synchronous pulsations of loudness and timbre, of such extent and rate as to give a pleasing flexibility, tenderness, and richness to the tone (1938, p. 33).

Another definition is:

Vibrato is repeated, voluntary rhythmical pulsation of tone used by vocalists, string instrumentalists and wind instrumentalists to impart an expressive effect in music (Weait and Shea, 1978, p. 56).

The term vibrato, in its current meaning, was not universally established until well into the nineteenth century, although many seventeenth, eighteenth and nineteenth theorists recognized its use for expressive purposes. Hearsay suggests that vibrato was denounced in medieval times and adversely compared with 'a horse's neighings'. Fillebrown offers this definition:

The *vibrato* is a rhythmic pulsation of the voice. It often appears in untrained voices, in others it appears during the process of cultivation. Some have thought it the perfection of sympathetic quality; others esteem it as a fault (1911, p. 80).

The phenomenon of vibrato contributes to perception of pitch, intensity, and timbre of the vocal sound. The term is used somewhat loosely to describe several kinds of pitch fluctuation that may occur during a sustained tone. Currently, singers employ it as a constituent of pleasing tone. However to the well-informed singer/teacher vibrato is a quality of a healthy, trained voice. Unfortunately, beginning singers, whose main ideas of singing may have come from pop and rock, are suspicious of vibrato. It has to be pointed out to them that as well as being healthy it is the domain of Western classical singing. It is generally accepted that a 'straight tone' or 'white voice' in singing has no vibrato and sounds 'dead'.[17]

The average pitch vibrato rate is between five and seven times a second and the average extent of pitch variation is a semitone.[18] According to Titze an acceptable rate of vibrato is 4.5 to 6.5 Hz (not all authorities agree on this) and plus or minus 0.5 semitone (1994, p. 291).[19] The vibrato extent increases with intensity, for example, in crescendo. Its frequency sometimes increases with pitch and the excitement level of the singer. Nervousness and tension may give a bleating sound in the 6–8 Hz range. Davis suggests that 'Vibrato extent decreases when negotiating runs so that pitch is more precise' (1998, p. 31). Lack of energy or fatigue resulting in wobble may be in the 2–4 Hz range. Physical fitness seems to aid acceptable vibrato. Caruso had a vibrato frequency near 7.0 Hz, whereas Pavarotti's average vibrato rate is near 5.5 Hz. Earlier researchers proposed that vibrato was an aerodynamic action. They based this research on fluoroscopic pictures, which recorded synchronized diaphragmatic vibrations and the vibrato rate of singers thus tested. Others proposed that vibrato was instigated by movement of the jaw or larynx. In fact, this movement is often observable in some singers. Another suggestion is that the rate of vibrato depends on neural impulses which change the tension on the vocal folds. The latest research has not shown exactly how vibrato is created, but the suggestion is that it involves combined laryngeal and respiratory action. Titze offers this suggestion:

The origin of vibrato is not well understood, but some evidence is beginning to show that vocal vibrato may be a stabilized physiologic tremor in the laryngeal muscles (Ramig & Shipp, 1987). It is conceivable, though speculative at this point, that a natural vocal vibrato can be cultivated from a 4 to 6 physiologic tremor in the cricoids and thyroary-tenoid muscles (1994, p. 289).

Faults allied with vibrato are: too fast or too slow a rate; too great a pitch variation, and irregularity of the vibrato. Many teachers suggest that faulty breath management, from different causes, contributes to this. Very often lack of vocal and physical exercise can be at the root of some of the problems, particularly in older singers who may develop the *tremolo* or wobble (when two distinct pitches are heard).

Whereas some singing teachers advocate the use of vibrato as a question of taste, Miller is convinced that its presence is the manifestation of healthy and efficient singing. Certainly without vibrato there is no *legato*, as we shall see in the next chapter. Marguerite d'Alvarez said, 'A voice without vibrato would be cold and dead, expressionless. There must be this pulsating quality in the tone, which carries waves of feeling on it' (cited by Brower, 1920, p. 15).

The last verse of a limerick by Titze will serve as a cautionary conclusion to this section:

On stage please follow this motto:
'Know the bounds of vocal vibrato!'
A voice with a wobble
Like a limp or a hobble
Can draw a rotten toma*t*o (1994, p. 304)

Agility

Fast moving musical passages – *fioriture, Rouladen*, rapid melismas, embellishment, and trill – are not decorations on the surface of vocal technique. The same umbilical-epigastric control that permits the precise onset, the staccato and the execution of velocity or coloratura passages also produces the sustained line in singing (Miller, 1986, p. 40).

Although agility and sustained sound (*sostenuto*) are opposing poles of vocal accomplishment, both are achieved by the same muscles. Agility exercises should be part of every singer's daily practice whatever the vocal type – bass or soprano. Without the ability to accomplish running passages and *melismas* easily, *sostenuto* passages will be difficult to produce with comfort.

Agility is as important for the male singer as for the female. His repertoire demands fast runs, skips and trills and the male voice is capable of this aspect of technique. In running passages of whatever type the same vibrancy must be present as in sustained passages. Caruso, who was a great exponent of practising with a closed mouth, had this to say, 'Vocal work with closed mouth is also a powerful auxiliary to vocal agility' (1909, p. 59). He believed that vocalizing with the mouth shut improved breathing and rested the voice. Perhaps Caruso was benefiting from humming as recommended by G.B. Lamperti: 'It is the rain-bow bridge connecting voice and breath' (cited by Brown, 1957, p. 105). On the other hand, any form of vocalizing uses the vocal mechanism, so rest would not be possible. However humming is often taught by speech language therapists to the vocal user displaying excess tension when phonating. It is also used in singing exercises to improve resonance – the tongue remains in its at rest posture, as the singer discovers *impostazione della voce* (desirable vocal timbre through sensation) by humming, prefixing [m] before a simple vocalize.

Resonance

Resonance can be defined as echoing; resounding; continuing to sound; causing reinforcement or prolongation of sound, especially by reflection or vibration of other bodies; filling the place with sound. To the singer it means carrying power and the quickest way to achieve it is through the understanding of the singing mechanism and acoustics.

One does not need a 'big' voice to fill a concert hall or opera house. Simply stated, resonance balancing is the relationship of the changing size and shape of the resonating cavities together with the surface characteristics which create the energy in the vocal spectrum which the ear perceives as vowels. The vibrating folds, on their own, make a minimal buzzing sound. The resonator tube extends from the vocal folds to the lips and is largely made up of the buccopharyngeal chamber. This chamber serves as a filter to the laryngeally generated sound. Richard Miller sheds light on the nature of resonance balancing as he describes vowel modification:

> The principle of vowel modification is that the initial vowel undergoes some migration as the scale ascends, by modifying toward a near neighbour. The laryngeal configuration changes for each vowel, and there should be a corresponding change in the shape of the resonator track. When the filtering aspects of the vocal tract are in tune with laryngeal configurations, the vowel is properly 'tracked.' Vowel modification in the ascending scale permits vowel tracking and balancing of the formants (areas of acoustic strength), thereby avoiding either 'open' or heavily 'covered' singing (1993, p. 41).

Titze has this to say,

> The vocal tract acts like a megaphone, or a pair of cupped hands, in 'magnifying' the sound that is produced at the glottis and radiated at the mouth. Although there is no actual power amplification (the vocal tract is a passive system that can only dissipate energy), certain select frequencies are given a boost over others ...Vocal intensity is boosted dramatically when Fo is high and a harmonic coincides *exactly* with a formant. This is called *formant tuning*. It can be exploited in singing and theatre speech ... (1994, pp. 230–31).

It has often been said by singers and teachers that resonance in the nasal passages and sinuses contributes to good singing. Experiments have been undertaken to investigate this claim. Austin describes how one experimenter filled the nasal passages of several singers with cotton wool; another filled the nasal passages with cotton wool and the sinuses with water. Their singing, with nasal passages blocked and unblocked, was assessed both by acoustical analysis and perceptual judgement. There was no difference. However Austin reminds us that the well-known peda-gogue Cornelius Reid insisted that the roots of teaching nasal resonance go back to Curtis who believed the use of nasal resonance relieved the vocal folds from excessive fatigue.[20] The conflict seems to arise because of localized sensations felt by some singers in the upper face, 'the mask'. These sympathetic vibrations may be confused with nasality. Tosi, in the eighteenth century, admonished:

> Let the Master attend with great Care to the Voice of the Scholar, which, whether it be *di Petto*, or *di Testa*, should always come forth neat and clear, without passing thro' the Nose, or being choaked in the Throat; which are two the most horrible Defects in a Singer, and past all Remedy if once grown into a Habit (1723, p. 22).

Sensations vary from singer to singer and cannot be imposed from one to the other. Concerning factors of resonation, most singers are so used to a feeling of sympa-thetic vibration that they are not aware of it. This is not a problem, so long as it is not the result of faulty technique, but is rather a matter of specific sensations, particular to the individual which cannot be transferred to others. Too much reliance on internal sensations suggested by the teacher, particularly concerning resonance ('placement') can be dangerous and harmful. It is an acoustically known fact that tone cannot be 'placed'. Once a soundly based technique has been established then singers develop their own reliable and consistent internal and external sensations.

Theories abound regarding the 'placement' of vocal sound. The cover on the dust jacket of the classic textbook, still popular in many conservatories in the United Kingdom, announces that this book aims 'to provide singers and teachers with a scientifically exact basis from which to work directly and objectively on the physical elements responsible for the production of the singing voice' (Husler and Rodd-Marling, 1983). Unfortunately, the authors proceed to ask the singer to 'place' the tone: at the edges of the upper or lower front teeth; on the upper edge of the breastbone, at the top of the head; in the forehead; at the back of the neck or down the back of the throat. They argue that, '"Placing", therefore, is not a fiction, as science would have it' (ibid., p. 69). The authors then attempt to justify these manoeuvres physiologically. Inasmuch as sound cannot be 'placed' as the acousti-cians inform us, these theories can only be based on sensations of sympathetic vibration that accompany singing. Since not everybody feels the same sensations this approach is unsound and can be vocally damaging.

Other 'placement' howlers may lead to tension and malfunction, for example: imagine a grapefruit or pear in your throat in order to keep it open; place the tone on the bridge of the nose; up and over; in the dome (of what?); at the back of the throat; in the head; on top of Nefertiti's hat – the list is endless. Ultimately singers will discover their own personal imagery for the sensations they feel when their singing is right. They will become aware that if it does not feel good, then it will not sound or look good.

Kantner and West describe how resonance patterns produce recognizable vowels:

> All vowels, per se, have resonance but each vowel has its own distinct pattern of resonance that is the result of the number, frequencies and energy distribution of the overtones that are present. It is by means of these differences in the overall patterns of resonance that we are able to hear and discriminate one vowel from another. These changing resonance patterns are produced by altering shape and size of the discharging orifice (cited, Miller, 1986, p. 50).

The shape and flexibility of the vocal tract allows for extreme acoustic variation. These extremes have to be balanced. For example, acoustic distortion of the vowel will result if the tongue is held low and flat when the acoustic shaping of the vowel is determined by a quite different tongue position. Similarly, acoustic distortion occurs if the tongue is held high when it ought to be low.[21]

Davis is very keen to point out that the auditor/teacher determines which is the student's best sound, and then encourages the student to remember how it felt and sounded so that it can be rehearsed and remembered. The reason for external guidance is that singers hear their singing sound through bone conduction of their skull and therefore do not appreciate the true sound. Most teachers would accept this point. However Davis goes on to say:

> … the air conduction of sound through the eustachian tube, and the air conduction of sound as it exits the mouth arrive at the ear as vastly different stimuli. For example, as the pitch of the voice goes higher, the upper partials of the voice become more directional and less heard at the ear while bone conduction remains the same. The result is confusion. Generally, the better your voice sounds to you, the worse it sounds to us (1998, p. 36).

I find the last sentence rather strange and Davis does not offer any evidence in support of this statement.[22]

Laryngeal Factors

The position that the larynx is asked to assume for singing has a direct effect on the resultant vocal sound. *Gola aperta* or 'open throat' is the aim to be achieved here and atrocities as to how to produce *gola aperta* have been, and still are, extremely common. As can readily be verified by any observant listener, a high laryngeal position produces distinct vocal timbres. An elevated head and chin thought to free the larynx for singing shortens the vocal tract because the distance between the glottis and the larynx and velum is reduced. This diminishes the depth of timbre resulting in a 'brighter, thinner' sound. A depressed laryngeal position produces other qualities of sound. The lowest possible position of the larynx is achieved with the full-blown yawn, during which action the vocal tract is elongated (the distance from the vocal folds to the velum is increased). These spreading sensations are mistakenly thought to 'open the throat'. But the effect is one of 'darkening' the sound. John Potter claims that the low larynx position is the norm for classical singers; rather, it is a product of the German school (1998, p. 53). It is vocally unhealthy as the larynx is being depressed unnaturally, causing tension and pressure on the vocal folds. The stabilized and freely moveable larynx, which is neither raised nor depressed, results in a free and balanced sound distinct from the first two.

Formants and the Singer's Formant

Appropriate balancing of formants results in 'good singing tone' that displays the 'ring', 'ping', 'focus' of the sound. Miller defines this, 'as the tracking of the laryngeally produced vowel by the resonator tube' (1986, p. 56). A formant is an area of strong acoustic energy (resonance) which determines the distinctive individuality of a vowel.[23] As we have seen above various tonal ideals exist yet they all demand certain qualities required for *crème de la crème* vocalism. The practised ear of the teacher determines when these qualities are present and they show up clearly on a spectrogram. The spectrogram reveals the fundamental frequency and its integral harmonic multiples as they occur within time.[24] In sung pitch the concentration of acoustic energy is not found at the fundamental frequency. Most acoustic energy is found above the frequency of pitch perceived by the listener. This distribution of energy is explained by the overtone series or harmonic series. The lowest note is known as the fundamental sound and the rest are the harmonics, upper partials or overtones; first, second, third, fourth and fifth formants. The first formant is an important region of acoustic strength. It is found at the bottom part of the spectrum, in the area of 500 Hz–800 Hz in the male voice depending upon category. This formant is responsible for 'depth' in the voice or the dark (*oscuro*) of the historical *chiaroscuro* (light/dark) – the balanced sound required of the professional singer.

A second important formant which can be seen in the spectrum is the one which defines vowel sounds. It produces a diagonal pattern characteristic of vowel definition from the lateral (front) to the rounded (back) vowels. Each vowel has its own specific configuration in the laryngeal tract and its own set of distinguishing formants. These formants result from the harmonic partials in the spectrum which determine the characteristic quality of each vowel. These partials are located between the first and third formants. The third formant produces the *chiaro* (light) tone of the *chiaroscuro*. The correct balance of the acoustic energy in the upper, middle, and lower parts of the spectrum plus vibrato constitute the resonance balance of the classically trained voice.

The singer's formant is an area of particular acoustical strength which allows the voice to be heard, for example, over and above the orchestra.[25] In the male voice this can be found at around 2,500–3,200 Hz and, usually, up to 4,000 in the soprano voice, but can reach up to 4000 Hz or 5000 Hz.

Articulation

Articulation is mainly by the lips, tongue and soft palate. Vowels are shaped mostly in the vocal tract, the lips also being used to some extent. The vocal tract is fashioned to change shape in order to assist in the formation of vowels and consonants; it remains flexible during the communication of language both in singing and speaking. The pharynx acts mainly as resonator. The tongue plays a major role in articulation. It is a proportionately large muscle connected to the styloid process on the temporal bone, mandible, hyoid bone, and soft palate.[26] Distortion or tension of the tongue results in very many problems for the singer. Lip movement changes the shape of the anterior part of the vocal tract. Tense lips adversely affect the muscles of the upper pharynx. Exaggerated, protruding lips pull the back of the pharynx forward diminishing the space needed for resonance. Miller argues against the maintenance of a basic posture and lists some pedagogical fallacies which are still promulgated, for example:

1. maintaining a low jaw position,
2. trumpeting the lips (holding the lips in the [u] position),
3. squaring the lips and jaw,
4. pulling down on the platysma muscle,
5. retaining the smile position,
6. maintaining an elevation of the upper lip,
7. covering the upper teeth with the upper lip (pulling downward on the upper lip), and
8. covering the lower teeth with the lower lip.

It is the vowel, the consonant, the tessitura, and the intensity level that determine the degree of mouth aperture (mandibular movement) (2000, p. 83).

The human voice is the only musical instrument that can communicate words. This is an added technical feat for the singer to achieve. If the words are not clearly articulated then the performance is a poor one, and the audience is dissatisfied. Again Freed has found us an apt inaccurate instruction: 'Enunciate with the lungs' (2000, p. 9).

Tetrazzini instructs the singer to have 'the sides [of the tongue] slightly raised so as to form a slight furrow in it' (Caruso and Tetrazzini, 1909, p. 18). She goes on to say, 'in ascending the scale the furrow in the tongue increases as we come to the higher notes' (ibid., p. 18). Many top grade contemporary performers demonstrate this technique. Unfortunately, contrary to popular belief, in this technique the back of the tongue becomes restricted because the bulk of the muscle thus displaced constricts the throat. Another well established tenor performer goes to the lengths of curling the apex of the tongue upwards towards the roof of the palate for assistance in reaching the high C's, which makes for a slightly more strident sound. Doubtless the reasoning is to remove tongue bulk from the resonating pharynx, but I suspect the stretching of the muscle adds tension, hence the stridency heard. In earlier days Domingo said:

> But I do have a basic problem which I discovered only lately. Sometimes I am recording ... feeling really fantastic ... and all of a sudden the voice starts to sound, from one phrase to another, different ... In many notes my tongue goes up. I do that very often, not constantly. You can hear the changes of sound in the microphone ... Now ... I want to put a mirror near my music stand, and I want to control that tone until the tongue will go down by itself automatically (cited by Hines, 1988, p. 105).

Marilyn Horne says of the raised tongue, 'That's terrible ... You've got to get a groove in it.' (ibid., p. 136). And, of course, a groove which runs from front to back of the tongue distorts the muscle and adds tension to its movement. Harry Evan Williams foolishly suggests that we might

> Imagine two pieces of whip cord. Tie the ends together. Place the knot immediately under the upper lip directly beneath the center bone of the nose, run the strings straight back for an inch, then up over the cheek bones, then down around the uvula, thence down the large cords inside the neck. At a point in the center between the shoulders the cords would split in order to let one set go down the back and the other towards the chest, meeting again under the arm-pits, thence down the short ribs, thence down and joining in another knot slightly at the back of the pelvic bone (Williams, 1920, p.127).[27]

This is bad imagery used for a completely wrong purpose. The teacher well educated in how the pharynx and larynx function has no use for such imagery. Nonetheless, there is good imagery as stated by Miller: 'the breath of expectation', 'the breath of joyous anticipation', 'the breath of quiet excitation' (1996, p. 80).

Unfortunately, handed down from one teacher to the next, is the opposing view made by Tetrazzini in 1909: 'As one great singer expresses it: "You should have the jaw of an imbecile when emitting a tone"' (Caruso and Tetrazzini, 1909, p. 25). And yet another howler comes from a teacher eighty-two years later:

> It is perhaps helpful to visualize a washing line, situated on the level of the cheekbones and continuing round each side of the head to the jaw hinges. The placing of consonants remain on that level, but all vowels hang totally loosely from the cheekbones/washing line, like clothes blowing in the wind, with absolutely no tension or holding of the chin (Sutton, 1992, pp. 35–6).

Vowel Modification

Vowel modification or *voce coperta* is sometimes called 'cover' or register unification. *Voce coperta* is the result of consciously modifying the vowel throughout the ascending scale in order to 'disguise' or eliminate the register changes. The aim is for an equalized scale without any perceptible timbre changes or vowel distortion. The vowel, although modified, remains recognizable in all but the most extreme points of the upper range. Conscious controlled adjustments are not applied directly to the larynx or vocal tract. The adjustments are made unconsciously in *voce coperta* by virtue of modification of the vowels according to the demands made by the trained ear. *Voce coperta* is a process of subtle adjustments (*aggiustimento*).

In both female and male instruments, most vowel modification in ascending pitch is in the direction of lateral to rounded vowel. For example, by opening the mouth (lowering the mandible) for ascending pitch, [i] approaches [ɪ]; [ɑ] takes on more of the character of [ɔ], although it may also be necessary to go in the opposite direction with certain voices so that [u] in those cases will actually approach [ʊ]. In some cases, modification may need to go even further. It is wrong to assume that there is one point in the mounting scale applicable to all singers. By opening the mouth with the ascent of pitch, vowel modification becomes a natural process. It also avoids the presence of shrillness on the higher pitches.

Vowel modification is also related to resonance balance. *Chiaroscura* (light-dark) timbre describes the well-balanced resonance throughout the range of the singing voice. In *chiaroscura* the harmonic partials throughout the spectrum have a balanced relationship. The skilful singer achieves *chiaroscura* from the lowest to the highest note of the scale. Although the physiological and acoustical explanation appears complicated, the technical performance of *coperta* is easy to explain, but the execution takes practice.

When Marilyn Horne was asked by Jerome Hines about the sensation she feels when changing registers to achieve higher pitch she says, 'It's like an hourglass, or its like two pyramids, one upside down.' To which Hines added, 'Their tips touching one another' (Hines, 1988, p. 139). This again is imagery, useful perhaps to Marilyn Horne and amazingly understood by Hines, but of very little use to any overhearing student.

Singing teachers approach the teaching of vowel modification and registration events in many different ways, some extremely complicated. For example:

> In my fifth article, I attempted to explain exactly what the *open* and *closed* tones really were. I showed that *open tones* were high extensions of a *lower* Column of Resonance, and the *closed tones* were *lower* extensions of a higher Column. I also introduced my Descriptive Vocal Symbols, which had been developed to communicate with the student more effectively … (de Peyer, 1994, p. 15).

The following rules for modifying vowels are much more straightforward:

1. Vocal tract lengthening and shortening. 'Formant frequencies decrease uniformly as the length of the vocal tract increases' (Titze, 1994, p. 165).
2. Lip rounding lengthens vocal tract, lowering formant frequencies. Lip spreading increases the formant frequencies.

The two following rules should be in mind when forming vowels:

1. Front half of vocal tract (mouth) is narrowed, lowers first formant and raises second formant.
2. Back half (pharynx) is narrowed, raises first formant and lowers second formant.

Sostenuto

As mentioned earlier, singers will be without freedom in their singing unless they are proficient in executing the onset, the brief phrase, the release, can sing with agility, and have precise fluid articulation – there will be a build up of tension and strain particularly when singing long sustained phrases. The best way to achieve *sostenuto* is to progressively lengthen the breath-pacing exercises of short duration mentioned earlier, followed by sustained vocalises. As proficiency increases, range should extend and slower tempos may be introduced.

Vocal problems also may result if the technically insecure singer is given songs and arias of a sustained character, coupled with a high-lying *tessitura* too early. Hence the great need for a wide knowledge of repertoire. Singing extensive sweeping lines is not a possibility if the torso collapses at inappropriate moments.

Dynamic Control and Messa di Voce

Without contrasting dynamics singing lacks expression and interest. An important part of good singing is the control of these dynamics. A singer who appears to be unimaginative in the use of dynamics may in fact be lacking in technique, not imagination.

To increase loudness or intensity an increase in subglottal pressure is necessary. 'The loudness of sounds corresponds to their acoustic intensity and for phonation is primarily dependent upon subglottal pressure' (Scherer, 1995, p. 87). Sundberg states:

> When the abdominal muscles contract after inspiration, the air pressure in the lungs, or the subglottic pressure is raised. How much this pressure is raised depends on the degree of contraction and also on the resistance against airflow provided by the glottis … [the] main tool for raising loudness of phonation is an increase in subglottic pressure (1987, p. 35).

The same tonal quality should be present and maintained both when singing loudly and softly. The airflow rate, although it must still be used efficiently, will be lower when singing softly. Singing *pianissimo* is one of the last aspects of singing technique to be learnt.

To encourage the wide use of contrasting dynamics the classic device is *messa di voce*. Here the student begins to sing at *pianissimo* level with a sustained tone, crescendoing to *fortissimo*, then decrescendoing back to *pianissimo*. The same tonal quality should be apparent throughout. It should be possible to achieve the whole dynamic range of *messa di voce* on every pitch within the entire vocal range. *Messa di voce* is usually the last aspect of technique to be taught and practised, as it requires the ultimate in technical stability. Its importance can hardly be over-estimated. It is the supreme test of a coordinated technique.

Hearing, Feeling and Seeing the Voice

To a great extent singers have to teach themselves, and teachers have to try to develop this independence. I have found that the three following self-help principles are useful. First, being able to *hear* the differences between differently produced sounds; secondly, *feeling* the differences between the differently produced sounds; and thirdly, *seeing* what is happening physically as the result of the various technical manoeuvres.

As previously mentioned, it is often said that one cannot hear oneself sing. We have seen that the sound one hears is not exactly the same as that heard by the audience or teacher. The singer hears the sound externally through the meatus (the passage leading from the ear-drum to the outer ear cartilage) and from behind the megaphone shape of the mouth opening from which the sound emanates. Internally the sound is heard through the sympathetic vibrations of bone conduction. But this does not mean that singers cannot assess the quality of their singing. Singers are aware that they can produce different qualities of sound (timbre) at every pitch level – some more beautiful than others – and can easily distinguish between the different kinds of singing sound they can make at these different pitches. It is the responsibility of the teacher to determine the most desirable sound. The preferred sound is determined by the efficient and healthy way the sound is produced. Teachers must be careful not to be influenced by their own personal tonal ideals or taste, and young singers in particular must avoid the temptation to imitate their favourite performer. When the voice is functioning healthily, efficiently and freely then that is the unique voice belonging to that individual and no one else.

Singers constantly monitor the effect of breath management, vowel modification and all other aspects of technique in order to achieve their most beautiful, efficiently produced sound. Students must be trained to listen carefully and critically and must not be easily satisfied. Teachers must regularly have students assess and reassess the sound being produced. Perhaps teachers of singing should be called teachers of hearing as well as teachers of singing. This hearing should always be linked with how it looks and feels when the sound is right. Hearing, feeling and seeing the acceptable sound will become a measure for consistency in production of the preferred sound and will be stored in the memory, so that this production of beautiful sound, with practice, will become habitual. Nonetheless, the critical ear of the singing teacher is always essential to the singer, hence the need for all professional singers to find time in their busy schedules for check-up singing lessons. This in no way detracts from the statement that singers should have a sound enough understanding of technique to enable them to be their own teacher.

Singers need to be able to repeat exactly, each time they sing, the healthy and efficient manoeuvres for breath coordination, laryngeal activity, and factors of resonation which produce their most beautiful timbre. Learning how it feels when the sound is correctly produced is indispensable, especially when linked with hearing and seeing.

An overall feeling of lightness, poise, balance, energy and joy results from correct bodily alignment that also can be seen with mirrors or the video recording. Correct breath management can be monitored by how it feels when the abdominal musculature releases at the end of the phrase in readiness for the air to refill the lungs, the freedom from any tension in the lower abdominal region while singing, the feeling of release in the head and neck area, and many other factors concerned with posture and breathing. It becomes more and more clear how much anatomical and physiological knowledge is required of the teacher.

The singing voice is sometimes called the 'hidden' instrument. However, much of it can be seen and, therefore, carefully monitored following soundly based instruction. Singers can only see inside their larynx with the aid of medical instrumentation such as fibreoptics and stroboscopy. However, wonderful vocal improvements have been known to be made when singers, under medical supervision, make subtle adjustments on seeing the inside of their larynx by videostroboscopy. Of course, such immediate successes cannot be predicted or guaranteed. Problems singers may have had for years can suddenly disappear when they see what is going on inside their larynx and they try to remember and reproduce this improved sound by how it feels or sounds when they are back on stage or in the studio.

However the larynx is not the only part of the instrument, and much of the rest is visible. We can easily detect incorrect posture, head movement, external musculature of the neck, sternum, clavicles, rib cage and abdomen. We can observe correct and incorrect movement of the mouth, tongue, lips, external facial musculature and even the position of the larynx itself – if we know what we are looking for. Indeed, as we saw in Chapter 1, vocal pedagogues relied exclusively upon such visible features before the advent of instruments capable of revealing internal visualization.

Wall mirrors, freestanding mirrors, hand mirrors, and hand mirrors used together with other mirrors for side-views are indispensable for the singer. The apex of the tongue, the various positions of the mouth, lips and tongue can be carefully monitored, together with facial muscles, laryngeal position and general posture.

The singer has to *look* into the mirror, and many are often reluctant to do this and find it quite difficult at first. Gentle encouragement is sometimes necessary on the part of the teacher. A similar reaction is often found when using video recorders or cassette recorders. Pupils protest, 'I can't bear to watch myself. I can't stand listening to my own voice'.

Singers often imagine and believe that what they are doing is correct, but teachers are seeing and hearing something quite different. Incidentally, it may be useful for singing teachers to have their hearing tested regularly. External posture and physical behaviour on stage needs to be learnt, and what better way of checking this than by the mirror or video recording. Feeling and imagination are not enough; singers need to be aware of how their body language and their facial expressions really appear to an audience.

The three proprioceptive stratagems, hearing, feeling and seeing the voice are extremely reliable checkpoints, given the parameters of healthy and efficient vocal function based on a systematic technique, and they should be included in all vocal pedagogy. If it sounds good, then it feels and looks good. If it feels good, then it looks and sounds good. If it looks good, then it feels and sounds good.

Warming Up and Cooling Down the Voice

'The ability to do subtle tasks with great strength and agility, without forcing, on a very consistent basis' is the definition of athletics suggested by William Riley, New York singing teacher and consultant to Lennox Hill's Department of Otolaryngology (no citation available). He goes on to say that this definition may just as readily be applied to singing.

Saxon and Schneider make it clear that, 'The exercise workout or session for athletic or vocal performance should consist of a progressive regime: warm-up, a conditioning phase, and a cooling down' (1995, p. 69).

The singer is the ultimate vocal athlete. Athletes warm up before an event, they do not suddenly throw themselves into strenuous activity. Most of them begin by performing stretching exercises that encourage gentle movement of the muscles. They may then slowly jog or run. But they never over exert themselves immediately before a race or sporting event. So, surely, this kind of approach must also be beneficial for the singer-athlete. Warming-up helps to strengthen and condition muscles, thus enabling the voice to function more efficiently. Cooling-down following athletic activity is equally important.

Warming-up and cooling-down are appropriate for all types of singing voice including, classical, musical theatre, jazz, blues, rock, popular, night club, gospel, and also for any other professional voice user.

It seems sensible that singers should go through a series of exercises to warm-up the voice first thing in the morning and to cool-down the voice following each intensive practice session, rehearsal or performance. Warm-ups not only help the voice function more efficiently, but also can encourage a feeling of relaxation and focus before a performance.

Whatever the type of singing session, it is advisable that it should consist of a progressive, organized regime. This should include warming-up, the main session or conditioning phase itself, which may be: technical work, learning new repertoire, a singing lesson, rehearsal or performance, and cooling-down.

The function of the *warm-up* is to increase blood flow to the working muscles and increase the muscle temperature, decrease the number of injuries to the working muscles, and increase muscle tissue temperature ... The warm-up activity should gradually intensify to prepare the muscles for the higher intensity conditioning phase (Heywood, V.H., cited by Saxon and Schneider, 1995, p. 69).

Martin, Robinson, Wiegman and Aulick studied the cardio-respiratory responses of subjects with and without warm-up prior to an exercise workout:

Compared to the no-warm-up group, the prior warm-up group reached higher oxygen consumption because warm-up facilitates oxygen's ability to break away from hemoglobin. Consequently, muscles with a higher temperature would increase the muscle enzyme activity and enhance the distribution of blood to the muscle, thereby dissipating the added heat within the muscle (ibid., p. 69).

I suggest that warming-up should be part of a systematic technique taught to the singer by the teacher. It should not be a case of dashing through a random selection of vocal exercises, but should become an established routine and may take between twenty and thirty minutes every day, maybe less time for the singer in peak condition. Having this consistent routine monitors the condition of the voice and may give a feeling of physical and psychological security. Warming-up should be part of the every day routine not only of the singer, but also of the teacher, the choral director and every other professional voice user, whether speaker or singer. Of course, responsible choral directors will ensure that their choristers are warmed-up at rehearsal and prior to performance.

It is advisable for singers to warm up before their singing lesson; otherwise much of the precious lesson time is wasted if the teacher has to work through the warm-up routine before introducing technical work. The teacher would be well advised to review the student's warm-up routine from time to time, checking on correct performance and the order of the exercises. And, of course, beginner singers will have to learn and be able to accomplish, healthily and efficiently, the exercises set before the routine can be established.

Individual programmes may be devised to suit particular needs. Light physical exercises for relaxation, energizing, stretching and releasing the whole body, should precede any vocalization. Exercises to be included are those which give a feeling of freedom and elasticity throughout the body, for example: gently running on the spot; swinging the arms in a windmill fashion; dropping the head and arms downwards and then returning slowly to an upright position; slow shoulder shrugs; gentle head turning from side to side on a level plane and slow forward head rolling. Strenuous exercise should not be attempted immediately before singing.

It is recommended to begin vocal warm-ups in medium vocal range with a graduated approach. Nothing drastic should be attempted. A suggested programme is as follows:

1. Gentle, brief onsets and offsets (attack and release).
2. Humming in a medium range.
3. Nasal and vowel sequences.
4. Exercises to encourage a flexible tongue and jaw.
5. Agility exercises, beginning with descending patterns in a medium range and gradually adding ascending patterns with range extension.

A short period of rest is advisable before proceeding.

6. Vowel definition and modification.
7. *Sostenuto.*
8. Registration and *passaggi* exercises.
9. Rapid, extensive range arpeggios and rapidly moving scale passages.[28]

In the warm-ups specific technical problematic aspects are not dealt with; these come later in the daily practice (conditioning) sessions. It is proposed that singers should beware of too long periods of warming up, particularly before performance.

Although the benefits of vocal warm-ups have long been understood, the benefits of cooling down have not been appreciated or widely used for as long. The same exercises should be used, but at a lower intensity level. Low intensity activity allows the blood to return to the heart, which staves off blood pooling in the extremities. It also prevents dizziness, the possibility of fainting, and it shortens the recovery time. Singers may apply these thoughts to their vocalizing.

At about midday on performance days (assuming an evening performance) after a leisurely morning, it is beneficial to work through the complete daily warm-up routine, including the few gentle physical exercises of the type suggested above. This session should, perhaps, last for about twenty minutes with short rests between each exercise. After this singing is best avoided until just before performance time when a few scales or arpeggios may be sung. Performers need to find a quiet place where they can warm up on their own without the distraction of others who may have idiosyncratic ways of preparing for performance. To use opening songs of a show or recital as a substitute for warming up beforehand is unacceptable, unprofessional, and potentially disastrous. Beginning a heavy singing role, either in rehearsal or performance without warming up is vocally unhealthy. To go straight from the stage to a post-performance party with one's friends and fans may be good public relations, but hard on a voice that has just been cooled down.

It is recommended that all singers have a reliable, consistent routine for warming up and cooling down. The benefits in terms of healthy and efficient vocal function and for a confident feeling of security will very soon be seen to be enormous.

The Spoken Voice

Although singers spend a great amount of time and money on their singing voices, very few seriously consider training for their speaking voices. Very often the

singer's vocal problem shows up in the voice clinic as a speaking voice problem. We have one larynx for both singing and speaking. However, there are significant differences between speaking and classical singing. Singing has requirements greater than those required for speech. The classical singer does not engage in sung speech. There are additional factors, among them: wide-ranging pitch; longer duration of the vowel; specific breath management adjustments, energy and control; and resonance balance. Some singers, in spoken dialogue in opera, speak with their singing voice technique – they continue to 'sing' as they speak. Rather, they should have training in speaking for the stage. It must be remembered that in non-traditional notation and extended vocal techniques we find vocal hybrids such as *Sprechstimme* and recitation, which may be considered as neither speaking nor singing.[29]

Ideally, the spoken voice should match the singing voice.[30] Work on the spoken voice is neglected in many singing studios, with the result that many singers have speaking voices which are misused and often sound like a completely different person. This can be particularly jarring, both for the singer's and the listener's ear when an opera singer is required to alternate between song and speech. There can be no question that a well-trained and well-used speaking voice will contribute to the longevity of the singing voice. As Rodenburg has rightly said:

> To speak a heightened text clearly to hundreds of people requires a huge vocal extension ... To speak and then to sing and then speak, are demanding activities that require skill and stamina (1997, p. viii).

This judgement is endorsed from the side of speech therapy by Morton Cooper: 'Misuse and abuse of the speaking voice may negatively influence and affect, if not destroy, the singing voice' (Hines, 1988, p. 48).

The following quotaton from Miller will both encapsulate the main findings of this chapter on technique and lead us forward to consider the multi-faceted subject of performance:

> Anyone who practices an art form must first learn to deal with all its components. That is why the singer needs to learn systematic coordination of the motor, the vibrator, and the resonator. Only then can the art of performance become a holistic event (2004, p. 248).

Notes

1   See further, White, Peta (2001), 'Long-term average spectrum (LTAS) analysis of sex- and gender-related differences in children's voices', *Logopedics, Phoniatrics, Vocology*, **26** (3), 97–101.

2   See further, Welch, Graham F., and Peta White (1993/4), 'The developing voice: education and vocal efficiency – a physical perspective', *Bulletin, Council for Research in Music Education* (119), Winter, 146–56.

3 See further, Harris, Lee D. (1993), 'An investigation of selected vocal characteristics in young male singers at various stages of maturation', *Texas Music Education Research*, 15–22.

4 See further, Sataloff, Robert Thayer (2000), 'Vocal aging and its medical implications: what singing teachers should know', *Journal of Singing*, **57** (2), November/December, 23–8.

5 See further, Richard Miller's clear description of the countertenor's vocal technique in *The Structure of Singing*, New York: Schirmer, 1986, pp. 123–5.

6 See further, Pleasants, Henry (1983), *The Great Singers*, London: Macmillan.

7 Vilkman and colleagues suggest that registers are biomechanical happenings and depend on several physiological and aerodynamic events. See further, Vilkman, E. and A.M. Laukkanen (1995), 'Vocal-fold collision mass as a differentiator between registers in the low-pitch range', *Journal of Voice*, **9** (1), 66–73.

8 See further, Miller, Richard (1986), *The Structure of Singing*, New York: Schirmer.

9 See further, Chapter 1 above.

10 See Appendix 4, Illustration 11.

11 For relevant exercises see Miller, Richard (1986), *The Structure of Singing*, New York: Schirmer.

12 Titze (1994, p. 74) goes on to recommend detailed discussions on breathing by Vennard, William, 1967; Proctor, D.F., 1980; Hixon, T.J., 1987).

13 See further, Chapter 1 above.

14 See further, Stark, James (1999), *Bel Canto. A History of Vocal Pedagogy*, Buffalo, NY: University of Toronto Press.

15 See further, McNaughton, Elizabeth (2002), *Breathing for Singing and its Vocal Pedagogy*, London: Phoenix Again.

16 See further, Bunch, Meribeth (2000), *A Handbook of the Singing Voice*, London: Meribeth Dayme (formerly Bunch).

17 For essays and scientific experiments concerning vibrato see further, Dejonckere, P.H., Minoru Hirano, and Johan Sundberg (1995), *Vibrato*, San Diego: Singular.

18 See further, Sundberg, Johan (1987), *The Science of the Singing Voice*, Dekalb, IL: Northern Illinois University Press.

19 Hz is a unit of measurement of cycles per second as in 440 Hz (current concert pitch) named after the physicist Gustav Hertz. See further, Miller, Richard (1986), *The Structure of Singing*, New York: Schirmer, 1986.

20 See further, Austin, Stephen F. (2000), 'Nasal resonance – fact or fiction?' *Journal of Singing*, **57** (2), November/December, 33–41.

21 See Appendix 4, Illustration 12.

22 See further, Zielinski, Shirley and Paul Kiesgen (2002), 'To listen or not to listen', *Journal of Singing*, **59** (2), November/December, 133–8.

23 See further, Chapter 3 above.

24 See further, Watson, Colin (1992), 'Higher partial enhancement and glottal source manipulation by the trained opera singer', *Voice*, **1** (1), 1–18.

25 See further, Sundberg, Johan (1987), *The Science of the Singing Voice*, Dekalb, IL: Northern Illinois University Press.

26 See Appendix 4, Illustration 13.

27 Richard Miller has the most telling example of all resonatory imagery, used in a lesson he once observed and which he demonstrates in public lectures, the full text being found in his *On the Art of Singing*, 1996, Oxford: Oxford University Press, pp. 41–3.

28   See further, Titze, Ingo (2001), 'The five best vocal warm-up exercises,' *Journal of Singing*, **57** (3), January/February, 51–2.
29   See further Mabry, Sharon (2002), *Exploring Twentieth-Century Vocal Music*, Oxford: Oxford University Press.
30   See further, Boone, Daniel (1997) *Is Your Voice Telling on You?* London: Whurr. Although mainly addressed to spoken voice users, the content is appropriate for all levels of singers.

Chapter 5

Performance

In this chapter I shall consider the preparation for performance, the occasion of performance, and the evaluation of performance. We shall see that in addition to specifically musical matters, psychological, philosophical and other considerations come into view. My case is that it is important that vocal pedagogues clearly understand how this happens and that they achieve a degree of mastery of the several contributory fields.

The Preparation for Performance

It goes without saying that performances are of many kinds, and take place in a variety of venues. In this chapter, without in any way denying the importance of performing at auditions and on the radio and television, I shall concentrate on opera and the concert platform.[1] Following some general remarks on each of these spheres I shall turn to some more specific matters which bear directly upon the preparation of literature for performance.

General Considerations

Opera

Opera singers are required to immerse themselves deeply, not only in the study of the character they will be playing, but also in the context from which the opera's plot emerges. As with the song, the text should be spoken aloud, read and re-read, and the singers should become increasingly familiar with the character to be played. The dramatic conflicts and their causes in the text ought to be considered. Scenes can be imagined and various questions asked: What is the national and domestic background? Are the actions of the character obvious or subtle? What is the character's physique, posture, manner? How does he or she behave? What would be the facial expressions in given situations? Acting is the art of reacting to an underlying cause in the plot. It is useful to improvise the role, using mime – actions often speak louder than words.

Opera often requires singers to act and react in a language not their own. In this case it is helpful to take the score and write a word-for-word translation. It is important that what is being sung comes across as a language, not as isolated syllables.[2] Singers have to realize dramatic possibilities when they explore vocally such theatrical devices as whispered lines, voices played in disguise, or even pauses in recitative for maximum dramatic impact. In *Cosi Fan Tutti*, for example, one of the biggest difficulties is found in the *secco* recitatives, which must move at normal speech tempo and sound like ordinary conversation.[3]

Opera singers have used the term 'third line' to refer to the unwritten interpretative line devised by the singer to accompany the text and music of an opera. Helfgot, with Beeman, clearly explains the meaning:

> The third line is, briefly, the interpretative line a singer adds to the other two lines in an operatic score. The first line is the text of the libretto. The second is the musical line. The third line is one the *singer* adds and consists of the body movement, eye focus, facial expression, and inflection that make the score leap off the page and into reality on the stage. The third line is the singers' considered conclusion as performers – their visual, physical, mental, and vocal answer to the tasks set for them by the composer and librettist (1993, p. 6).

In opera (as in oratorio) we find that there are three kinds of recitative: *recitativo secco* (dry recitative), *recitativo accompagnato* or *arioso* (accompanied recitative), and *recitative drammatico* (dramatic recitative, sometimes a combination of *secco* and *accompagnato*). Clarity of diction is a basic requirement in all recitative and particularly in *recitative secco*.[4] Recitative is generally concerned either with story telling, explaining ideas or describing feelings. The singer has a little more freedom in expressing the meaning of the text than in a song or aria. The story needs to be moved on; the thoughts and feelings need to be expressed as if they had been thought of just at that moment, not rehearsed and memorized – of course, this aspect of immediacy applies to songs and arias too.

Once it was not required of an opera singer to act. Nowadays they are encouraged to be as convincing as actors in the theatre. They have to consider the composer's intentions and interpret them in performance. Acting assists in communication, creating a reality on the stage.

There are two main schools of acting: classical or technical (mainly Western European), and method acting (sometimes linked with America) which is based on the teaching of Stanislavski. To these must be wedded the specialized training of actor-singers.[5] While much could be written on acting methods it will suffice here to note that opera singers will need to understand stage directions; appreciate the importance of relevant gestures as contributing to characterization; be at ease with stage properties; and be able to project from recumbent positions. They should also be able to speak lines as convincingly as they sing them – and do so in character.[6]

Becoming accustomed to one's costume is an important part of the opera singer's preparation. Particular attention is required to period and historical costume, such as winged collars or corsets, to ensure that these garments allow rib movement and do not instigate clavicular breathing or restrict the breathing mechanism. Technical exercises may be practised to counteract this and rehearsal in costume as soon as possible is advisable. High collars should not be so high that they make singers throw their heads back. Hats and wigs must be securely fitted so that singers are not spending effort balancing them with resulting neck tension. Moustaches and beards must be securely fixed; additional weight on the head may restrict movement and facial hair can alter points of tension. Shoes with high heels or platforms will alter body balance and alignment, so work will be needed to maintain correct postural alignment. Masks may constrict the head and neck, leading to inaudibility and reduced sight lines; it is best to redesign them where possible, and to rehearse wearing the masks as soon as possible.

Concert Platform

Traditionally a recital included: Italian or English song of the seventeenth and/or eighteenth century; German lieder; French *mélodies*; folk or contemporary English song. Sometimes opera arias were inserted. However the introductory 'old' pieces may be fraught with dangers for the inexperienced singer, for many are technically difficult, particularly for insertion at the beginning of the programme when the singer is settling and developing rapport with the audience.

There is much to be said for opening a recital with two or three shorter songs, rather than something longer; audiences may be rather more restless at the beginning of a recital, and some may intrude as latecomers, thereby disturbing a longer work. As first impressions count, it is recommended that the first songs be chosen carefully and executed with great finesse. A more modern longer piece with opportunity to warm up, emotionally as well as technically, might also be a sensible choice at the beginning of the recital. This 'warm-up' is not the regular daily routine (see Chapter 4). Opera arias are often best programmed sparingly, especially in the case of a beginning performer.

In order to provide adequate resting time for the singer, three groups might be sung in the first half of the concert and two groups in the second. The first half of a recital is usually longer than the second half. It is advisable to have the total length of singing time not more than an hour and a quarter. Less music is better than too much – in performance, tempo usually goes slower than in rehearsal – the accompanist often begins a little slower for safety reasons and the singer tends to put more expression into the actual performance.

The second group may be in a different language from the first, and in a different style. Something with an obbligato instrument would give additional colour to the programme, for example, Schubert's *Der Hirt auf dem Felsen* or perhaps something less familiar. An operatic aria could come in the third group as a climax to the first half of the programme. After the interval, a lighter approach might be more suitable and a change of language. Traditionally, the last group was in English and often consisted of national folk songs or sometimes comedic songs. For encores the pieces should be light and familiar. If too many encores are demanded and the singer is becoming tired then a quiet song will usually put an end to the proceedings.

The accompanist usually writes the programme notes, but there is a tendency, nowadays, for singers to introduce their own music; thereby helping to create a bond between the audience and singer. It is recommended that these introductions be rehearsed and presented so that the voice carries to the back of the auditorium. Also to be considered are printed programme notes and song translations. These are expensive to produce and the rustling of programmes as the text is followed can be as disturbing to the singer as to the audience. An anecdote tells of Toscanini ordering programme notes of gold silk to reduce noise, however even they rustled. For programme notes to be read easily some house lights need to be on; this, unfortunately, may nullify the theatrical atmosphere. In general, it is suggested that each half of the concert begin in lighter mood and moderate tempo gradually building up to a dramatic and emotional climax, and finally the recital ending with a complete change of mood, possibly humorous, thus leaving the audience in a bright and cheerful mood, and the singer feeling good about the performance. There is much to be said for balance, proportion and variety.

The success of a song can depend on where it is placed in the programme. Chronology is not important. Singers would do well to plan carefully contrasts between styles, tempi, keys, rhythmic patterns in piano accompaniment, mood, and expression. Pauses between songs in song cycles should be varied and therefore planned in advance.

It follows from what has just been said that in devising a programme the likely performance impact and entertainment value should be borne in mind. Students are well advised to avoid the performance of songs that contain technical or interpretative pitfalls that they have yet to overcome. They may have their own preferences – those songs they think they perform well, and that have been successful in previous recitals. On the other hand, some of this repertoire may display habitual faults because of over familiarity, which will need correcting. It may be wise to learn something new. A programme consisting of difficult numbers piled on difficult numbers will exhaust the singer by interval time. It is recommended that easier songs follow difficult ones, not only in view of preserving the vocal health of the singer but also in order to avoid audience exhaustion. 'Avant-garde' scores may appear strange at first, but are often relatively simple to perform.[7] A debut recital should show the singer at his or her best – a future career may hang on this. In the big cities, unfortunately, critics may dash from one recital to another, staying for only a small part of the performance. Something unfamiliar or new may be inserted in the programme to attract the critic's attention, although some critics like to hear familiar music in order to be able to compare one performer with another. Conscientious critics will decide what they wish to hear, and time their appearance accordingly.

It is highly desirable that the singer who performs recitals regularly has a large repertoire of programmes, which do not become routine, but are constantly revised, with new material added. The experienced singer may present a one-language recital and sometimes a one-composer recital – sometimes with the composer acting as accompanist.

At the present time themed programmes are in vogue: Shakespearean poems; Goethe settings; an evening of Romantic songs; a single language programme; twentieth century; songs for children or about children. The Song Makers Almanac has many varied themed programmes, among them, 'Night and Day'.

A discussion may be had about choosing the material according to the likely audience. However, it takes a lot of experience to judge the psychology of an audience. Should the programme be different for large cities, for example, London, where self-selected audiences are more likely than in the provinces where a diverse audience needs to be attracted? Generally, and unfortunately, popular appeal wins the day. This perpetuates the problem of what to present. Mabry makes bold to say:

> Today's media-addicted, channel-surfing audiences will no longer sit for long periods through a passive performance. They crave variety, excitement, and passion in short doses. This societal change has many negative implications for the vocalist (2002, p. 20).

As Emmons and Sonntag says:

> It is imperative to recognize that the song recital, however aesthetic and refined it may be, is meant to be enjoyed. The prime purpose of a recital cannot be educational, although its educational value is an inherent factor (Emmons and Sonntag, 1979, pp. 21–2).

It is quite a different situation if the audience is made up of interested persons, for example, managers, agents, personal and press representatives.

Plunket Greene recommends ten essentials in programme planning:

1. Variety of Language.
2. Change of Composer (except in the case of a group).
3. Chronological Order.
4. Change of Key.
5. Change of Time.
6. Classification of the Song.
7. Style of Technique.
8. Change of *Tempo* or Pace.
9. *Crescendo* and *Diminuendo* of Emotion.
10. Atmosphere and Mood (1914, pp. 223–4).[8]

In a song recital there is a degree of intimacy, therefore a minimum of extra musical gesture must communicate subtle and evanescent emotions expressed in the poems and music. Piano parts are often as expressive as the vocal line and may convey in the music more essential elements immediately than the words in the text. Smaller halls are frequently the best setting, though some singers with larger than life personalities can cope with larger venues.

Student recitals may be used as a measure of their progress and comparison with their peers. Ideally, such recitals might be held twice a year. They give experience of performing and afford opportunities of experiencing, and constructively handling, performance anxiety.

Concerts range from more informal ventures in the voice teacher's studio, through festival finales to large-scale concerts with full orchestra. Increasingly fashionable are holistic concerts in which the art song is integrated with other performing arts, notably speech, dance, painting and fragrance. Venues are equally varied: from stately homes, villages and church halls to major theatres. All of which throws into relief the wisdom of Oren Brown's words: 'In presenting a song, nothing should be taken for granted either sociologically, psychologically, or physically' (1996, p. 135).[9]

Specific Matters

It is a prominent argument of this work that sound vocal technique is the foundation for successful performance. Not, indeed, that technique is all. Bunch has rightly remarked:

> To elevate technique into an art there must be co-ordination that allows freedom in performance, spontaneity that springs from confidence and knowledge and lastly personal magnetism to attract the listeners (1995, p. 139).[10]

Accordingly, we now turn our attention to some further specific matters that bear upon preparation for performance. Our first concern must be with the songs or arias to be sung.

Learning Songs

There are three main approaches to learning songs which apply to both children and adults: immersion and phrase-by-phrase, and a combination of the two – the whole/part/whole (WPW).[11] In the WPW approach the piece or a significant proportion is experienced first before any details are worked out. The piece may be sung through or a recording listened to, the point being to create a starting point and to show the context of the piece. The second stage is the 'part' of WPW where smaller sections are rehearsed. Finally the whole piece is sung through, bringing together the details rehearsed, as they relate to the work as a whole, and thus giving a sense of accomplishment.

There is much to be said for treating every song as a whole. Plunket Greene is adamant about this:

The composer wrote it as a whole; the singer must sing it as a whole. A musical phrase is made up of a number of notes. The singer does not think of those notes separately; he thinks of the phrase as a whole, and the song is to the phrase what the phrase is to the note. The mind absorbs the picture, and the detail fits into the perspective of itself (1914, p. 13).

It is a good idea to encourage singers to discover how the music is constructed. What is the form of the piece? What is the most obvious rhythmic characteristic of the piece? How would you describe the overall feel or rhythmic flow? Where is the point of arrival for this phrase? How does the composer set the text to convey its meaning? Lilli Lehmann suggests that the text comes before the tone; get 'an entire picture' of the text before singing it (1924, p. 204). Garcia agrees with her:

The pupil must read the words of the piece again and again till each finest shadow of meaning has been mastered ... The accent of truth apparent in the voice when speaking naturally is the basis of expression in singing (1894, p. 59).

In the historic Italian school of singing the advice to singers, as we saw and which could be applied here, was '*cantare come parlare*', 'sing as you speak'.

Repetition of pitches and rhythms is meaningless without the study of the score (including, among other things, dynamics) and text. It is valuable to have thinking musicians taking an active part in their music making. Repeating phrases over and over again without correct dynamics, phrasing, or intonation breeds poor and incorrect performance habits, which have to be undone if the detail is added later.[12]

The inherent repetitiveness of a strophic song clearly poses problems for the singer. As Whitton comments, 'It is undoubtedly a limiting, even limited form, and without a great interpreter ... it can readily lead to boredom' (1984, p. 8). On the other hand, paradoxically, the very repetitiveness of strophic song gives scope for variety and complexity, in the interplay between a poem which progresses, with music which repeats. We hear the textual meaning in each poetic strophe, which is then connected retrospectively with each repeat of the music. However there must be some legitimate artistic reason for varying the mood, dynamics and tempi when the music is repetitive.

Textual and musical dissonance occurs when the text does not match what the music expresses. This has sometimes been considered a weakness in the composition, but some would say that it highlights that particular part of the text. Much has been written on this aspect of interpretation.[13]

Each note must have its vowel sustained for its entire length, no matter how short it is, particularly on unstressed syllables and notes which are not on the beat, and especially if a song or phrase begins on an anacrusis, otherwise the *legato* line is lost. Silences and rests are music and, therefore, sung through silently to maintain movement, pace and rhythm. Careful breathing adds to both musical and literary effect, and dynamics should be scaled carefully within the song as a whole.

Miller usefully cautions us against the following:

scooping into important words (beginning the note slightly under pitch), with gradual arrival at the tonal center

starting the vocal tone straight and then letting it 'wiggle' with vibrato

introducing rubato where the composer never intended

detailing and underscoring each long note in every musical phrase

negating the vocal legato on notes of short duration

removing vibrancy on notes of short duration

changing the dynamic intensity of each note in a phrase

using exaggerated 'vocal coloration' and 'word painting' to the detriment of vocal timbre (1999, p.16).

Practice is vital.[14] It is sensible to have a flexible approach to practising, where methods can be adapted according to the individual piece. There is much to be said for working hard in short bursts. Problems requiring extensive work may be isolated: the same stumbling occurs in the same place if only run-throughs are prac-tised. Analytical bar-by-bar scrutiny without voice, including phrasing, notation and text is helpful. Necessary beats should be marked. It is useful when speaking the text aloud, to encourage awareness of percussive and *legato* elements in the syllables as well as in the overall meaning. Singers would be well advised to learn the accompa-niment thoroughly. A certain caution is advisable when publishers supply accompa-niment tapes with the score; such tapes may become crutches, contributing to imitation, a restriction of the singer's imagination and a 'quick-fix' approach.

As with the beginning of the song, the ending is immensely important. According to Plunket Greene it should be executed without recourse to sentimental tricks such as a *rallentando* plus *portamento*. He goes on to make helpful suggestions, for example, the use of the *Kunst-pause* (artistic pause); emphasis on the first consonant of the final word and the appropriate use of anti-climax (1914, p. 178).

With a view to classifying a song and visualizing its context, Davis suggests grouping questions, 'who, what, where, when and why' (1998, p. 62). Here is a selection of questions that might be asked:

1. Who are you? (age, status, gender). What do I want? How am I going to get it? Why am I here? To whom am I speaking?
2. What are you saying in the song?
3. Where are you when you sing it? Where is the listener?
4. When does the song occur? What happened before the song and what follows?
5. Why are you singing the song? What use is it in the programme or opera?

We next have to consider the choice of repertoire for student singers. The treasure chest of vocal music contains folksong, ballad, art song, lied, recitative, aria, arioso, *scena*, song cycle, opera, comic opera, grand opera, music drama, operetta, hymn, sacred solo, anthem, cantata, oratorio, mass, passion. How can the teacher go about choosing repertoire for students, when the material available is so extensive? The following are a few suggestions:

1. Select music of good quality.[15]
2. Select teachable music – generally speaking good quality music will be teachable.
3. Select music appropriate to the context: age appropriate, with cultural setting suitability; appropriate range and *tessitura* and level of difficulty; respect for the student's taste at first, followed by the presentation of a broader and more diverse repertoire; choice of song that singer enjoys singing.

Rhythm

Rhythm is the most basic element in music, yet probably the most difficult to teach or define. Songs may be sung with the correct time values but they do not sound right if the feeling of rhythmic progression is absent.

> Music do I hear?
> Ha! ha! keep time: – How sour sweet music is,
> When time is broke, and no proportion kept! (Shakespeare, *Richard II*).

This feeling of rhythmic progression comes from within the singer; it is not just feeling the beat. There are ways to help: as a phrase or section is practised, the singer may stop for at least a beat on the first pulse of every bar (stops can be determined in different places in shorter or longer bars); all music before the strong beat must be felt as leading to it. These suggestions may be practised several times and then the music can be sung again with no stops, but with the singer still leading in the mind towards those strong pulses. This will help to encourage rhythmic progression. Plunket Greene again gives timely advice:

> ... wherever breath has to be taken *in spite of* a phrase – *i.e.* where no pause is marked – *the time-value must be taken from the note that is left, not the note that is approached*; it is the place you land on, not the place you take off from, which matters (1914, p. 62).

Languages

Much of the great song literature is composed to poems in a language other than English. In order to communicate it is essential that singers completely understand the text. It is recommended that every student study foreign languages and not just take a course in foreign diction. Communication consists not only of words but of an exchange of thoughts or ideas between the singer and the audience. This is not possible if students do not understand the language in which they are singing. Some teachers will not assign songs in a foreign language that has not been studied by the student.

The singer should have at least a reading knowledge of the language in which the song or aria is written. This will promote a fuller understanding of the text.[16] When faced with Russian text a mastery of the Cyrillic alphabet is essential. As if the challenge of other languages were not enough, English singers often give the impression when singing *English* texts that they are singing with their mouths full of marbles; their vowels are often distorted and the meaning of the text is lost.

Working with a vocal coach/répétiteur helps the singer to understand foreign texts and improve pronunciation. The vocal coach and répétiteur do not teach singing as such. Their function is to ensure that singers move on from the répétiteur to the conductor and orchestra secure in what they are singing. The répétiteur guides the singer towards accuracy coupled with interpretation, good intonation, a pleasing sound and a high standard of diction. There is a very thin dividing line here between teaching technique and performance. Répétiteurs' keyboard skills (which are different from those of the concert pianist, to whom the score is sacrosanct) allow them to create the atmosphere of the orchestra and take liberties with the score in order to produce dramatic effects.

Diction

Diction is not the same thing as articulation. Articulation is the physical process of making the sounds or as the *Oxford English Dictionary* defines it, 'the adjustments and movements of the speech organs involved in pronouncing a particular sound'. The same dictionary defines an articulator as 'an organ in the mouth or throat which when moved, helps to give speech sounds their characteristic acoustic properties'. Diction is an individual's way of pronouncing words. Considerations for the performer are:

1. Being understood by the listener.
   Good diction should not be sacrificed for beauty of tone, or production of high pitches. A vowel held on a long note should retain its integrity. Diphthongs and triptphongs should be analyzed carefully so that the correct vowel receives the stress and importance required. A composer sometimes creates a musical phrase with the important word sung on a high pitch – for example, for emphasis or dramatic effect. Incorrect pronunciation must not be allowed to destroy this effect. The listener may misunderstand colloquial or local pronunciations. Dictionaries that incorporate IPA are invaluable.
2. Deciphering the difference between the way a word is spelt and the way it is pronounced.
   When performers are not fully familiar with a language, reliance on a phonetic approach can have its dangers. For instance, a performer may not realize that in English the word *palm* has a silent *l*, or that the final consonant of the German word *und* is pronounced as a *t*.[17]
3. Recognizing that there are more than five or six vowels.
   All vowel sounds in whatever language should be identified and practised separately, in order to maintain their unique qualities. Vowel modification helps to

eliminate the 'problems' of high notes without sacrificing the identity of the vowel.[18]

4. Knowing when and which form of consonant to use.

Consonants are classed as Voiced, where the consonant is produced by sounding the consonant vocally, for example, [b] as in 'baby'; or Voiceless, where the consonant resonates by the air passing through the vocal folds, for example, [p] as in 'puppy'.

Singers are always being admonished to 'sing on the vowels and shorten the consonant'. One might gather from this that consonants are the enemy. Of course, badly enunciated consonants will destroy not only the understanding of the text but the whole musical line. On the other hand, many teachers, such as Garcia II, Marchesi, Vennard and Miller, have written about using consonants to improve sound quality, to induce sensations and for resonance balancing.[19]

5. Determining the correct pronunciation of a word.

Students should have a good knowledge of IPA and have easy access to a dictionary with a good pronunciation guide. IPA is considered a basic tool of vocal pedagogy, but there are perils to avoid. There can be discrepancy in symbols between authors, author preference or pronunciation discrepancies. Some language sounds, for various linguistic reasons, do not correspond easily to the finite symbols set by IPA. Some composers set texts from outside the Western tradition, such as, native American, Maori, Zulu, and European folk traditions. Some compositions involve extended vocal techniques or a non-language text and they employ IPA symbols for sound colours, for example, *Stimming* by Stockhausen.

However the delivery of sung text depends also on grammatical and syntactic structure of a language, the 'feel' or 'taste' of words, the spoken intonation and stress patterns, what a word implies as well signifies and not only good enunciation and diction.[20] A strict adherence to IPA transcription can lead to the interpretation sounding stilted and mechanical. Nevertheless one of the greatest strengths of IPA is that it compels students to look at what actually is happening to the sounds as they speak or sing.

Improvement in diction does not come about by the study of IPA alone. The symbols must be understood for what they are and related to the actual sounds of the language to be performed. Individual coaching in the language still needs to be given to the student by the teacher. If the song is to be sung in a standard version of the language IPA is helpful. It is also useful for the acquisition of a regional accent and in an historical approach to diction, for example, Britten's *A Ceremony of Carols*, or Debussy's *Trois Chansons de François Villon*.

Care must be taken that extra vowels and consonants are not added to words, for example, 'that love of mine' should not have a schwa [ə] added to the end of 'mine'.[21]

Again, the lyrics of Gilbert and Sullivan may help singers to learn how to deliver dialogue. Some critics and commentators have a disdain for Gilbert and Sullivan and some singers think that their music is of a low status. But singing their works provides much practice in delivering clear diction and in articulation.

It goes without saying that for effective training of the student in optimal communication of a song it is imperative that voice teachers have complete knowledge of the movements of the muscles in the vocal tract required for the phonological system of the language being sung.

Phrasing

Giovanni Lamperti said of phrasing, 'Phrasing is simply musical punctuation, which frequently coincides with that of the words' (1905, p. 31).

Legato is essential to achieve a beautiful and smooth phrase or musical line. Originally the words *legato* and *portamento* were used interchangeably. We recall that Lamperti's theory was that

> portamento signifies the gentle carrying-over (not dragging over) of one tone to another. In doing so, the second tone is barely audibly anticipated at the end of the first (1905, p. 21).

Today *portamento* means the consciously perceived gliding between neighbouring notes of more than a major second.

Miller has this to say: 'Perhaps the most expressive device is the *legato*, which permits continuous sound that then can be sculpted into eloquent phrases' (1996, p. 108). The term *legato* stems from the Italian verb *legare* meaning to 'bind' or 'tie'. In singing *legato* is the result of binding one sound to the next. It is the progression of uninterrupted sound. Continuous vocal sound will move the phrase and gives it its direction. If the singer changes from sound with vibrato to a non-vibrato sound then both *legato* and the flow of the phrase is interrupted. If a false assumption is made that it is artistically desirable to customize each syllable or word in order to enhance it, minutely detailed and conscious shaping of a phrase can be counterproductive, in effect destroying the contour of the phrase. Some singers treat syllables and words like long swags of sausage links (Miller, 2004, p. 201). Thus, we hear notes not phrases, and words not sentences. In this preoccupation with detail we find the singer making a *messa di voce* on every syllable, in the hope of being artistic, but this results in mannerisms and musical naivety. Of course, there has to be dynamic variation throughout the song or aria. Diction will be clearer when constant *legato* and quickly occurring consonants allow a flowing singing line:

> A combination of subtleties of rhythm and dynamics such as I have been describing creates that priceless musical ingredient which is called 'line'. A phrase must not be just a series of tones, they must be related to each other organically. The whole must be greater than the sum of all its parts. Each tone must seem to grow out of the preceding tone … (Vennard, nd., p. 28).

Bernac believes that '… it is the musical line, above all, that the singer must serve and respect' (1978, p. 4). He, seemingly, interchanges the term *legato* with *cantabile* (ibid., p. 4). A phrase must always have a main word and with it a musical highpoint; it can be found by reading the text aloud emphasizing what is important and giving less importance to the surrounding words.

Often it is appropriate to use the device staccato. Staccato being the opposite of *legato*, Kirkland suggests:

> Departure from the *legato* is not to be made merely for the sake of departure, nor for the sake of singing a passage in another mode, but to emphasize the emotion being expressed at the moment (1916, p. 126).

Tone Colour

In catechetical style Garcia II asks:

> Q. Is the great variety of timbres of any practical use?
> A. They are the physiognomy of the voice. They tell the involuntary emotions which affect us, and assume a more clear or covered tint, a timbre more brilliant or more obscure, according to the nature of those feelings (1894, p. 45).

In Plunket Greene's opinion, 'Tone-colour is part of the physical *response of the voice to the play of feeling* … ' (1914, p. 19). He goes on to describe two kinds of tone-colour; one being *Atmospheric* where the tone-colour reflects the mood and *Dramatic* where the voice reflects a character or characters (ibid., p. 20). It may thus be concluded that the text itself determines tone colour, a technical manipulation of the tone is unnecessary.

Aural Skills, Theory, Composition and Listening

In my opinion a thorough understanding of the elements of music is essential for the full and satisfying performance of a piece. Theory is a very practical matter, inextricably linked to the performance and composition of music. The complex system of symbols concerned with pitch, rhythm, dynamics, meter, tempo and form is a form of shorthand to express the core elements of music, a vital component in the learning process of the musician.

Aural and sight-singing abilities vary with the individual and are often a 'cross to be borne'. Ottman suggests:

> An important attribute of the accomplished musician is the ability to 'hear mentally', that is, to know how a given piece of music sounds without recourse to an instrument. Sight singing, together with ear training and other studies in musicianship, helps develop this attribute (1986, p. xvii).[22]

Eric Taylor goes so far as to say, 'What is being trained or tested is the musical intelligence' (nd., p. 5).

The best teachers treat weaknesses in a positive way. To this end the first essential is fear elimination by confidence-building and regular experience of sight singing. A little aural training and sight-singing practice done regularly goes a long way. Students, usually grow accustomed to the practice, lose self-consciousness and keep their aural senses alert.

Memorization

Memorization was not practised in the early part of the nineteenth century, but in the twentieth century David Clark Taylor says, 'In studying a song the first thing to do is to try and memorize it, so that the mind will not be taxed with trying to recall the words and melody' (1914, p. 26). Many methods to aid memorization may be gleaned in literature written for the concert pianist, who traditionally has inordinate quantities of scores to remember.[23] Among these are the repetition and the subsequent linking of phrases. Singers have an advantage over pianists in that they can learn to associate text with musical phrases. It should however be noted that there is much still to be learned about the process of memorization. As Richard Davis has said, 'For text memory we will rely upon processes as yet undefined by neuropsychologists, and some research data from the field of information processing' (1998, p. 83–4).

Hempel sees point in having the score with her in a concert performance in order to avoid the constant posture of hands clasped as though in supplication:

> This attitude becomes somewhat harrowing when held for a whole program. For myself I prefer to hold in hand a small book containing the words of my songs, for it seems to be more graceful ... I never refer to this book ... but I shall always carry it, no matter what the critics may say (cited by Brower, 1920, p. 77).

Since a singer engaged to appear with an orchestra is generally allowed very little rehearsal time it is necessary that the singer is well rehearsed and has mastered the programme. In opera, at the first rehearsal, which is usually musical without staging, singers are expected to know their part from memory and sing it with musical understanding.

Communication

Singing is communication and communication needs someone on the receiving end. It is desirable that all singing be animated in the sense of 'Listen to this, just listen to this'. Plunket Greene believed that to be successful singers must have magnetism:

> Magnetism is the indefinable *something* which passes from singer to audience and audience to singer alike; for the audience which the singer holds in the hollow of his hand, holds him as surely in its own (1914, p. 9).

and that magnetism is a 'pure gift' (ibid., p. 8). Eighty years on, Bunch replaces the word 'magnetism' with 'dynamism':

> Dynamism comes from true mental receptivity and sensitivity. Being dynamic implies a body that moves gracefully; a technique that is ever changing within the framework of vocal production and emotion; awareness of what one's senses are conveying from within and without; a sense of unconfined space and certain imperfections which add uniqueness to the performance (1995, p. 147).

In every song the singer is portraying a character who is singing the particular words of the song. There are at least three possible relationships which may fit the situation and the text of each particular song. First, the song may be sung to another character (real and onstage or imagined); secondly, the song may be sung to oneself; thirdly the song may be sung to the audience.

Singing to a character onstage is easier than singing to an imagined one; we are used to communicating to another human being in real life. Singing to an imagined character is rather more difficult as an illusion has to be created with which to respond dynamically. One helpful suggestion in creating this illusion is by rehearsing with a live partner who gradually moves out of view of the singer, thus weaning the singer off the permanent presence.

Singing to oneself is as valid an act as talking to oneself, as when we try to gain control over circumstances in order to cope. In spoken theatre these occasions are sometimes called monologues or soliloquies. Usually we talk to ourselves silently, so how do we sing to ourselves out loud? One needs to create a mirror image of oneself, or a twin and literally sing to 'myself'. This twin fulfils all the reactions of the real or imaginary partner on stage and can be placed anywhere in the theatre where the impact of performance needs to be directed. Stanislavski had this to say as he was coaching a young singer:

> 'For whom are you singing this?'
> 'I am talking to myself. I am alone.'
> 'You mean you are reflecting? When a man reflects, when he communes with himself, there is nonetheless a kind of dialogue; it is as though his mind is conversing with his heart. Consequently, the monologue will contain hesitancy, doubts, firmness, weakness, and stubbornness – all the elements of an ordinary argument' (1975, p. 32).

Michaela, in the third act of Bizet's *Carmen* singing 'Je dis que rien ne m'épouvante' is an example of a character singing to herself.

When singing to the audience one very rarely makes eye contact, the singer is singing to the imaginary partner once again. An exception, for example, is in the finale of Mozart's *Don Giovanni* when, after the demise of the Don, the remaining members of the cast sing directly to the audience the moral of the opera. But, usually, the audience plays the role of spectator not partner. Singing to someone, imaginary or otherwise gives our singing a focus. The song has a destination or a place to go and this sensation will help bring the song to life.

We are obliged at all times to consider the audience. Words have to be transmitted with both colour and conviction. The singer has to convincingly 'tell a story'. To make the words come alive the singer may be encouraged to look for the adverbs and adjectives and give emphasis to these to help create colourful and suggestive descriptions. Correct stress and shading must be given to individual syllables in words. Length and stress of consonants and timbre used in vowel formation are important in giving effective colouration to the words. Looking at the words which fall on accented beats of the bar to give a clue as to what the composer intended. The poem itself when read or spoken gives the most important lead; surely, this is what initially inspired the composer of the music. Some singers advocate the use of body language; others find facial expression, eye contact and overall presentation sufficient.

In communicating emotion singers have to use their imagination to enter into the mood of the specific feeling to be portrayed. Singers do not need to be murderers to understand hatred; to commit suicide in order to interpret *suicido*. These emotions must be thought about and then recalled in an impassive (to the performer) way, such as being brought into voice and face subtleties. Beyond this singers must not lose themselves.

The vexed question of gesture in concert performances falls now to be considered. How may we deal with the problem of gesture? Should the singer make a full gesture, a half gesture or none at all? In the half gesture it appears that singers feel they must do something and then embarrassedly and awkwardly make pathetic arm movements, very often with rigid muscles. Wildly gesticulating hands are equally to be avoided. Hands can, however be placed in a relaxed position at the sides of the body. Balk describes the singer's common predicament,

> Instinctively, many singers sense the necessity of sustaining the gestural energy in response to the music. At the same time they do not have the freedom to commit themselves to a full gestural statement. So they end up with a sustained half-gesture which defeats both purposes and neither makes a statement or structures it … Many singers, having been told that the only good gesture is no gesture, allow the hands to hang freely at their sides (1985, p. 128–9).

60–70 per cent of our communication is non-verbal, hence the desire to gesture. The purist argues that gesture detracts from the sound – the sound is all. Balk opines that 'the rejection of gesturing is in obvious defiance of life itself, which is filled with gestures of every size, description, and destination' (ibid., p. 261). Some would suggest being selective. According to Stanislavski:

> Unrestrained movements, natural though they may be to the actor himself, only blur the design of his part, make his performance unclear, monotonous and uncontrolled (1989, p. 73).

Regarding choice of gesture: *cielo* seems always to gesture up to heaven; *amore* has the hands placed over the heart. Stanislavski was aware of this; it still continues today:

Operatic performers quickly learn how to make a declaration of love, to suffer, to meditate, to die, and so on, and they repeat these forms in all analogous situations that they happen to be in. These are well known rubber-stamp effects. Nearly everyone knows them all, and speaks of them scornfully, yet ... a majority of singers go right on using them (1975, p. 217).

Lotte Lehmann had this to say about gesture,

How great is the power of expression conveyed by the eyes and hands! I do not mean that you should ever make a gesture which would disturb the frame of concert singing ... Be careful that you do not cultivate the possibilities of expression with the body from the outside, so to speak, – I mean by artificial movements ... (1985, p. 13).

Facial gesture and expression should be unconscious and appear automatic but must be rehearsed. When rehearsing, a mirror is needed to see if the intention of the singer is, in fact, being achieved.

Working with an Accompanist

Accompanist and singer are equal partners, and both are well advised to use a notebook and/or a tape recorder when working together. It is amateurish for accompanists to suggest that they will 'follow' the singer's singing or for singers to demand that the accompanist just 'follow' them. Having decision making recorded will save disagreement later as to what decisions were made at a particular time. It is important to carefully note rehearsal time, plus specific direction and agreement regarding fees and payment of the same. The responsibility for the training and remuneration of a page-turner when used usually falls to the accompanist. If no page-turner is employed then accompanists should rehearse the page-turns and turn the pages quietly. It is recommended that the singer be able to follow the pianist's score and the accompanist should speak the singer's words aloud in order to know what the singer is doing. It is also more professional for singers to be familiar with key signatures rather than requesting a piece to be played 'a little higher' or 'a little lower', if the song is unsuitable for their vocal range. In recitals accompanists should keep their eyes on the singer and the singer should be alert as to what is happening in the hall/room – piano benches have been known to disappear, music has fallen off the piano, light-bulbs have exploded, but the 'show has gone on'. Accompanists should keep their hands on the keyboard at the end of a song in the middle of a song cycle, as a signal to the audience that the piece is not over; be knowledgeable of cadence in case a song has to be suddenly curtailed; be ready to prompt in case of memory lapse on the part of the singer, and be able to extemporize in the face of mistakes.[24] Singers should be flexible and willing to listen to the opinions of the accompanist in matters of interpretation or pronunciation or even incorrect notes or rhythm.

Ideally, rehearsals might include protocol policy, for example: rehearsing in the recital hall; checking the tuning and action of the piano; noting the acoustical balance of the hall; giving instructions for backstage personnel; checking the lighting in order to ensure adequate exposure. The accompanist might like to count four or five seconds before following the singer onto to the stage, observe the audience, place the music on the piano and prepare to begin. At the conclusion of the group of songs the accompanist may carry the music off after the singer has walked towards the wings. It is necessary to carefully rehearse the acknowledgement of applause and the taking of bows with the accompanist. The singer should give appreciative recognition to the accompanist at appropriate moments, perhaps after each group of songs, or after an especially difficult accompaniment. Singers and accompanists are partners and collaborators in music and not as C.P.E. Bach wrote in Part 2 of his 'Essay on the True Art of Playing Keyboard Instruments' (1762) ' … the soloist takes all bravos to himself and gives no credit to his accompanist … ignorant custom directs these bravos to him alone' (cited by Solomon, 1981, p. 12).[25]

Interpretation

Numerous authors have expressed themselves on interpretation, and on occasion their views seem to cancel one another out. Thus, for example on the nature and importance of good interpretation Henderson observes:

> One may have a perfect attack, a beautiful legato, a ravishing portamento, a noble messa di voce and an elastic fluency of delivery, yet sing ineffectively. If the singer bestows all his thought on the perfection of each phrase as an individual entity he will never sing eloquently, though here and there he may rise to heights of extraordinary beauty … The singer must grasp his aria or his recitative in its entirety … Only in this way can he arrive at a proper conception of the delivery of his music, for only thus can he determine the distribution of vocal effects (1906, p. 254).

On the other hand, Bassini takes a less intellectual approach, 'The singer's mind should always be rather on the sentiment he is uttering than on the execution' (c. 1857, p. 18); while Kofler warns against abandoning all technical facility to the emotions:

> The advice commonly given to singers and actors to feel the emotions they express, is not quite right … Were he really to feel, to experience these emotions, not only would he be unable to sing or to recite, but his voice would be spasmodic in action, tremulous and irritated from nervous excitement (1889, p. 28).

For his part, Santley defends individuality in interpretation:

> The interpretation depends greatly on the idiosyncrasies of its interpreters; if they are experienced artists, though the mode of carrying out the interpretation be in each case different, the result will be clear, forcible and logical (1908, p. 67).

More broadly, Plunket Greene emphasizes the personality of the singer, 'Personal magnetism, the ability to hold an audience, is also to a great extent a gift of the imagination' (1914, p. 18).

What shall we make of such remarks? Henderson's advice that performers think of their piece as a whole is well taken, though in rehearsal each phrase will need to be practised individually. Bassini rightly focuses on sentiment over execution at the time of performance: it is psychologically disruptive, in the middle of a passionate love song, to be thinking 'Here comes that top C – how shall I achieve it?' The technical work should have been so thoroughly done that such a mid-performance question would never arise. Kofler does well to underline the point I made earlier, namely, that the singer is to *convey* emotion rather than experience it, while Santley and Plunket Greene return us to the performer's personality and imagination. It is not necessary to have had personal experience of the emotions to be conveyed; the memory of a similar experience helps one to identify with the words. As Bernac reminds us one of the main perils in any given recital is the switching of emotions demanded by a varied programme:

> But far more subtle is the task of the concert singer who, in the course of an evening, must be not one but twenty different characters, who, at times within the compass of just a few measures, and without any visual aid, must succeed in creating an atmosphere, evoking an entire poetic world, suggesting a drama – that is more often than not an inner one – expressing one after the other the most varied feelings: sadness and joy, quietness and passion, tenderness, irony, faith, casualness, sensuousness, serenity, and so on (1978, p. 6).

The neurologist, Critchley, writing about ecstatic performance mentions an incident quoted about the famous soprano Pasta:

> According to a critic who attended her performance of Paisiello's *Nina*, ' ... not only did this enchantress hold her listeners spellbound; she was herself so seized and carried away that she collapsed before the end. She was recalled, and duly appeared; but what a sight! Too weak to walk alone, supported by helping hands, more carried than walking, tears streaming down her pale cheeks, every muscle of her expressive face in movement, and reflecting as touchingly as her singing, the depth of her emotions! The appearance rose to the highest conceivable pitch – and she fainted!' (1983, p. 37).

From this extreme of interpretative exertion McKinney will bring us to earth with a bump:

> In the final analysis interpretation cannot be taught. If the student does not have enough creative imagination to react aesthetically to the text and the music, and enough freedom of personality to express what he feels, no amount of instruction can redeem the situation (1994, p. 29).

While, as McKinney suggests, the singer's personality and imagination are key factors in interpretation, the voice teacher can nevertheless *facilitate* a student's

performance and stimulate the imagination. It is desirable that singers love literature. Teachers can help here by suggesting reading material. One has too
frequently heard it said that few young singers are interested in the poetry of the
songs they perform, or in the books and plays which have inspired operas. We also
hear that full-time vocal students have no time to read because of heavy timetables.
A short cut, although far from ideal, for the opera student may be to study in detail
just within the framework of the libretto itself. Very often composers modified play
texts and characters to suit their own purposes. For example, the plot of Verdi's
Otello stays very close to Shakespeare's *Othello*, but the operatic characters are not
quite the same as their Elizabethan counterparts. It might therefore seem that study
of the original play will not help with characterization. However songs usually gain
new depth when the verse that inspired the music is studied. Understanding the
word and sentiments of poems leads to changes in dynamic levels, volume, accents,
rubato and an overall understanding of the entity will add vitality and warmth.

Kivy makes clear that 'the question of what a musical performance is assumes as
its first principle only that a musical performance must be compliant with a score'
(2002, p. 224). There are two main aspects in the performance and interpretation of
a song or aria. First, a careful study of the literary text and secondly, a careful study
of the music: 'No musical notation can be interpreted outside the background
knowledge required for its interpretation' (ibid., p. 228). In agreement with this I
recommend that music and text are always seen as a whole. But how do we get from
a lifeless mechanical rendition to a meaningful interpretation? Kivy replies:

> The performer is under contract to play *what* the composer has written. But the contract
> also enjoins the performer to exercise his or her artistry as to the manner in which what the
> composer has written is played (ibid., p. 239).

Composers have their own ideas concerning the interpretation of their music, but
they do not have the means to set all these ideas on paper; it is up to the intuition,
trained imagination and artistry of performers to bring the music to life, adding
aspects of their own imagination and personality with integrity. This involves
scholarly investigation, awareness of style, and detailed knowledge of performance
practices.[26] Donington describes interpretation as

> that element in music made necessary by the difference between notation (which
> preserves a record of the music) and performance (which brings the musical experience
> itself into renewed existence) (1980, p. 276).

Bernac states at the beginning of his book on interpretation of French song that after
the sight of the text 'The performers' first task is [therefore] to decipher this notation
and embody it in sound, with the utmost care and scrupulous accuracy' (1978, p. 2).
Tom Sutcliffe has this to say on hearing a wonderful performance:

> You can feel the gorge rising in your throat, swelling up, as you hear a certain kind of voice making sense in its special totally personal way, creating a sound which to you as an individual resonate spiritually (perhaps physically) like a sympathetic string on a viola d'amore. You just want the sound to go on forever. It's inexplicable. It's infatuation. And it's one on the most powerful engines of engagement in the whole operatic business ... (2001, p. 14).

The musical quality of a performance depends on the singer's ability to listen, think and feel, to make imaginative and sensitive decisions about how a song is to be sung, and to translate all this into practice, given the understanding and command of technical skill. Paul Harris says:

> When musicians read music they hear it in their musical ear, they understand key and rhythm, they perceive balance and sonority, structure and meaning. When they hear music, they instantly know about it (Harris, 2001, p. 14).

He goes on to say that 'effective teaching can help ... bring about development of true musical thinking' (ibid., p. 14).

It follows from what has been just said that singing should be inspired, alive, expressive and intelligent. These features cannot be taught in isolation, nor can they be checked off as individual, specific achievements; they are too closely and complexly inter-related. But when they are all in place we have a musical performance, and when they are not, it is quite easy to recognize an unmusical one. Lotte Lehmann advises singers thus:

> Do not build up your songs as if they were encased in stone walls – no, they must soar from the warm, pulsing beat of your own heart, blessed by the inspiration of the moment. Only from life itself may life be born (1985, p. 10).

The question as to where the line can be drawn between the subjective and objective aspects of the performance process has been much debated. The teaching of sung musical performance ought always to be based on awareness of music as sound to be created and listened to – with, of course the added bonus of words. Some have said that musical performance cannot be taught, but that it can be cultivated in most people. From the fact that singers wish to learn how to sing, one can assume some interest which might suggest some basic interpretational senses on which to build, and on which the teacher might concentrate. Specific periods might be allocated where the singer is a given a task, such as receiving a letter containing good news; bad news; a threatening letter or a funny letter, observing their own reactions alongside their teacher. There is no limit to this type of exercise; and new powers of observation may thus be aroused, and then related to song.

In a beginner, an apparent lack of musicality may be due to lack of experience. In such cases it may be helpful to afford plenty of time, to let beginners have opportunities to make their own musical decisions. Being constantly told what to do, and to be rushed through the learning of skills, deprives musicians of their full potential. Time is needed to practise and to develop ideas, awareness and the ability to think in the medium of singing.

Encouragement should be given, from the very first lesson, to engage with the songs, some aspects of which are given and some to be decided about. Awareness of different musical possibilities may be awakened by talking about and trying alternative interpretations, although composers' clearly stated wishes should not be disobeyed. Good intonation, phrasing, rhythmic interpretation, tone quality, among other things, determine how the music will sound, and technical skill becomes the necessary means of producing different and controlled sounds and of finding new ones. These are the unique touches, which make each performance individual and interesting. No two performances are alike, because no two performers are alike. Neither will the performer sing the same song identically on successive occasions. Mood, environment and the changing temperament of the performer will influence the performance.

For a satisfactory performance the singer must know the work well, so that there may be complete freedom of expression, otherwise the performance will be wooden and lacking in imagination. Having the student become creator by composing encourages thought about the elements of song construction.

There are no hard rules or laws to be applied to expressive singing, though useful suggestions may be offered. While the detail of expression cannot be taught, the various methods of producing expressive effects and the application of these methods may be studied before inward emotions can be displayed in artistic singing.[27] This is largely a matter of having efficient technique and wide knowledge of time changes, for example. The time change may need to be gradual and in steps, working from semi quavers to crotchets; a gradual but even decrease may be indicated by *ritardando* or *rallentando*; a sudden immediate slowing of the tempo may be indicated by *ritenuto* or 'holding back'. A more permanent change would be indicated by a switch from *allegro* to *allegretto*. These terms are best not limited to the theory lesson, important though that is, but may be demonstrated to the student by the teacher.

Similarly *fermata* should be clearly explained and demonstrated. Students cannot always understand the need for a pause. They may wonder why the composer did not just increase the value of the note. The explanation may illustrate that the *fermata* is a way of telling performers that they have complete control over the duration of a particular note or notes. There is more to artistry than simply following the instructions given by the composer: a pause may be a breathtaking moment of suspense or just a space; a *crescendo* may be an exciting build-up of tension or just a getting louder.

One impediment, which may stand in the way of sensitive interpretation, is a lack of knowledge relating to the type or style of a song or aria. Here, once again, we see the necessity of a well-rounded multi-disciplinary education for the teacher/ singer.

Intuition and experience are the best teachers. Students will find it beneficial to listen to the performances of other reputable musicians (but not, of course, to imitate them; they should be encouraged to develop their own ideas for interpretation) and to study scores. Frank Battisti quotes Wilhelm Furtwängler on the process of studying a score:

> First the actual notation, through it the performer gets to know the work. He traces backward the steps of the composer, who gave life to his music before putting it down on paper … The heart and marrow of this music is therefore like an improvisation which he tries to write down. Whereas, to the performer, the work appears like something exactly the opposite of an improvisation, as a thing written with fixed signs and unalterable shape. Next the performer must guess the meaning and work out the mystery of this music in order to get to the work itself, which it is his business to bring to life (1996, p. 13).

In the same article Battisti quotes Carlo Maria Guilini:

> A composer can write down on paper only part of his thought. Our problem is not just how to study the score and learn the notes but how to read between the lines (ibid., p. 14).

Although, as I have argued, the use of analogy, metaphor and simile is less than helpful in teaching singing technique, when teaching interpretation these devices may stimulate the imagination.[28] We can permit Edidin aptly to conclude this general discussion of interpretation:

> The artistry of classical performers is exercised in activity whose point is focussed on bringing to sound the artistry of composers. The varying success with which they do so testifies to the importance of the details left to their keeping (2000, p. 325).

Performing Practice

When contemplating a performance it is helpful to reflect on the contribution offered by performing practice. Performing or performance practice means, according to H.M. Brown, 'the way music is and has been performed (especially as regards the relationship between the written notes and the actual sounds)' (1980, p. 370). It is concerned with 'authenticity' in performance.[29]

'Authenticity' begins with the study of music notation as a set of instructions to be interpreted. Notation has become more detailed as the centuries have passed. However no matter how detailed the instructions they can be read and interpreted by different singers in differing ways. As we have already seen, for various reasons (habit, training, temperament, acoustics), and no matter how much detail is written into the score, no two performances – even by the same person – are the same. Bridger rightly points out:

Even in so-called 'authenticity', much guesswork and invention is involved, often with only a veneer of solid, definite historical evidence. And in the actual notations available for the performing arts much is omitted – the inflections of speech, actual stage movement in drama, gesture, fine details of musical dynamics and articulation ... Approximation rather than pre-determined precision is the main characteristic, and it is for this reason that the role of the performer is so creative and diverse (1996, p. 64).

Many performers over the centuries have taken advantage of the various ambiguities in the score, for example, the excesses of ornamentation at certain points in history. Pitch level has been raised over the years and must be taken into consideration. Then there is the question of changing taste. But with the advent of sophisticated recording a definitive performance is being pursued by some. Unwritten conventions are problematic and some would say that you can read musical treatises alongside musical scores for ever but that even the treatises themselves are open to various interpretations, probably conditioned in part by our accumulated musical heritage, and the advice may be inappropriate for modern performing environments.

Obviously, we can never know how performances sounded before the advent of recording, but it seems a pity to ignore the possibilities offered by sources on historical performing practice for stimulating our musical responses and challenging stylistic habits.[30] Therefore, historical research is essential. What is the music is trying to say? For example, J.S. Bach is often thought of as being solely form, plus a collection of musical ornaments, but singers need to learn how the music of his time was received, otherwise performances of his work will become anachronistic, very often with nineteenth century romantic idiosyncrasies.[31] Singers will never be able to discover the whole story because they are too removed in time. But it is possible to study the music on its own terms using a 'clean' edition with, if possible, no additions to the composer's work. Often the composer worked with the singer in performance and ornaments were left to the singer to devise in what were the traditions of the day. The more recent the composer the less he or she leaves to the singer's discretion. Improvisations can be sung within what is thought of as acceptable parameters of the period.

Over the last hundred years some composers have set out to invent new ways of notating sounds and concepts. Certain notations are generally accepted but otherwise there are very few rules, and the singer is best advised to read the explanation with which the composer may preface the score.

I have found it beneficial, when seeking to determine the expressive shape of a piece of music, to study the philosophy of the composer. And, of course, the singer's own musicianship developed from experience and conditioning is layered over all. Here we may remind ourselves of the importance of a good standard of general education, vital for the singer, as mentioned at the beginning of this section.

The Performance

Promoting the Performance

Promoting oneself as a successful artist and performer takes time, money, and patience. Apart from performing, some of the things needed are event organization, publicity material, and establishing contacts. There are a few marketing and communications companies, as distinct from agents, who help and support artists in their professional development, taking the pressure off, and allowing the singers more time to perform. Among other things they organize publicity and assemble portfolios of work, teach their clients marketing skills and act as mentors. There is good reason to suggest that advertising should be completely honest, truthful, and unexaggerated.[32]

The Location of the Performance

Performers should carefully investigate the physical environment in which they will be working, and to do their best to familiarize themselves with the acoustics, and with any amplification system that may be in use.

Amplification helps in an acoustically appalling venue. Such a venue may be bedecked with fabric and furnished with thick carpet. Then there are over-reverberant rooms with high ceilings, marble walls, many glazed areas and hard floors. In a stadium or outdoors, it is taken for granted that the singers will be amplified. Rumour has it that more top opera stars wear microphones in their hair than is publicly acknowledged. Some companies have enhancement systems installed which, without picking up individual voices, can create sound reflections in areas where none had existed before. Microphones can sometimes seem to interfere with the natural communication between singer and audience. Much of this amplification is done in secret. The bass, John Tomlinson said:

> There is one significant practical move that could be made; namely, the complete honesty and openness of opera companies with their audiences on this subject of amplification. ... At least, then we would know what we were listening to, and we would end this conspiracy of silence (2000, p.13).

Concern is thus raised about the fact, not that amplification is occurring, but that it is being done dishonestly. Tomlinson goes on to say:

> And what about the future for the opera singing voice? Opera singers sing the way they do – with purity, clarity, strength and projection – because it has always been necessary to do so in order to carry over the orchestra and communicate with a large audience. But if you bring in mikes, slowly but surely singers will lose this projecting skill, and the whole of the art of opera singing, and the musical style associated with it, will never be the same again (ibid., p. 12).

Some directors are in favour of the use of amplification in difficult acoustics, though they would prefer to have the acoustics in the theatres improved. Many designers say that, even with state of the art technology the most efficient acoustic is the one to be found in the centuries old horseshoe shape. This design permits the greatest number of people to be as near as possible to the performers and allows the shape of the auditorium to be narrow. The narrowness allows for sound reverberation coming at the audience from the sides of the auditorium. Another important consideration is the design and position of the orchestral pit. In larger theatres the orchestra needs to be more in the open, but in smaller theatres a stage overhang dampens the sound of the orchestra. Balconies are vital, as they tend to reflect sound down into the expensive seats in the stalls, although it is not always the case that the most expensive seats have the best acoustic.

Performance Anxiety

'Nerves' are normal. Stage fright is no respecter of persons. Anyone, whatever their level of accomplishment or experience, can succumb to performance anxiety. It can be handled. It is a normal response to a pressurized situation. However if it becomes so severe that performances have to be cancelled then professional help is necessary.[33] Psychologists who treat performance anxiety are generally of two types: psychoanalysts or cognitive/behaviourists. Psychoanalysts tend to assume that anxiety is interpsychic; their treatment is lengthy and endeavours to uncover trauma and/or inhibitions that may be contributing to the anxiety. Behaviourists aim to modify a stimulus-response pattern that may do us harm. Amongst some of the different therapies used by the behaviourists are: systematic desensitization, implosion, behaviour rehearsal, attentional training, autogenic therapy, cognitive therapy, stress inoculation, and thought stopping. Humanistic therapists have great rates of success but lead to managing performance anxiety in very different ways. Some singers have recourse to rituals, superstitions, fate and religion. As a last resort there are pharmacological therapies. It is best to try to learn how to channel the adrenalin and use it positively.

The bodily response in performance anxiety is caused by the effect of increased adrenalin on the system, producing what is known as the 'flight or fight' reaction. It is inherited from our biological ancestors who literally had to flee or fight when confronted by danger. In this situation the heart beats faster to send more blood round the system, the muscles tense ready for action, the body sweats so as to lose heat when running, and digestion is inhibited so that blood can go to the muscles where it is needed. But for singers, rapid heartbeat makes for uneasiness, tense muscles cause poor 'fine' control and poor digestion makes for a sick feeling or nausea.

These symptoms can be controlled to a certain extent, accepting that it is just 'a pre-performance thing' and that the heart will go back to normal once the performance begins, that it is a 'buzz' or a positive feeling of elation.[34] It is a question of changing one's belief system or attitude either by self-help or counselling. Experience suggests that there are three causes of negative beliefs: conditioned responses, fear of fellow performers, and motivation problems. Conditioned responses involve performance anxiety resulting from previous performance disasters – if it can happen once it can happen again. This may be dealt with by confronting the fear as irrational using a sense of scale in relation to catastrophes such as wars, fires and floods. The counter measure to fear of fellow performers and their criticisms is to cultivate a spirit of generosity to yourself and to other musicians around you, others will then perhaps like you; if not then that is their problem. Then there are motivation difficulties, which include: how fellow musicians see us, inferiority dilemmas, apologizing or giving an excuse for not doing well, feeling that nobody understands us, or the inner conviction that we are frauds.

There are various positive steps, which may be taken to overcome stage fright and, usually, the results are good. Included in the remedies are many alternative therapies: beta-blockers, computers, bio feed-back machines, autogenics, hypnosis, meditation yoga, Alexander Technique, body engineering, reflexology, reikki, aromatherapy ... [35] Often relaxation is suggested, however the body is never totally relaxed, and for the performer who needs to be poised, balanced and ready to go, relaxation, as I said earlier, is a misleading term.

It is sometimes useful to imagine the actual performance. After all, the performance begins in the imagination, and it may be looked upon positively and not as something to be dreaded; one cannot communicate freely in an anxious frame of mind. To see the entire performance as a great occasion where the performer is confident, well prepared, physically fit and enthusiastic will contribute to a beautiful presentation. Singers might try to imagine their involvement in the music (it goes without saying that the music must be meticulously prepared), the meaningfulness of the performance and the feeling afterwards. This pre-performance imaginative reflection helps eliminate tension. If we think of issues in performance, for example, musicianship, attitude of the performer, we might ask, what impression do I wish to convey in the several items in the programme: fiery, passionate, authoritative, commanding, well-prepared, proficient, inspired? What is the aim of the performance: to impress the audience, agents, adjudicators, record producers, to achieve personal satisfaction, or a combination of these?

It can be helpful to visualize the programme in its broader context: the choice, type and order of the music; the warming-up period; the time and place of the performance; the performer's dress. One imagines oneself walking on to the stage, greeting the audience (if appropriate, with well prepared words), and beginning to sing (with eyes on the audience, no nervous lip-wetting, no floor-gazing). It is far easier to keep the audience's interest than to regain it once it is lost. Other questions, which may be posed in imaginative preparation, are: How should one leave the stage? What use should be made of the interval? Every specific detail, no matter how small, contributes to the outcome of the performance. Most of this preparation also applies to all singing projects.

After the performance some may suffer post-performance depression. It is possible, however, to prepare imaginatively for a positive feeling after performance, hopefully a proud feeling. This will influence the performance itself.

It is suggested that more than adequate preparation for performance is required. Kemp makes this suggestion, which applies to singers as well as other instrumentalists:

> ... many teachers advise their students: if they are prone to performance nerves, they should make sure they have a good margin of safety within which to operate. In other words, they should not play pieces in public about which they have doubts concerning their technical proficiency (2000, p. 97).

The following is the kind of guidance which is frequently offered to performers by way of allaying or reducing performance anxiety:

1. Visualize yourself in a positive light: walking onstage, opening the mouth to begin to sing or speak, hear the beautiful tone that flows out, feel the exhilaration, see the warmth in the audience; hear them clapping; and shouting 'Bravo'; bowing; coming back onstage for curtain calls; encores being demanded.
2. Resolve to enjoy the performance, mistakes and all – it is enough to do my best; strive for excellence rather than perfection, it is normal to feel nervous, vulnerable or fearful; a few mistakes are no big deal and many in the audience may not notice them; keep going whatever happens; learn through experience.

Kemp expresses a positive view:
> ... there is a body of research that suggests that, for some, anxiety can *facilitate* higher levels of standards of musical performance. This facilitative role appears to be particularly manifest in more experienced performers who may have learned to control the more debilitating effects of anxiety (ibid., p. 107).

Harris and Crozier recommend a good night's sleep the night before a performance, 'Cognitive ability and concentration are both dependent on an appropriate number of hours' sleep' (2000, p. 107). They put forward very basic ideas to relieve stress, for example, rehearsing previously the journey to the performance venue, allocating adequate time for the journey, checking the parking situation, and having the correct money for the meter (ibid., p. 107).

Since dehydration can result from performance stress, it is as well to increase water intake, not only on the performance day but also during previous weeks. Slow deep breathing helps. Beta-blockers have potential side effects: dizziness, light-headedness, hallucination, lethargy, and insomnia among them. Homeopathic drops may help and may not have side effects; Dr Bach 'Rescue Remedy' aids may be useful, and Australian 'Performance Plus' is said to be non-sedative and will not cause drowsiness.

In cases of dry mouth, it is advisable to beware medications that might worsen the problem. Over the counter liquid spray solution that creates artificial saliva (it is recommended to test this product well before the performance) may be helpful, gently nibbling the tongue tip to create saliva and subtle sucking movements to promote saliva can be tried.

Finally, it is encouraging to remember that positively used, the rush of adrenalin before and during singing adds extra excitement to the performance.

The Evaluation of Performance

Whether we think in terms of the theory of art, or, which is wider, of beauty (for the natural order, mathematical formulae etc. may all be said to be 'beautiful'); or whether we are thinking of that philosophical aesthetics which analyses the logic and presuppositions of aesthetic discourse, the fact is that many people, from 'ordinary' listeners to paid critics, evaluate music without ever having examined such theoretical matters. Clearly, there is an overlap between general and analytical aesthetics; indeed the latter is in a sense parasitic upon the former. For whereas the adjudicator or critic may say of a performance, 'That was beautiful', the analytic aesthetician will step backward and ask what is the analysis of this assertion. Indeed, *is* it an assertion or just an expression of emotion?[36] Is an objective claim being made, or a subjective judgement – or, perhaps, both?

It is highly desirable that vocal pedagogues acquaint themselves with aesthetic discussion, especially as it bears upon music because they are constantly evaluating performance not only from the point of view of technique, but aesthetically. Similarly, critics and adjudicators (roles which the voice teacher may from time to time fill) should ponder carefully the grounds of their judgements and the meanings of their utterances. Over and above all this there is the question of how far vocal pedagogy contributes to aesthetic education – and what is meant by 'aesthetic education'? Leonhard contends:

> Music education as aesthetic education is education in the realm of feeling ... [it] frees the human spirit and allows it to soar as a result of two types of experience. 1. Projecting the expressive import of music as a performer and as a composer. 2. Reacting in a feelingful way to the expressive import of music as a listener (1971, p. 6).

General Aesthetic Considerations

It has been said that the whole of philosophy consists of footnotes to Plato, and certainly he introduced lines of discussion in aesthetics which are being pursued to this day. Among his important concepts is that of *mimesis* (imitation, representation of reality). This has given rise to a vast discussion of how far all art is, or should be, representative; and this in turn has prompted that realization that in important respects music is unlike those arts such as painting and sculpture which can be (though they need not necessarily be) more obviously representational.

Plato believed that the aspect of reality imitated in the music was automatically imitated by the performer; consequently if the music was imitating unworthy things then the performer too was imitating unworthy things. It would then, Plato implies, follow that music has a moral influence:

> rhythm and harmony sink deep into the recesses of the soul and take the strongest hold there, bringing that grace of body and mind which is only to be found in one who is brought up in the right way (cited by Cornford, 1951, p. 88).

Building on Plato, the Italian philosopher Croce (1866–1952) went a stage further and introduced a distinction between representation and expression: representation as by narratives, stories and descriptions, and expression as existing without the stimulus of these. The present day philosopher, Kivy argues that music is sometimes representational and refers to Honegger's *Pacific 231*, in which the sound and movement of a train is imitated,[37] while Scruton points out:

> It is one thing for a piece to be *inspired* by a subject, another for it to imitate the subject, another for it to evoke or suggest a subject, another for it to express an experience of the subject, and yet another for it to *represent* the subject (ibid., p. 134).

In addition there are theories of non-mimetic or non-conceptual music. Wilkinson asks:

> What kind of art can this be?
> The theories of musical aesthetics, which attempt to answer this question, fall into two broad classes:
> (a) *heteronomist theories* which try to explain the aesthetic value of music in terms of its relations to something outside the music, and this 'something' is usually emotion; and
> (b) *autonomist theories* which maintain that the aesthetic value of music depends on nothing outside itself, but solely on features intrinsic to the music (1995, p. 195).

The contrast between programme and absolute music is indicated by (a) and (b) above.

While music may be written in such a way as to stimulate the imagination (in which case the title of the piece may assist the imagination), it does not represent to an audience a linear or three-dimensional shape. If bees are brought to mind when Arthur Askey performs 'The Bee Song', it is nevertheless Arthur Askey that we see, not visual representations of bees. The same applies to Vivaldi's *Four Seasons*, and Debussy's *La Mer*.

Some have argued that music can convey, or represent the emotions. Scruton believes that

> we should not attribute the expressive content of a work to the artist who created it ... Mozart was deeply unhappy when he wrote the "Jupiter" Symphony, K. 551; but what higher expression of joy than the last movement of that work? (1999, pp. 144–5).

This view is countered by Hanslick, and by such contemporary philosophers as Derrida, who deny that the meaning of any 'text' is stable and, accordingly, do not dwell on the possibility of evaluation. Hanslick rejects the representational in music: 'The representation of a specific feeling or emotional state is not at all among the characteristic powers of music' (1986, p. 9). According to Wilkinson, theories such as music being the expression of people's feelings are '"heteronomist" because they rely on something *other* than the work' (cited by Hanfling 1995, p. xvi). Dodd's idea follows that of Plato in that music is eternally conceived and then discovered by the composer (2000, pp. 424–40). This view is rejected by Trivedi who defends Levinson's conception 'of musical works as creatable indicated types' (2002, p. 73).[38]

Others, who think in instrumental/utilitarian terms that the objective of musical performance is usefulness to society, will also query the importance of the individual's emotions. Examples of this can be found at various points in history.

In the fifteenth century the main aesthetic principle was that the music should be fitting to the occasion, for example the music should be suitably mournful for a funeral and joyful for a banquet. Wegman tells us that Tinctoris (c. 1435–1511) felt that

> However pleasing sound may be … there ought to be more to musical experience than acoustic sensation alone … If one is to take true delight in music, then one must exercise the internal faculty of understanding and appreciate 'proper composition and performance' (2002, p. 52).

Agricola (c. 1443–85) affirms, 'In order to pass informed judgement on the quality of a work, and the skill of its composer, one needs to exercise understanding' (ibid., 2002, p. 52).

Knieter is adamant that 'the quality of life in any community is directly related to the quality of music available to that community' (1983, p. 33). He goes on to cite Plato's philosophy 'that the study of music could improve health, affect morality and cultivate good citizenship' and continues by pointing out that these claims 'support the study of music for nonaesthetic (non-musical) reasons' (ibid., p. 35). However he concludes that these views 'fail to communicate the virtues and uniqueness of music … and are susceptible to attack by any well-educated member of the community' (ibid., p. 35). Following Plato, we have other instances throughout history of musical aesthetics of the individual's behaviour being influenced by music.[39] Tarry cites Martin Luther: 'Music was to Luther " … a mistress of order and good manners which makes the people more moral and reasonable, that is, more active and sensible in the faculties of wise and true thought"' (1973, p. 356). As Sim points out:

> the definition of art has often been connected with questions of value, and according to some writers, the questions 'What is art?' and 'What is good art? are inseparable (1992, p. viii).

As we come to more recent time, we find Adorno, favouring Schoenberg as a composer breaking with the past, seeing 'arts value as lying in its ability to challenge tradition and the established order' (cited by Sim, 1992, p. 147). What Adorno considered false were traditional tonal combinations. Writing in the light of Marxist theory he paid particular attention to the current social context and argued that only such music as the dissonance of Schoenberg reflects the way in which society is. Others have questioned whether 'society' is in all respects as decadent as Adorno seems to have supposed. Scruton repudiates two ideas of the Frankfurt school with which Adorno together with Horkheimer and Bloch was associated. These ideas are that of

> mass culture as a 'bourgeois' product, and of modernism as the only available answer to it. The first of those ideas is based in a sociological theory, the second in philosophy of art (1999, p. 469).

Rowe, in a review of Scruton's book mentioned above was delighted to write about the section headed '"Thoughts on Adorno", [it] made me want to walk round the room with pleasure' (2000, p. 424).[40]

On the other hand, Dickie contends that a work of art is simply that which has been deemed to be such by a person or persons competent to make the judgement. This, as Sim points out, 'presupposes nothing about the intrinsic qualities of the work, or about the experiences or attitudes of those who view or hear it' (cited by Hanfling 1995, p. xiii).

Turning more directly to the assessment of performance we find that Putman leans towards assessing performance less on the emotions and more on the content of the music:

> The professionalism of an outstanding orchestra does not lie in the members' emotive potential but in their ability at any given performance to understand what the structure of a work implies, emotionally and otherwise, and to express that work well (1990, p. 362).

Putman goes on to say that this sensitivity is

> not then a re-enactment of the composer's feelings nor primarily an expression of the performer's feelings. It is a fusion of intellect and emotional capability focused on the artefact itself (ibid., p. 363).[41]

Sparshott aptly illustrates the above:

> The following situations may all be realized, though they may well be indistinguishable in practice in the absence of specific information:
> (a) someone skillfully sings a sad song, not feeling sad at all;
> (b) someone sings a sad song and happens to feel sad in the way the song expresses, but their singing is not affected by their sadness;
> (c) same as (b), except that the sadness the singer feels is not the sort of sadness that the song expresses;

(d) a sad singer sings a sad song, intending the song to have the meaning of expressing that sadness to the hearer;

(e) a sad singer sings a sad song, using the song to express that sadness for the singer but not intending it to have that significance for the hearer;

(f) a sad singer sings a sad song, meaning it to be taken as evincing the singer's sadness (that is, its sadness is to be taken as caused by the singer's sadness), but meaning it not to be meant to be recognized as intended to express it;

(g) a singer sings a sad song, not knowing it to be sad, so skillfully that its hearers recognize its sadness (1994, p. 32).

But if the emotion of a song is adequately to be conveyed the performer must be guided by the words. To 'jazz up' a lachrymose aria would sound false, inadequate, because 'unfeeling'. But to say this presupposes that we have access to the composer and writer's intentions – something which a number of philosophers deny. At the extreme this leads to a situation in which no rational discussion of alternative evaluations is possible, for subjective relativism rules. Honouring the composer's intentions can be taken to extremes while disregarding musical aesthetics. Wimsatt and Beardsley's paper 'The intentional fallacy' (1954) took to task (albeit referring to literature) much of twentieth century criticism based on what the author intended, saying that what the author intended 'is irrelevant to the act of critical interpretation' and 'They make a sharp distinction between internal and external evidence for the meaning of a literary work' (cited by Sim, 1992, p. 334). On the other hand, if one has the opportunity to work with composers then one may suppose that what they intended in their composition is made clear and that defines the interpretation. However, Ross and Judkins would say:

> While we admit the artists' beliefs and intentions are relevant to the interpretation of their works, we do not *privilege* those intentions. That is, we do not claim that the meaning of a given work is whatever its artist intended in creating it. Such an approach would be too limiting, since the artist may have failed to achieve her intentions, or may have unknowingly created a work with a certain significance (1996, p. 18).

They go on to insist that musical interpretation demands knowledge of structure and content of the music to be performed. Kivy also claims that authenticity in performance demands more than just trying to define the composer's intentions and cites re-understanding of performance conditions as they relate to the contemporary situation.[42]

The traditional discussion as to whether beauty resides in the object, or is in the eye of the beholder, takes a particular slant where music is concerned. For although in a sense the music exists when composed, and prior to performance, each performance is a unique work of interpretation; when it is over the work of art comprising the union of composition and execution, though it may linger in the memory and (unlike a piece of sculpture or a painting) is repeatable (though never absolutely exactly – even by the same performer), is 'gone' – or imprisoned in a recording. On the occasion of musical performance there may be some who find the beauty inherent in the work, while others judge the beauty or otherwise of the piece in terms of their subjective response to it. Langer has argued that musical patterns are analogous to human feelings, and that 'music articulates forms which language cannot set forth' (1957, p. 223). It is not clear, however how such extra-linguistic forms are intelligible.[43]

Even if it could be shown that specific emotions somehow inhere in specific musical forms, the link between such forms and the frequently diverse emotional responses of individuals to a given performance is by no means clear. Kivy says:

> Sad music emotionally moves me, *qua sad* music, by its musically beautiful sadness, happy music moves me, *qua happy* music, by its musically beautiful happiness (1999, p. 13).

That artistes are not alone in bringing emotion to bear upon a performance is clear when, for example, a tenor is booed by members of the audience; 'Call that singing?' 'You're faking' and 'You're finished' (Mason, 2001, p. 6). Mason continues:

> Perhaps it is not surprising that an extravagant art form which expresses such powerful emotions, attracts an audience that is not afraid to make its feelings felt about some of these issues (ibid., p. 6).

The tenor, Schade, and the baritone, Braun, have clear ideas about their own music making and interpretation and, 'Both agree that there's a misguided modern tendency for audiences to treat loud as good because people think volume is emotional' (cited by Carlin, 2000, p. 38).[44] Moreover, some disjoin the expressiveness of music from the emotional response of the audience.[45]

But need we draw a hard and fast distinction between the subjective and the objective? Confronted by the subject-object distinction, Kant sought a fresh approach. In *The Oxford Companion to Philosophy*, the article on aesthetic judgement makes much of Kant's influence:

> aesthetic judgements are distinguished both from the expression of subjective likes and dislikes, and from judgements that ascribe an objective property to the thing that is judged. Like subjective preferences, they must be made on the basis of an experience of pleasure; but like property-ascribing judgements, they make a claim with which other subjects are expected to agree (Honderich, 1995, p. 9).[46]

This remark is echoed by Scruton:

> In one sense aesthetic judgement is subjective – for it consists in the attempt to articulate an individual experience. But in another sense it is objective, for it aims to *justify* that experience, through presenting reasons that are addressed impartially to all beings with aesthetic understanding (1999, p. 376).

Earl William Jones expresses this opinion:

> … the perception of beauty in the beautiful singing is the confirmation of a multi-layered experience; a unity of physical, intuitive, and intentional acts; the artistic exploration of the silent, sound, signal, and symbol modes, integrated, fused into song (1989, p. 197).

Evaluating Vocal Performance

It seems that however much a Platonist (Croce and Collingwood come to mind) may hold that all music is already eternally written and in that sense exists before and apart from human beings, a performance is given at a specific time and place, and such performances are in fact evaluated by singing teachers, critics, agents, examiners, and adjudicators. Over and above the considerations in the preceding sections, it will be helpful to approach the evaluation of performance with Lonergan's classification of mental capacities in mind: attentiveness, intelligence, reasonableness and responsible decision (Meynell, 1995, pp. 7–8). Meynell goes on to say, 'The principles which I have sketched need no further foundation; they establish themselves by virtue of the fact that any attempt to argue against them is self-defeating' (ibid., p. 8).[47] With the foregoing theoretical considerations in mind we proceed now to reflect upon a diverse group of evaluators.

The Critic

From a critic we expect the response of a broadly educated person who may or may not be a practitioner of the art form under review. In some cases a critic may display ignorance of the singing voice, and may hunt down his prey with gossip and titbits which make an otherwise boring column interesting to the non-discerning. The critics can build a singer's reputation or destroy it overnight. Steane on Carreras:

> He sang, as before, within severe limitations of range, repertoire and expressive resources … he still has them [the audience] held. He offers no high notes, no operatic arias, no tricks of personality or presentation; his voice is now by no means beautiful in quality or strikingly individual in timbre (2000, p. 94).

This would seem to be little more than the emotional outburst of one who probably has little if any technical knowledge of the aging voice. Steane writes, '[she] left one wishing that she would assiduously avoid the tendency to an edgy shrillness …' – what does he mean by edgy shrillness? (ibid., p. 96). Of yet another singer, he says 'the singer was able to infuse her well-defined tones with some smiling warmth'; again, what does this mean? (ibid., p. 96). He continues, 'There is a thrill in her voice, which is capable of the gentlest tenderness and also catches the rhapsodic ecstatic note never far below the surface' – technically, what does this mean? (ibid.,

p. 96). Should the critic express a point of view without justifying it? Siepman comments, '[Brahms] described by one of history's greatest musicians [Tchaikovsky] as a "scoundrel", a "self-inflated mediocrity" ... The only interesting thing about Tchaikovsky's opinion of Brahms is that it came from Tchaikovsky – and it tells us a lot more about Tchaikovsky than about Brahms' (2000, p. 3).

But where does one pitch a review? On the one hand, it should be encouraging, but on the other hand, it should be honest – not everything is always wonderful. Swanwick makes certain suggestions that could be used by critics as a basis for their assessments:

> If we are really listening to music, we are bound to attend to sonorities, to the management of sounds: the secure control of instruments – the quality of tone itself; we are also conscious of the character of music ... we also look for coherence, ways in which musical gestures 'hang together', evolve, relate, contrast, find a sense of direction, where the music is 'going' (1991, p. 140).

The Agent

The Cardiff Singer of the World is among many competitions which attract agents; they are saved time and money by having such a wealth of talent in one place at the same time. Will it sell? is their question, and they may well be guided by audience reaction as much as by anything in the performance as such.

The Festival Adjudicator

For students some kind of assessment is appropriate, even essential, particularly with regard to self-esteem, motivation, knowledge of achievement and awareness of success. Apart from the encouraging teacher, peer group performances, concerts and examinations, competitive festivals have a place. Some pupils are more competitive than others and derive more benefit from festival competitions.[48]

I have dealt with the ethics and psychology of this, but now we are concerned with the evaluations offered. Competitors rely on the adjudicator for help and encouragement – it is not a 'pass/fail' situation. The principal aim is celebration, with the bonus of some education through performance and listening.[49] Personal feelings, on the part of the adjudicator, should not influence professional assessment. Here we move into the realm of tangential 'aesthetics'. This is more than a musical matter: assessors of performance may be swayed by the personal appearance of the candidate; race and gender may be included here. But what is a person's attractiveness? Is it physical characteristics, behaviour, dress, personality?[50]

The adjudicator's written report should be constructive, containing some praise and encouragement. One or two areas can be dwelt on in the case of a totally disastrous performance, though not everyone will take the advice offered. Criticism of the teacher must be avoided and also criticism of the venue. Cohen quotes Nelson as saying:

> Most competitions fall down on the quality of the adjudicators ... they pay very little money to adjudicate at festivals, so the standard varies. The adjudicator is not God. I have heard people tell students 'you are just unmusical' (2001, p. 6).

However Bonney comments on competitions such as Cardiff Singer of the World that, 'This gives these kids a chance to have a platform – it's a matter of just being seen' (cited by Flind, 2001, p. 96). From the agent's point of view, no doubt it is. But it may be hoped that some participants will regard the occasion as an opportunity to hear experts comment on their work. It may be doubted whether they always receive this. Indeed, the question how far adjudicators of voice need to be experts in the field is a vexed one. While a clarinettist may have no difficulty in deciding whether or not he or she enjoyed a vocal performance they may well have no appreciation of the mastery of technique required to negotiate the vocal registers in a tricky piece – any more than a voice teacher may understand the challenges of negotiating the break in the clarinet or the alternative fingerings available in *presto* sections. Where singers are concerned there is a more sombre consideration to be pondered. Since so many professional singers drop out of the profession in their thirties, having ruined their voices, one would hope that at festivals, like Cardiff, where budding professionals perform, tell-tale signs of trouble ahead would be noted by at least one adjudicator. There is no record of this ever being done, yet the signs, for example, head and neck tension and incorrect breathing, are there for those in the know to see.

As stated above, the principal aim of the festival is celebration but such occasions also contribute towards aesthetic education. Leonhard says that there is a crying need for aesthetic education through music,

> Aesthetic education is taking place when human beings (and students are human beings) have experiences with music that enliven their spirits, touch their hearts and enable their feelings to soar (1971, p. 6).

Festivals are not problem-free zones if, for example, the competitive element is over emphasized. There can be cut-throat rivalry between contestants, teachers (and/or their parents); too much attention may be paid to the marks and too little to the adjudicator's comments; the adjudicator may over-or under-praise; there may be pressure on the adjudicator to mark highly.

Most of the above considerations apply to the conduct of workshops and master classes, though in these a more intentionally educational emphasis is normally expected.

The Examiner

It is vital to remember that graded practical examinations are a means to an end and not an end in themselves. The main purpose is to encourage the development and further the skills and musicianship of students. As with competitions, the preparation helps motivation, concentrates the mind and should result in success. Thus examinations and competitions can be justified.

It goes without saying that examiners should be persons of knowledge, experience, perception, sensibility, and sound judgement, able to put candidates at their ease, and adept at making a positive contribution to the situation. Impartiality is the keyword for Associated Board of the Royal Schools of Music examinations. This particular examining board uses non-specialist examiners for Grades 1–8 in order to assess the musical outcome of a performance rather than the means by which it is achieved. Guildhall School of Music and Drama employs examiners in a specialist capacity who examine only candidates in their own discipline.

Examiners are able to influence teachers by providing independent advice, for although the examiner's report is written as to the student, such a comment as 'Take care over your diction' should serve as a clue to the teacher.

But there are always examiners with pet ideas: those who wax lyrical about releasing the creative impulse – an admirable idea, but one seldom demonstrated. Some confine themselves to only one aspect, which is frustrating for the candidate who has gone to great lengths to produce a 'whole' performance.

Jenkins cites a music teacher who was concerned with the marking of grade examinations. She had provided the piano accompaniment for the pupil of a colleague in the examination. On later receiving a copy of the examination report, 'she was startled to find that the candidate had been given full marks for pieces, scales and arpeggios. The pupil had done well – but surely not *that* well, she thought' (2002, p. 5). Beniston makes it clear that:

> The aim is to learn to play the instrument, and the exam is a way of sampling the process against the carefully worked out standards and criteria. The service provided by the examiner is to decide if the sample of work heard has yet reached that set out in the criteria (2001, p. 4).

This applies equally to singing.

The Teacher

It may be hoped that voice teachers will increasingly understand the ramifications of performance evaluation. As has become clear, this is a multi-faceted activity which ideally turns upon a sound knowledge of anatomy and physiology (not least because the adjudicator must watch as well as listen). Some understanding of the acoustic properties of the venue is called for, because these may assist or hinder the performer. (In particular teachers should be aware of, and prepare their students for, the adjustments which they will have to make when transferring their performance from the confines of a voice studio or practice room to a larger hall). Detailed knowledge of the songs performed is required, in relation to their type, structure, historical context, and language; and in regard to the technical challenges which they pose. In offering a performance evaluation regard should be had to the insights derived from developmental psychology in so far as these relate to the age and experience of the performer. The psychology of inter-personal relations also comes to the fore, especially since the voice belongs to the person in a way that no other instrument does. Closely related are the ethical considerations posed by the question, 'What *ought* I to say?' – a question which concerns both the content and the manner of the verdict expressed. Finally, philosophical questions arise as teachers reflect on the grounds of their aesthetic judgments and the meaningfulness or otherwise of the language in which they are expressed. Properly conducted, the act of performance evaluation will contribute in terms of content and example to the aesthetic education of students.[51]

It is not too much to say that such evaluation at its most competent is fertilized by all of the disciplines with which this study has been concerned. This consideration ushers in my Conclusion.

Notes

1   For suggestions concerning auditions, radio and television, see Appendix 3b.
2   More will be said regarding languages below.
3   See further, Goldovsky, Boris and Arthur Schoep (2002), *Bringing Soprano Arias to Life*, London: Shelwing.
4   See further, Greene, Harry Plunket (1914), *Interpretation in Song*, London: Macmillan.
5   See further, Wilson, Glenn D. (2002), *Psychology for Performing Artists*, London: Whurr. An excellent summary of the acting schools is given here. See also, Benedetti, Jean (1990), *Stanislavski: An Introduction*, London: Methuen. Stanislavski, Constantin (1989), *Building a Character*, London: Methuen; (1990), *Creating a Role*, trans. E.R. Hapgood, London: Methuen; (1992), *An Actor Prepares*, trans. E.R. Hapgood, London: Methuen. Following Stanislavski's training of actors and singers came the renowned teachers, Walter Felsenstein, Boris Goldovsky and Wesley Balk.
6   See further, Berry, Cecily (1993), *The Actor and His Text*, London: Virgin; Rodenburg, Patsy (1992), *The Right to Speak*, London: Methuen.
7   See further, Mabry, Sharon (2002), *Exploring Twentieth Century Vocal Music*, Oxford: Oxford University Press.
8   See further, Emmons, Shirlee and Stanley Sonntag (1979), *The Art of the Song Recital*, New York: Schirmer.
9   See further, Appendix 3a.
10   See further, Bunch, Meribeth (1995), *Dynamics of the Singing Voice*, Wien: Springer-Verlag; Hemsley, Thomas (1998), *Singing and Imagination*, Oxford: Oxford University Press.
11   See further, Klinger, Rita; Patricia Shehan Campbell, and Thomas Goolsby (1998), 'Approaches to children's song acquisition: immersion and phrase-by-phrase', *Journal of Research in Music Education*, **46** (1), Spring, 24–34.
12   See further, Davis, Richard (1998), *A Beginning Singer's Guide*, Lanham, MD: Scarecrow.
13   See further, Eliade, Mircea (1954), *The Myth of the Eternal Return*, trans. Willard R. Trask, Princeton, NJ: Princeton University Press; Feil, Arnold (1988), *Franz Schubert:*

die schöne Müllerin, Winterreise, trans. Ann C. Sherwin, Portland, OR: Amadeus Press; Stein, Jack (1971), *Poem and Music in the German Lied from Gluck to Hugo Wolf*, Cambridge, MA: Harvard University Press; Whitton, Kenneth (1984), *Lieder: An Introduction to German Song*, London: Julia Macrae Books.

14   See further, Sloboda, John A., Jane W. Davidson, Michael J.A. Howe, and Derek G. Moore (1996), 'The role of practice in the development of performing musicians', *British Journal of Psychology*, **87** Part 2, May, 287–309.

15   See below on aesthetics.

16   See further, Marshall, Madeleine (1953), *The Singer's Manual of English Diction*, New York: Schirmer; Colorni, Evelina (1970), *Singers' Italian*, New York: Schirmer; Cox, Richard G. (1970), *The Singer's Manual of German and French Diction*, New York: Schirmer; Cox, Richard G. (1990), *Singing in English*, Lawton, OK: American Choral Directors Association; Wall, Joan (1989), *International Phonetic Alphabet for Singers*, Dallas: Pst ... Inc; Wall, Joan, Robert Caldwell, Tracy Gavilanes, and Sheila Allen (1990), *Diction for Singers*, Dallas: Pst ... Inc; Piatak, Jean and Regina Avrashov (1991), *Russian Songs and Arias*, Dallas: Pst ... Inc; McGee, Timothy J. (ed.), A.G. Rigg and David N. Klausner (1996), *Singing Early Music: The Pronunciation of European Languages and the Late Middle Ages and Renaissance*, Bloomington: Indiana University Press.

17   See further, De'Ath, Leslie (2002), 'The hazards of reflex: caveats of a voice coach', *Journal of Singing*, **59** (1), November/December, 155–9.

18   See further, Chapter 4 above on vowel modification.

19   See further, Garcia, M.A. (1847 and 1872), *A Complete Treatise on the Art of Singing, Part II*, trans. and ed. Donald V. Paschke (1975), New York: Da Capo; Marchesi, Mathide (1970), *Bel Canto: Theoretical and Practical Vocal Method*, New York: Dover; Vennard, W. (1967), *Singing: the Mechanism and the Technic*, New York: Carl Fischer; Miller, Richard (1986), *The Structure of Singing*, New York: Schirmer.

20   See further, Phillips, Gerald L. (2002), 'Diction: a rhapsody', *Journal of Singing*, **58** (5), May/June, 405–9.

21   See further, Leenman, Tracy E. (1997), 'A closer look at DICTION', *Chorus* **5** (1), August, 34–5, 42.

22   See further, Telfer, Nancy (1992), *Successful Sight Singing*, San Diego: Neil A. Kjos; Harris, Paul and Richard Crozier (2000), *The Music Teacher's Companion*, London: ABRSM.

23   See further, as one example written for pianists, Matthay, T. (1926), *Memorizing and Playing from Memory*, London: Oxford University Press; Wood, David (1988), *How Children Think and Learn*, Oxford; Blackwell.

24   See further, Bean, Matt (1998), 'Manipulate the accompanist', *Journal of Singing*, **54** (3), March/April, 41–3.

25   See further, Adler, Kurt (1907), *The Art of Accompanying and Coaching* (1965), rep. edn, New York: Da Capo.

26   See further, Ivey, Donald (1970), *Song: Anatomy, Imagery, and Styles*, New York: The Free Press.

27   See further, Miller, Richard (2002), '(1) Imaginative singing', *Journal of Singing*, **58** (5), May/June, 415–16.

28   See further, Stollak, Mary Alice and Lois Alexander (1998), 'The use of analogy in the rehearsal', *Music Educators Journal*, **84** (6), May, 17–21.

29   See further, Dart, Thurston (1967), *The Interpretation of Music*, London: Hutchinson.

30 See further, Stevens, Denis (1997), *Early Music,* London: Kahn and Averill; O'Dea, Jane (1994), 'Authenticity in musical performance: personal or historical?' *British Journal of Aesthetics,* **34** (4), October, 363–75.

31 See further, Donington, Robert (1982), *Baroque Music: Style and Performance,* London: Faber Music.

32 Cf. the discussion of ethics in Chapter 2 above.

33 See further, Ching, James (1947), *Performer and Audience,* London: Keith Prowse; Wilson, Glenn W. (2002), *Psychology for Performing Artists,* London: Whurr.

34 See further, Grindea, Carola (2000), 'The phenomenon of "Peak Experience" or "The Flow" in musical performance', *ISSTIP Journal* (10), November, 7–11.

35 See further, Haid, Karen (1999), 'Coping with performance anxiety', *Teaching Music,* **7** (1), August, 40–41, 60; Harris Sandra R. (1988), 'A study of musical performance anxiety', *American Music Teacher,* **37** (4), February/March, 15–16; Steptoe, Andrew (1989), 'Stress, coping and stage fright in professional musicians', *Psychology of Music,* **17**, 3–11; Senyshyn, Yaroslav (1999), 'Perspectives on performance and anxiety and their implications for creative teaching', *Canadian Journal of Education,* **24** (1), 30–41.

36 For the historical context of musical aesthetics see Lippman, Edward A. (1992), *A History of Western Musical Aesthetics,* Lincoln, NE: University of Nebraska Press; Barwell, Ismay (1986), 'How does art express emotion?' *The Journal of Aesthetics and Art Criticism,* **35** (2), Winter, 176–81.

37 See further, Kivy, Peter (1991), *Sound and Semblance: Reflections on Musical Representation,* Ithaca, NY: Cornell University Press.

38 See further, Berenson, Frances (1994), 'Representation and music', *British Journal of Aesthetics,* **34** (1), January, 60–68; Trivedi, Saam (2002), 'Against musical works as eternal types', *British Journal of Aesthetics,* **42** (1), January, 73–82.

39 See further, Mark, Michael L. (1982), 'The evolution of music education philosophy from utilitarian to aesthetic', *Journal of Research in Music Education* **30** (1), 15–21.

40 See further, Edgar, Andrew (1990), 'An introduction to Adorno's aesthetics', *British Journal of Aesthetics,* **30** (1), January, 46–56; Paddison, Max (1993), *Adorno's Aesthetics of Music,* Cambridge: Cambridge University Press.

41 See further, Robinson, Jenefer (1994), 'The expression and arousal of emotion in music', *The Journal of Aesthetics and Art Criticism,* **52** (1), Winter, 13–22; Kivy, Peter (1980), *The Corded Shell,* Princeton, NJ: Princeton University Press and (1990), *Music Alone,* Ithaca, NY: Cornell University Press.

42 See further, Kivy, Peter (1995), *Authenticities: Philosophical Reflections on Musical Performance,* Ithaca, NY: Cornell University Press.

43 See further, Åhlberg, Lars-Olof (1994), 'Suzanne Langer on representation and emotion in music', *British Journal of Aesthetics,* **34** (1), January, 69–80; Wilkinson, Robert (1995), 'Art, emotion and expression', in Hanfling Oswald, *Philosophical Aesthetics,* Oxford: Blackwell, 179–238.

44 See further, Allen, R.T. (1990), 'The arousal and expression of emotion by music', *British Journal of Aesthetics,* **30** (1), January, 57–61.

45 See further, Robinson, Jenefer (1994), 'The expression and arousal of emotion in music', *The Journal of Aesthetics and Art Criticism,* **52** (1), Winter, 13–22.

46 See further, Weatherston, Martin (1996), 'Kant's assessment of music in the *Critique of Judgement*', *British Journal of Aesthetics,* **36** (1), January, 56–65.

47 I draw this summary from Meynell, Hugo (1995), 'On Nietzsche, postmodernism and the New Enlightenment', *New Blackfriars,* **76** (889), January, 4–18, who in turn follows

Lonergan, Bernard (1971), *Method in Theology*, London: Darton, Longman and Todd, Chapter 1.

48 See further, Kay, Graeme (1996), 'Competitions', in Ford, Trevor (ed.), *The Musician's Handbook*, London, Rhinegold Publishing.

49 See further, Cunningham, Sara (2003), 'Judge and jury', *Classical Music: Competitions Supplement*, 9.

50 See further, Wapnick, Joel; Alice Ann Darrow, Jolan Kovacs, Lucinda Dalrymple (1997), 'Effects of physical attractiveness on evaluation of vocal performance', *Journal of Research in Music Education*, **45** (3), 470–79.

51 See further, Plummeridge, Charles (1999), 'Aesthetic education and the practice of music teaching', *British Journal of Music Education*, **16** (2), July, 115–22.

Conclusion

The Introduction to this study took as it starting point what actually happens in a voice studio. It became clear that a constellation of disciplines is involved in classical singing pedagogy. We further noted that while a considerable amount of research has been undertaken within each of the disciplines, the implications for vocal pedagogy are not always drawn out. This was not an adverse criticism of specialist works devoted to, for example, ethics, science, and aesthetics, but it did suggest the desirability of bringing the relevant disciplines together for the first time within one study with a view to showing that, how, and at which points they contribute to classical singing pedagogy, and frequently do so in mutually supportive ways. The reason for undertaking this study was that if the disciplines in question are indeed relevant to singers and their teachers, if there is more to educating singers and teachers than simply training their voices, then the several disciplines should take their place in the curriculum to which prospective singers and singing teachers are exposed.

Underpinned by substantial personal experience over many years I critically analysed a considerable body of published material relevant to each of the disciplines under discussion, with the aim of demonstrating the thesis 'that an holistic education entailing multi-disciplinary study is essential if classical singers and vocal pedagogues are to be prepared adequately for performance, for their teaching role, and for cooperation in inter-professional relations'.

It remains to draw the the findings together with a view to noting some of the practical implications which flow from them.

In the first chapter the historical roots of the many teaching methods available today were explored. It was apparent that some of them paid greater heed to a freely functioning vocal mechanism than others. Knowledge of traditions of technique can be a useful aid when faced with a singer in distress; the particular damaging aspect of technique can easily be spotted. However personal and anecdotal experience show that many traditional methods are being taught indiscriminately, without considering whether they are soundly based in theory and conducive to vocal health. So many of the conventions have been passed down by imitation and, as we have seen, what is physically appropriate for one person may be damaging for the next. Similarly we have found that the imagery, useful and appropriate in interpretation, can be meaningless and damaging when teaching technique. Voice teachers should be encouraged to realize that some understanding of the history of vocal pedagogy and its traditions and legacies is an important part of their equipment.

In exploring the scientific and medical aspects of the history of vocal pedagogy, we found that while some things have changed, others have not, and yet others have developed from very sound scientific roots. Immediately, we found the disciplines overlapping and interweaving.

It became clear that ethical considerations impinge upon vocal pedagogy at a number of points. Indeed the very first question, 'Ought I to teach?' is an ethical question. Accordingly, an understanding of the basic principles of ethics was shown to give the teacher a sound basis on which to make moral judgements in business, in relationships with students, parents, professional performers, other musical colleagues and other professionals.

It is easy to appreciate the value of the knowledge of general psychology as a basis for the more specialized branches of that discipline applicable to vocal pedagogy: an understanding of emotion in its physiological, cognitive, social, and personality aspects; cognition and all its branches; physiological and social psychology; developmental and musical psychology. Practical application of this information is vital in the teacher's relationship with pupils of all age groups, parents and other professionals. We have seen that a grasp of basic psychology can also alert the teacher to possible psychological problems in the student which may need help from a practitioner qualified in that field – the teacher here acting as an early warning signal. It goes without saying that in such situations tact, sensitivity and understanding are called for; at no point should teachers attempt to deal with problems for which they are unqualified: we are back to the close connection between ethics and psychology once again.

Turning to the contribution of science, it was encouraging to find that polarization between voice studio pedagogy and voice science is on the wane although there are areas of debate still to be found. With a wealth of information about the physical function of the singing voice teachers are more easily able to diagnose and remedy vocal faults, and advise the student to consult a medical practitioner if a potentially serious problem is presented. I emphasized that problems should be handled with discretion and confidentiality, and, unless also medically qualified, voice teachers should not offer medical diagnoses. Brandfonbrener worries that,

> some teachers who appear to feel that with reading, and a workshop or two they have suffi-
> cient information to themselves make medical judgements. It is critical that we, as medical
> practitioners and they, as performance teachers learn to operate within the limits of our own
> area of expertise. Neither should oversimplify the material from each other's domain.
> A therapeutic alliance is the ideal solution and while often it may require equal doses of
> diplomacy and hard work, it is a goal well worth the effort to promote (2002, p. 41).

We have discovered how important adequate knowledge of anatomy and physiology is as an aid in determining what is an efficient and non-damaging vocal technique. The implications are far reaching; they concern correct posture, competent breathing technique, correct use of the laryngeal area and the resonators. It would be a great pity if teachers and singers were to ignore the value of state-of-the-art scientific instrumentation which is becoming more readily available. As we have seen, this assists in the assessment of vocal performance and progress and may sometimes reveal a problem not noticed by the singer or teacher. Advice on general health care surfaces during the study of vocal science, in particular, how to care for the vocal instrument. We should do well to remember the testimony of those otolaryngologists who say that they have fewer singers in their clinics from studios where the teachers have been adequately educated in basic vocal health and hygiene.

Turning to vocal technique, the most important result of this study is to note the overriding importance of efficient, healthy technique. The message coming over loud and clear from medical practitioners who have to deal with serious vocal abuse is, 'Change your teacher'. Without a sound technique artistry is inhibited and a short career predicted. To whom does the singer look when this choice has to be made? Surely, the obvious answer must be that the singer chooses the teacher who has the necessary soundly based knowledge, which a multi-disciplinary training has provided.

A number of specific points of technique, among them, onset and release, breath management, and resonating factors, were discussed with a view to showing how results consistent with anatomical and physiological realities can be achieved. Without efficient vocal technique, a performance may be disappointing both to performer and listener. But technique alone is not enough; in the preparation for performance there is much to be learnt. Preparation (among other things, history, performance practice, languages) and positive, useful practising are vital. Imagination has to be stimulated and cultivated, the conveying of emotion has to be learnt – at which point psychology comes in again; so too does history, because knowledge of a song's period, and style further stimulates the imagination.

So many skills have to be acquired for dealing with the actual performance, the programming of recitals, and working with an accompanist. The teacher needs to know how to teach the song or aria accurately, including rhythm, languages, diction, phrasing and tone colour. Without an education in aural skills, theory, composition, listening and performance studies and standards, it is difficult to see how this can be achieved. Appropriate repertoire for the individual student has to be chosen. The pupil has to learn how to memorize, how to communicate, how to deal with auditioning, publicity, performance venues, radio and television, and importantly and commonly, how to deal with performance anxiety.

More and more we began to see the broad scope of the education of the singer and singing teacher. More and more frequently we found that the several disciplines mutually inform one another.

Finally, there is the evaluation of performance. We saw that teachers are constantly evaluating the performance of their pupils, and reacting to the assessments of examiners, adjudicators, critics, and agents. They may also be called upon to serve in these latter capacities from time to time. How useful, therefore, to have a basic background in aesthetics, particularly, of course, music aesthetics, in order to contemplate the language of, and basis for, the assessment of the performances they witness or criticize.

Implications for Educating the Singer and Singing Teacher

If all the disciplines referred to above are pertinent to the education of singers and singing teachers then they should be included in the training of singers. However Freed has this to say:

> The conflict between the scientific and empirical may also continue because of the hiring policies of departments or schools of music. Read the latest advertisements for job listings in voice. Some institutions place an emphasis on pedagogy and scholarship in addition to performance. Other institutions have advertisements like this: 'Associate professor of voice. National reputation; outstanding singer with a professional performing career; must be dedicated to teaching.' Singers with the performing careers, having little training in pedagogy, may be able to sense what is right in singing for themselves, but what about teaching the beginning student? (Freed, 2000, p. 10).

Kemp delineates the problem with which this thesis is concerned:

> That the processes of learning to sing are so subjective seems to encourage a plethora of contradictory theories, which may leave singers, at best bemused, and at worst, highly anxious and constantly unsure about whether they are performing correctly or doing themselves untold damage. Singing students may well find themselves moving from teacher to teacher in constant search for a 'guru' who, by use of a particular form of metaphor, somehow manages to 'speak their language'. This whole process may be very anxiety provoking (2000, p. 174).

Happily, there are ways to go about improving the education of singers and singing teachers. Courses which include all of the above disciplines could be established. Some conservatories and universities are attempting this, but none, as yet, includes all the disciplines. Admittedly, conservatories do not have medical schools, but most have universities as their validating bodies, and there could be interchange of medical students to vocal pedagogy classes and singers to anatomy and physiology classes. Similarly, there could be facilities for singers to attend psychology and aesthetics classes in other departments. The plea that there is no time for all of this does not hold if one accepts the conclusions of this study, namely, that efficient, healthy vocal function is paramount for all singers and that a wide spectrum of inter-acting disciplines is vital to achieve this.

Many professional societies in Britain, in Europe and the United States are leading the way in the study of vocal health and its application for the professions. For example, The International Society for the Study of Tension in Performance is pioneering a diploma course to train *Music, Medicine Therapists*. It is offered to singers, instrumentalists, and medical practitioners. This course is the most holistic of all available at the moment; faculty consist of specialist medical practitioners (rheumatologists, neurologists, laryngologists, orthopaedic surgeons), psychologists, musicians, a voice consultant, an actors' coach, a Feldenkrais teacher, an Alexander Teacher, osteopaths, physiotherapists and a podiatrist. While some disciplines are unrepresented, the overall range of expertise is exceptional. Refresher courses for practising teachers are also available. For example, in the United Kingdom, the Association of Teachers of Singing holds an annual short summer course for teachers; the Associated Board of the Royal Schools of Music offers a Cert ABRSM course; and the University of Reading in collaboration with the Incorporated Society of Musicians offers a Diploma Course in Music Teaching in Private Practice. Some of these lead to a formal qualification, but to date none of them covers all of the required disciplines. There is an extremely valuable contribution being made by the staff of voice clinics, some of whom encourage participation in assessment and healing practices by other professionals, including voice professionals, and are extremely successful in rehabilitating the sick voice. However, unfortunately, by the time the assistance of such professionals is sought the damage has frequently been done, and very often the singer is at a loss to find a teacher who can effectively build upon the good work done at the clinic.

In the light of the argument advanced in this book I am now in a position to frame some specific training suggestions. A comprehensive study of theory, harmony, aural skills and language training is taken for granted. In addition, a scheme of study for singers and voice teachers (for the roles frequently overlap) might include:

1. The acquisition of an efficient, healthy, freely functioning singing voice based on sound technique.
2. The history of vocal pedagogy which reveals the fact that a scientific approach to the voice is not a late twentieth century novelty and which includes the several vocal techniques and their tonal ideals.
3. The ethics of professional practice.
4. General psychology and those branches of the discipline which directly apply to vocal pedagogy, especially developmental psychology.
5. The anatomy and physiology of voice.
6. Vocal science, including acoustical science as it relates to the voice, and the acquisition of familiarity with scientific equipment related to voice.
7. Vocal health and hygiene, including attendance at relevant courses in medical schools and observation at multi-disciplinary voice clinics.
8. The study of voice techniques for all age groups.
9. The preparation for performance, including: interpretation inspired by general musical appreciation, knowledge of skills, styles and other distinctive attributes of the various composers; the subtleties and sensibilities of poetry; rhythm; languages; IPA; performance practice (the authenticity debate); diction; aural skills; theory; composition; communication skills; working with a conductor and an accompanist.

10. Business and management skills for performing: performance venues; advertising; auditioning; working with an agent; recording; radio and television performance.
11. Dealing with performance anxiety.
12. Training in Alexander Technique.
13. Attendance at concerts, recitals, opera, listening to recorded music, visits to multi-disciplinary voice conferences, singing conferences and courses, master classes and voice workshops.
14. Immersion in philosophical aesthetics and musical aesthetics as a basis for well-grounded evaluation of performance, for example by critics, adjudicators, examiners, and teachers.
15. Student recitals during the course of study, the performance accompanied by pedagogical/programme notes. In this way the student would see how the several contributions of many of the disciplines are brought to bear on performance and pedagogy.

In the light of the foregoing suggestions we may now conclude that if voice teachers are required to handle psychological, ethical, and aesthetic questions; to have a sound knowledge of anatomy, physiology and voice science as it bears upon vocal pedagogy; to have a grasp of developmental psychology in relation to curriculum planning; to be well versed in musicianship, interpretation, and communication – all of which entails a knowledge of history, theory and language; and to be competent in performance for the purposes of demonstration, then these ingredients should be present in the training of voice teachers and singers generally, many of whom also teach, or take up teaching following a performing career.

Implications for Inter-professional Cooperation

Since singing teaching is an unregulated profession, an endorsement of competence by such professional bodies as the British Voice Association or the Association of Teachers of Singing in order for singing teachers to be able to work alongside other voice professionals would facilitate a greater degree of inter-professional cooperation and give other professionals confidence in their singing teacher colleagues. Such endorsement would be based upon the presentation of full course transcripts (to ensure that all relevant disciplines have been covered), and not simply upon diploma or degree certificates.

For their part doctors and medical students should be encouraged to be aware of performing arts medicine as a specialty. Ten years ago Hewer and others argued the case for 'multi-disciplinary, directly-interactive teams' in the diagnosis and treatment of voice disorders in professional singers (1993, pp. 25–6). The special perspectives and skills of the otolaryngologist, speech-language therapist, voice scientist, nurse and singing teacher are complementary and necessary for the successful rehabilitation of the singer. There is such a wealth of knowledge on the various voice specialisms published each year that it is impossible for anyone to know all the information in another's specialist field.

It is recognized that at present voice science laboratories and fully staffed voice clinics are not to be found in all areas, and that the lack of funding is a serious impediment to developments in these fields. It is also the case that problems of confidence in voice teachers as professionals cannot but arise from scientific and medical quarters when persons can set up as voice teachers with a pass at Grade 5 – or lower (all otolaryngologists have done more than scrape through GCSE Biology). It would be well to have a separate compulsory paper on vocal pedagogy in every examination for a voice teaching qualification. It is highly desirable that all voice-training establishments offer a sound pedagogical course grounded in vocal science. If the reply is that funding and/or availability of personnel will not permit this for just a handful of singers, then the benefits to be derived from a voice course by wind instrumentalists whose breath management may be inefficient may be explained. Furthermore, if we wish to foster a culture of inter-professional cooperation, we ought seriously to consider the possibility that as an essential element of their training, voice students in music departments, conservatories and private studios, together with students in such cognate disciplines as voice science, medicine and speech and language therapy, learn together in team-taught voice laboratory sessions.

Coda

When the initial training is complete the learning process is barely begun. It is vital that singers and voice teachers continue to study: new discoveries are frequently reported in the professional journals, in new books, and in papers presented at conferences. The benefits of constant study and practice in one's own performing and in one's own teaching will increasingly be manifest.

As we saw at the outset, almost three hundred years ago Pier Francesco Tosi wrote,

> It may seem to many, that every perfect Singer must also be a perfect Instructor, but that is not so; for his Qualifications (though ever so great) are insufficient, if he cannot communicate his Sentiments with Ease, and in a Method adapted to the Ability of the Scholar … (1723, pp. 160–61).

Today there is more understanding of the disciplines contributing to vocal pedagogy than ever before. One can only hope that training courses for singers and singing teachers will reflect this fact, and that aspiring performer/teachers will approach their multi-disciplinary studies with zeal.

Appendix 1

Supplement to Chapter 1

a

Historians of vocal pedagogy have proposed various ways of dividing the subject. For example, von Leden specifies 'four cultural phases' of voice production. First comes 'the fictitious or mythical stage' including folklore, magic, supernatural and religious phenomena; secondly, 'the metaphysical stage ... knowledge was based partly on observation, but mainly on speculation'; thirdly, 'the traditional stage' where information was 'based on tradition or revelation, on the great authorities of the ancient world, and on the great Fathers of the Church'; and lastly, the realistic stage, beginning with the Renaissance, in which 'Knowledge was based on actual observation, experimentation, and coordination' (1997, p. 7). Presumably the final phrase concerns the relationship of voice production and medicine. While such a scheme has some credibility, it must be understood that the categories suggested by von Leden are not absolute. There are always time lags and overlaps in the development of any discipline.

Solo singers have always been to the fore: cantors in the chant, Minnesingers, troubadours, trouvères, followed by Meistersingers, and the English singer-lutenists. Then came the 'birth of opera' at the beginning of the seventeenth century with each decade making increased technical demands on the singer, mainly determined by the composer, but often by the audience. Vocal scores show the evidence for this. Thus Miller says:

> The Mantuan Monteverdi of *Orfeo*, 1607, is not the same as the Venetian Monteverdi of *Il Ritorno d'Ulisse*, 1641, nor of *L'incoronazione di Poppea*, 1642 ... The vigor and intensity, particularly of the *Poppea* roles, are reflected in the mounting vocal demands of range, agility, and sostenuto, far exceeding those of the first decade of the century (1997, p. xv).

As history moves on, the demand for ever greater technical ability continues to be made, as we shall see; hence the need for impeccable voice teachers.

Early History

Pre-history is inevitably based on inferences drawn from anthropological, ethnological and archaeological studies. These leave us to surmise that the historical tradition of singing handed down was oral: for example, mothers singing lullabies to their babies and children copying their elders in tribal, ritual and religious chants. The oral tradition may have continued for thousands of years. Only with the advent of literacy can we be a little clearer as to what was demanded of a singer, and even then scholars are in disagreement as to how the music sounded. Accounts of singing performance written before the nineteenth century have to do with the authors' tonal preferences rather than with the technique required to achieve the desired sound.

All that we can discover about the music of ancient Greece and Rome is from some fragments of Greek music. Scholars are not in total accord as to how this music sounded. From Rome there are no authentic remains; we have to deduce from accounts of performances and certain literary sources what the music and singing was like. Duey (1980) suggests from the literary evidence of Homer and Hesiod that the singing was improvisatory.

The writings of Plato (427–347 BC) and Aristotle (384–322 BC) tell us that music and vocal art played an important part in education, although there does not seem to be any concept of singing technique as such. Many of the terms used to describe poetry are applied to singing, as might be expected given that poems were often recited accompanied by the lyre, and that the word 'ode' is derived from the Greek word which means 'to sing'. It has been suggested that orators moved from spoken sound into singing sound in order to be heard. Plato was concerned that there should be a certain amount of decorum in the production of singing; it must not be too florid or showy. He suggested that rhythm and harmony should follow the words and not the reverse, 'song consists of three elements: words, musical mode, and rhythm', and in answer to the query, 'the musical mode and rhythm should fit the words?' he replied, 'Of course' (*Republic*, III, 398). He did not want the enjoyment of singing for its own sake, but rather that the music should encourage an uplifting of the soul. Elsewhere he declared that 'the figures and melodies which are expressive of virtue of soul or body, or of images of virtue, are without exception good' (*Laws*, II, 655).

As early as the fourth century BC Aristotle had appreciated the relationship of breathing to phonation. In his opinion:

> Voice is a sound made by an animal, and that with a special organ ... everything that makes a sound does so by the impact of something (a) against something else, (b) across a space, (c) filled with air; hence it is only to be expected that no animals utter voice except those which take in air ... The organ of respiration is the windpipe, and the organ to which this is related as means to end is the lungs ... Voice then is the impact of the inbreathed air against the windpipe, and the impact is the soul resident in these parts of the body (*De Anima* II, 8).

He goes on to explain his theories of differing voice qualities as follows:

> Not only structural variations in the organs of speech make a difference to the voice, but also their condition. When the lungs and windpipe are full of moisture, the breath is impeded and does not pass out continuously, because it is interrupted and becomes thick

and moist and difficult to move, as happens in the case of a catarrh and in drunkenness. If the breath be absolutely dry, the voice becomes rather hard and dispersed ... (*De Audibilibus*, 801a).

In addition to its Greek and Roman inheritance, vocal pedagogy is greatly indebted to the Judaeo-Christian tradition. Thus we find that the Old Testament contains numerous references to singing, and that parts of it were sung, particularly the psalms: 'the singers sang and the trumpeters sounded' (2 Chronicles 29: 28); again, 'I got for myself minstrels, male and female' (Ecclesiastes 2: 8). There is the Song of Deborah (Judges 5) and Miriam's song of triumph (Exodus 15: 21). The singers were often accompanied by dancing and by musical instruments.

Reliable sources find that the earliest Christians sang the great New Testament hymns in their worship, for example, the Magnificat, the Nunc Dimittis and psalms, hymns and other songs: 'speak to one another in psalms, hymns and songs; sing and make music from your heart to the Lord' (Ephesians 5: 19). The melodies were probably Hebrew as used in the synagogue. In the book of Revelation there are many references to singing, not least in connection with John the Seer's vision of the New Jerusalem: 'and they were singing a new song' (Revelation 5: 9).

According to Falkner, by the time of Plutarch (46–120) 'technical facility was by then apparently in decline'. He goes on to quote Plutarch, '... our men of art ... have brought into the theatre a sort of effeminate musical prattling, mere sound without substance' (1983, p. 3).

The early theologians of the Christian Church were mostly responsible for the preservation and transmission of what is now called Western music (Wilson-Dickson, 1992, p. 26). They, like Plato, warned against the vagaries of excessive vocal display, Clement of Alexandria was particularly keen to advise Christians to 'reject superfluous music, which enervates men's souls, and leads to variety, – now mournful, and then licentious and voluptuous, and then frenzied and frantic' (*Stromateis*, VI. xi). Eventually, owing in the main to the Christian chant style, objectives in relation to pitch and tone colour were specified, though without guidance on how to achieve the desired sounds (Potter, 1998).[1]

With the growth of church music, in particular plainsong, a school of singing was founded in Rome, supposedly by Sylvester (Pope 314–336). Congregational singing had been prohibited by the Council of Laodicea in 367, hence the rise in importance of trained choral singing in church services. The establishment of more singing schools by monks followed, in which candidates for the priesthood received vocal training.

There was a certain amount of theorizing which tended to demote the performer and promote the philosopher. Boethius (c. 524), along with other theorists, protests that the philosopher who contemplates is the real musician with the composer and performer ranking second and third. Duey (1951) suggests that this view was in vogue for almost one thousand years. Nonetheless, Pope Gregory the Great (c. 540–604), drawing upon influences from other Mediterranean music, particularly Jewish, developed what became known as Gregorian Chant. He founded or reorganized the first singing school, the Schola Cantorum in Rome. Here priests and monks were taught how best to sing the music of the Christian church. It has been suggested that the aim of the teachers was to achieve a mellow sound that blended readily with other voices. Eventually, Charles the Great (740–814) founded singing schools in most of the European monasteries, cathedrals, greater churches and chantries.

Isidore of Seville (570–636) wrote in his *Etymologiarum sive originum libri*, XX (7th century) of what he considered to be unpleasant singing voices. He compared them with the tonal qualities of musical instruments, 'penetrating voices, like the sound of trumpets ... sharp voices, as we observe in strings ... a hard voice, like the sound of an anvil' (cited by Jander, 1980 p. 339). His 'ideal' singing voice was, 'high, sweet, and strong', as it has been the 'ideal' of many critics throughout history (ibid., p. 339). The achievement of this ideal was a prominent objective of the voice teachers.

Duey tells us of the attention the ancients paid to vocal hygiene and gives many examples (1951, p. 19). For medicines Gordon Holmes refers to Galen (130–200):

> They include tragacanth, squill, turpentine, styrax, horehound, myrrh, poppy-seeds, pepper, frankincense, cassia ... mixed with wine or honey and were sometimes boiled down, cooled, and made into lozenges to be held under the tongue and dissolved (1885, p. 49).

Careful diets and careful living were important: 'Quintillian [b. 30–35] mentions the fact that an easy digestion is essential both to the singer and orator' (cited by Duey, 1951, p. 20).

Middle Ages and Renaissance

Before the ninth century music notation was undeveloped, and consequently the singer's entire repertoire had to be learnt from memory. It is suggested that it took ten years to train the monastery singer in the unison singing of the liturgy. When Guido Arezzo (c. 991–1033), a legendary pedagogue who trained singers in monasteries, devised his famous system of precise pitch notation, singers were able to sight sing their parts accurately, at greater speed, and much less memory work was necessary. All these aspects contributed to a shorter training period, and more especially, the development of polyphony was encouraged because singers were able to identify pitches accurately, probably aided by the fluidity of monodic melodies. But there was a sting in the tail, for Arezzo's simple method became extremely difficult if the range of the melody was beyond a hexachord, so he devised a system of four different related pitch hexachords through which singers could move by 'mutation' or 'modulation'. His system can be compared with the movable 'doh' used in tonic solfa today. This complicated table, known as the *Gamut,* had to be learnt from memory, both backwards and forwards, before singers could progress to singing melodies.

Pedagogical treatises were rare until the middle of the sixteenth century. Until that time they were for the most part limited to such basic theoretical matters as notation, scales, intervals and rhythm. There is pictorial and literary evidence of singing, although pictorial evidence is difficult to interpret. According to Falkner 'Voice registers were recognized, chest, throat and head, but much of vocal music handed down to us covers only an octave, occasionally a twelfth' (1983, p. 5).[2] This is a very narrow range similar to the vocal compass of sung folk music. Many medieval writers were quick to criticize the shortcomings of the voices they disliked and the Church objected, yet again, to over-embellishment by singers.

The eleventh century singer/poet/composer troubadours of the south of France and the trouvères of the north were followed by the Minnesingers and the Meistersingers from Germany and the minstrels and gleemen in Britain. Many of their songs were improvised and comprised, for example, love-songs, political songs, pastourelles, romances and puzzle songs. These were often accompanied by the singer on a single instrument, either viol or harp. Sometimes the singer would alternate voice with instrument. The role they played in medieval life was that of itinerant entertainer, females included; they might even be called professional entertainers. They continued into the early sixteenth century alongside the madrigal singers from the fourteenth century. Unfortunately, we have no literature on actual teaching methods, and nothing is known about tonal qualities or interpretation.

There is, in the twelfth century some reference to breathing, but mainly in the context of phrasing – where to take a breath. But, as is usual throughout the centuries, there was much literature concerning incompetent singers: 'In the barking of their brawls they roar higher than the ass's braying, and blare out more terrible than the uproar of beasts, and spew out bedlam' (cited by Duey, 1951, p. 35). These are words by the ecclesiastic Arnulfo in the twelfth century. There was much conflict between the clergy who wanted music to be part of divine worship and the singers themselves who regarded music as an art form in its own right and wanted the freedom to compose and perform rather more artistically with the improvisation of embellishment and ornamentation. This made much greater demands on vocal technique in many aspects, particularly those of agility, breathing efficiency and imagination. Raynard, Abbot of Citeaux (1133–1151), declares that 'It becomes men to sing with a masculine voice, and not in a feminine matter, with tinkling, or as is popularly said, with false voices to imitate theatrical wantonness' (ibid., p. 41). Is this an early comment upon the male falsetto voice?[3]

Music theorists suggest that the range of the voice in the thirteenth to fourteenth century was expected to be two octaves, possibly in the male voice F2–F4 (USA Standards Association).[4] Between the latter part of the thirteenth century and the beginning of the fourteenth century notation was refined. The new art of motet writing, Ars Nova, utilized more short notes per bar than hitherto. Fifty years or so later, more items, such as time signatures and the transference of the fourteenth century semi-breve and minim to crotchet and quaver became the norm.

With the passage of time expression became uppermost in the minds of composers. What was heard in the voice was believed to reveal the feeling in the mind – interpretation was coming to the fore. Alongside the beginnings of the Renaissance in the fifteenth century, the art of the singer/composer became increasingly sophisticated and the average musician found great difficulty in reading the complicated music notation of the song literature. Hence a simpler notation was necessary but this was slow in its development.

Günter proposes that the first printed book about singing was the German Conrad von Zabern's *De modo cantandi choralem cantum* (1474). He was professor of theology and choral director at the University of Heidelberg, and Günter quotes him as saying:

> After having read this book the teacher will give better voice lessons in the future ... It is not enough if the singers sing the right notes and the correct intervals. To sing well requires more and only expressive qualities make good singing (1997, p. 9).

According to MacClintock, von Zabern lists

> Six requirements for good singing:
>
> 1. Concorditer (to sing with one spirit and accord)
> 2. Mensuraliter (to sing in proper measure)
> 3. Mediocriter (to sing in the middle range)
> 4. Differentialiter (to sing with discrimination)
> 5. Devotionaliter (to sing with devotion)
> 6. Satis urbaniter (to sing with beauty and refinement) (1979, p. 12).

As the fifteenth century progressed, although the vocal folds were not yet studied, much was discovered about the mouth, throat and lungs in relation to voice production. Adam de Fulda (c. 1490) says:

> Voice is the sound formed by striking the teeth with the tongue as a plectrum, by striking the two lips like symbols, by the hollow of the throat and the lungs which aid in the formation, and which, like a pair of bellows take in and send out air (cited by Duey, 1951, p. 32).

What is noticeable here is the beginning of an advance upon the phoniatrics and vocal science bequeathed by the first laryngologist, Galen (130–200) thirteen centuries earlier.

Stevens suggests that, 'the appeal and personality of a fine solo voice was as great in those early centuries as at any other time' (1971, p. 70). Gaffurius in his *Practica Musicae of* 1486 writes of the kind of singing not admired:

> Singers should not produce musical tones with a voice gaping wide in a distorted fashion or with an absurdly powerful bellowing ... moreover they should avoid tones having a

wide and ringing vibrato, since these tones do not maintain a true pitch and because of their continuous wobble cannot form a balanced concord with other voices (cited by Jander, 1995, p. 345).

As today, bellowing and a widely oscillating vibrato was deemed an example of poor technique and unpleasant to hear. On the other hand, it appears from music written in the period from Dufay (1400–1474) to Palestrina (1525/6–94) that there were also trained singers who were highly accomplished in breath control, passing through the register changes smoothly, and with vocal flexibility.

As acknowledgement of the arts, most particularly amongst the nobles, broadened with the Renaissance and self-expression in all art forms became a widely held aspiration, many composers broke away from the rather more formal approach of motet writing to a freer form of melody writing which encouraged rather more emotional depth. Such melodies were sung by soloists with accompaniment on the lute. The art of singing developed as more importance was given to individual singers/performers, and as increased technical demands were made upon them.

The German, Hermann Finck, in his *Practica Musica* (1556) writing about polyphonic singing, demanded sweetness, 'elegant' and *legato* singing, 'elegant' meaning the execution of some of the long white note-values of the melody by breaking them down into shorter black notes – hence the term 'divisions'. This was also practised at about the same time in Italy, by Bovicelli, and Zacconi, among others, and by the Frenchman des Prez and the Flemish Coclico. It is interesting to note that the term *coloratura* resulted from the vernacular usage of the words 'blackening' and 'whitening' in relation to the shortening and lengthening of note-values. *Coloratura* means vocal runs, passages of agility and ornamentation.[5] Finck states bluntly that

> no song is embellished by roaring and screaming … the higher a voice rises the quieter and lovelier should the note be sung; the more it descends, the richer the sound (cited by MacClintock, 1979, p. 62).

b

Notable among them in the eighteenth century were: Farinelli, Caffarelli, Carestini, and Senesino in the 1720s and 1730s and Rubinelli, Pacchierotti and Luigi Marchesi in the 1780s. It has been suggested that at this period seventy per cent of all opera singers were castrati. They sang both female and male roles. In other roles, the emphasis was upon the low unchanged male voice rather than the tenor voice, which, however, regained importance by the end of the eighteenth century. In the eighteenth century female singers were becoming more common in secular contexts. They were taught by castrati and sang the same roles. It was accepted that men sang women's roles and vice versa. This could cause much confusion for the audience.

In the eighteenth century we find a predominance of treatises which deal mainly with the altered voice of the castrati and the female soprano voice, and fewer concerned with the normal male voice. However much of vocal pedagogy, for example, breath management and articulation applied to all types and genders of voices. Male and female larynges are affected differently by puberty. The castrati's larynx was altered by removal of part or the whole of the genitals between the ages of seven and twelve, and hence the effects of puberty were largely avoided. The castrato became a full-grown male, often above average in height, and sometimes having ungainly movement. He retained the range and quality of a boy's voice (the larynx remained in a higher position and the vocal tract would probably have different proportions in relation to the vocal folds than that of the normal male or female). His voice was enhanced by maturity, having the power of large lungs that could sustain extraordinarily long phrases, and the resonating capabilities of an adult, features that manifested themselves as a 'beautiful' big sound. It has been estimated that out of four thousand boys per year castrated in Italy very few became famous. The first castrati to arrive in Italy were from Spain and one of the last in the line was Alessandro Moreschi (1858–1922) who can be heard on recordings.[6] He was not numbered among the great, but the recording does give a very rough idea of what they sounded like. The female soprano's popularity often rivalled that of the castrati, and during the eighteenth century the low female voice gradually became accepted.

Notes

1   See further, Potter, John (1998), *Vocal Authority: Singing Style and Ideology,* Cambridge: Cambridge University Press.
2   See further, Reid, Cornelius L. and Donna S. Reid (2000), 'Eighteenth-century registrational concepts,' *Journal of Singing*, **56** (4), p. 31. The Reids write of Johannes de Garlandia (c. 1193–1270) who spoke of *vox pectoris, vox guttoris*, and *vox capitas* (chest voice, throat voice, and head voice).
3   Ibid., p. 31. Marchettus de Padua describes two distinctive and different 'voices': *vox integra* and *vox ficta* (chest voice and falsetto). The meaning of 'falsetto' is not made clear. Over the centuries there have been many differing understandings of the word 'falsetto'. Here I use the term as descriptive of the countertenor or male alto sound.
4   Pitch indications follow those recommended internationally by the Acoustical Society of America where middle C is C4, as opposed to the Helmholtz system which has middle C as C1.
5   See further, Celletti, Rodolfo (1991), *A History of Bel Canto*, Oxford: Clarendon Press.
6   *The Record of Singing* (1977), EMI, Vol. 1 (RLS 724). It is accompanied by an illustrated book of the same name by Scott, Michael (1977, 1979), London: Duckworth.

Appendix 2

First Impressions in the Voice Studio

Psychological considerations apply at many points in vocal pedagogy. In order to show this let us envisage a voice studio.[1]

From the moment that the student/parent lifts the phone to make enquiries about lessons, voice teachers are selling themselves and their skills, and a social psychological 'atmosphere' with the building of relationships is being created. We find teachers dealing with their own self-concept, self-image, self-esteem, self-perception and self-efficacy and that of others in the contact with students, parents and other professionals.

The response to the phone call should be warm, welcoming, friendly and enthusiastic, but not overbearingly so. Similarly when the student/parent comes to the studio the response should be the same. Dressing in a professional manner increases the chances of getting the respect deserved.

What is the impact on the student of the studio itself? It should be tidy, well organized and bright, with a piano that has been tuned regularly. If finances permit, good quality audio recording equipment is extremely useful for instantaneous playback of singing, so too is a video recorder with immediate visual and audio playback for the same purpose. If video recording is not available, then the humble mirror is essential, together with a small hand-mirror for close-ups of, for example, tongue, lip and mouth positions. There should be an adjustable music stand, appropriate pictures, flowers, and a waiting area nearby, with easy access to a lavatory. A computer is a further desirable piece of apparatus.

The teacher should give the impression of an efficient, helpful and knowledgeable professional. However the prospective student should not be made to feel intimidated; humility on the part of the teacher never comes amiss.

Singing teachers need business skills and sales skills. There are three parts to a sale: the approach, presentation and close. During the approach the student becomes interested in buying through referral, advertising or public relations. It is therefore important for teachers to publicize their wares in the community, such as inviting people to recitals (both the teacher's and the pupil's), special seminars and open houses. For the presentation, it is vital to make sure the student/parent is listening and maintain full control of the interview all the time. It is useful to have a logical sequence in mind or written down, and to be prepared for resistance. The teacher should try to recognize the enquirers' dominant needs and respond to them, for example, if they mention 'quality' more than once, then the teacher can use the same word. There is much to be said for the teacher being alert to body language.

Honesty and enthusiasm are significant. Closing means that the sale is being confirmed.

Attention to seemingly small administrative points will engender confidence in the teacher's competence. For example, the teacher should keep records of students' addresses and telephone numbers both on cards, computer, notebooks or ring binder, have a copy of the timetable by the piano, and keep the waiting list up to date. It should go without saying that thank-you letters for gifts received from students should always be written.

Teachers should reassure parents/students that music other than that specified in the examination syllabus will feature in the repertoire to be mastered. They should be familiar with the offerings of each examination board and explain that the board will be matched to the student's needs, similarly the number and level of grades to be taken. It is not necessarily wise to plough through each successive grade. Teachers should be so well prepared that they never get the syllabus wrong or fail to cover required items.

The preliminary interview with a prospective student is of great importance from the psychological point of view not least because the assessment of teacher and prospective student is mutual. On both sides first impressions are significant, and *both* parties will not only be seeking information, but will, consciously or otherwise, be concerned to discover whether or not there is a basis for constructive inter-personal relations which will assist the learning process. Hence the importance of mutual questioning of which the following, drawn from my experience, are examples:

1. Questions a singing teacher might ask the prospective student or parent may include: 'Why do you or does your child wish to learn?' (an adult student should be asked, 'What is your goal?' Goals work best when both teacher and student agree upon them, and they should be realistic and attainable). 'Have you always sung since you were tiny? Are you giving it a go for your Mum's sake or because your best friend has singing lessons? What do you want to sing – Classics, Musical Theatre, Pop? What music do you like? What do you listen to at home? Does your child want lessons or is it *your* wish? Are you willing to buy a music stand, mirrors? Are you prepared to tolerate daily practice (shift-workers may find the practising of singing unbearable as they try to sleep)? Will you keep an eye on progress by asking your child to sing for you? What other activities has the child, and is there sufficient time for regular practice? Will you ensure constant and punctual attendance? Will you agree to periodic graded exams?'

    The questions above can mostly be adapted, according to the age of the student. It is sometimes a good idea to have a moment alone with an accompanied child, particularly if the parent takes a dominant role in the interview.

2. The following questions are designed to elicit information from the teacher, in order to assist prospective students, *whether they are beginners or opera stars seeking an occasional vocal 'check-up'* (or even complete re-training following

the onset of vocal problems), in selecting a teacher. The same information may
be sought of teachers in conservatories.

(a) *How do you describe your approach to the teaching of singing?*

The answer will reveal whether the teacher favours the tonal quality
produced by one of the main singing techniques, and, if so, on what physiological, acoustical and aesthetic grounds. Do you advocate or use, for
example, Alexander Technique, Jacques Dalcrose, Kodály, Orff,
Comprehensive Musicianship (an American technique and philosophy for
teaching music)?

(b) *What formal qualifications do you have?*

The answer will enable the prospective student to judge whether the
teacher is able to provide a rounded musical education.

(c) *Do you teach to diploma level and beyond?*

This question is related to the last, but here the point is to beware of such a
reply as, 'Well I have only Grade V myself, so I specialize in beginners'.
But beginners need the most expert care and attention, and if a teacher has
not mastered the relevant disciplines, then we may question whether there is
a sufficient basis in anatomy and physiology, for example, to permit the safe
and responsible training of another person's voice. Let us bear in mind the
ancient medical dictum '*Primum non nocere*' (the first thing is not to do
harm). One may also wish to probe a private teacher who says, 'I take only
advanced students', for such a person may have tumbled off the performing
stage into the teacher's studio after many years of singing (or even having
ruined a promising performing career by damaging the voice) with little or
no pedagogical knowledge or skill. It is worth dwelling on this matter.

(d) *Are you still performing professionally?*

The question, which may appropriately be asked of teachers under the age of
sixty, assumes that those who teach singing will be able to perform too. The
answer may indicate whether or not (sickness or accident apart) the teacher's
own vocal technique has permitted performance over a number of years. If it
has not, the question arises whether the teacher's vocal pedagogy is sound.

(e) *How do you respond to demands made upon your students to others in the
profession?*

The point here is that members of choirs and choral societies can be at the
mercy of directors who make unrealistic and/or premature demands upon
the voices in their charge.

(f) *What are your fees?*

Are they fee per lesson; per term; group lesson fees; single or consultation
fees? There should be a clear statement of payment policy *apropos* missed
lessons, holidays and withdrawals.

Other questions to be anticipated may concern demonstrating, accompanying, and
practising. The teacher should be prepared for any type of question: Would the first

five lessons be a trial period? What are your views on exams, which board and why? Is entering music festivals a positive action to take? Do you include aural and theory in the lesson? How far do you want parents to be involved? Can I come to the first lesson? Can you recommend any books to study? Do you issue periodical period reports? Do you allow pupils to take part in choirs, school musicals where you have no control? Are there opportunities for students meeting together? Who is the best performer to listen to? If the answer is not on the tip of the tongue, then information should be easily accessible from such bodies as the Musicians Union; the Incorporated Society of Musicians; the Association of Teachers of Singing; the British Voice Association; and also from amateur operatic societies, local church organists and choirmasters and music periodicals.

Many different types of pupils with widely contrasting personalities will present themselves for an initial interview. There are the easily discouraged; the worrier; the perfectionist; the procrastinator; the musically sensitive but technically limited; the technically facile, but musically uninvolved; the detail obsessed, with slow progress; the intuitive, but detail negligent and others too numerous to be listed here.

Some people appear confident when they are not, whereas others who may appear to be of a retiring disposition may in fact be determined to the point of obstinacy. The teacher's ability to 'read the signs' is here at a premium. In this connection the observation of body language in the light of well-researched studies of that phenomenon is extremely helpful. For example, prospective students with low self-esteem may present as having poor posture and stooping, retreating into themselves, unable to make eye contact, fidgeting, being tense or appearing lethargic. On the other hand students who stand well, have brisk, erect walk action, and who maintain eye contact suggest confidence.[2]

There are many factors which contribute to the student's appeal to the teacher. These factors may include physical attractiveness, to which we tend to respond positively. Some teachers tend to favour those who are like themselves in attitude and thought, perhaps in order to avoid misunderstandings disagreements or direct confrontations. In contrast there are many people who are attracted to complete opposites of themselves.

It is hardly necessary to dwell upon the teacher who conducts interviews in hair-rollers; who keeps an ashtray overflowing with cigarette butts on the piano; who offers no written contract; who accommodates a cat on every chair – so one might go on. The psychological impression received is dire, as it is in the case of those who seem all at sea on theoretical matters.

Notes

1 See further, Mackworth-Young, Lucinda (2000), *Tuning In: Practical Psychology for Musicians who are Teaching, Learning and Performing*, Swaffam: MMM Publications.

2 See further Diagram Group (1999), *Collins Gem Body Language*, London: Collins; Wainwright, Gordon (1999), *Teach Yourself Body Language*, London, Hodder and Stoughton; Blakemore, Colin, and Sheila Jennett (2001), (eds), *The Oxford Companion to the Body*, London: Oxford University Press.

Appendix 3

Additional Performance Considerations and Contexts

a

To Oren Brown's list of considerations we might add the sartorial. It is advisable that on the concert platform female singers wear simple clothing and jewellery in order to avoid audience distraction away from the music to the singer's attire. A check of the appearance from front and back, when walking and standing, and the effect of raising the arms may be made by a colleague or friend. Old-fashioned, drab, bizarre outfits do not add to the presentation. It is well to record what clothing was worn at each venue. Various options to be avoided are: bright orange gowns for Handel's *Messiah*; and prints, unless they are very subdued. Some colours are more suitable than others for the concert stage. Looking at the dress from afar as though visualizing it as the audience will see it and taking care with skirt length (females) – the audience will be looking from about knee level – needs the help of the observant friend. For informal concerts it is suggested for the male performer that he wears solid colour suits, although, on some occasions, a blazer may be acceptable. He will be well advised to check that his trousers are long enough to hide his dark coloured socks and that the socks are long enough to hide leg skin when seated; to wear a conservative tie and have well polished shoes coordinated with the suit. The wearing of a white shirt is the most elegant, a pale blue shirt is better than white for television, cuffs might be one centimetre below the sleeves. For formal occasions, the tails or tuxedo/dinner jacket may be worn.

b

Auditioning

There is much to be said for learning to whom one's talent is to be sold; it may be to a panel of judges at a competition or festival, an agent, representatives of a music society or orchestra, or an opera company. The act of auditioning is a positive one. The judges, agents, administrators, producers and conductors are bursting to find an exhilarating and exciting singer. There are many reasons behind adjudicators' decisions, positive or negative, and some probably not what the singer may imagine.

Opera singers should know the entire role of the opera for which they are auditioning, and not rely on just learning one aria from the work. A long aria is not a good choice; the panel is likely to be experienced and will be able to judge very quickly whether the singer is suitable or not. It may be suggested that the singer wear something flattering but not too flashy, and noiseless, comfortable shoes. The panel will be able to visualize singers in costume if they wear something simple. Singers are usually watched, both before and after the audition and need to be prepared for this. It is advisable to communicate emotion and thought with the voice and use low-key gestures. Knowing the market differences will aid the aim of the singer. If it is a basic competition the judges will be adjudicating what they hear at the present moment. For the 'big' prizes plus recital, the judges will also be looking for someone who will be able to sustain a programme of an hour to an hour and a half. Colleges will be looking for ability, above all potential; some even include a session with a teacher to see if the student is 'teachable'. An audition for a broadcast or recording may look for a voice that is distinctive without the physical presence of the singer. Opera companies look for adaptable competent musicians and increasingly consider visual as well as vocal suitability when casting.

A few brief suggestions as to the auditioning singer may be appropriate here:

1. Be on time.
2. Dress appropriately.
3. Have all materials prepared (where necessary include up-to-date biographical notes for inclusion in a programme, a clearly presented CV, first-class photographs, previous testimonials).
4. Be courteous and accept instructions.
5. Be as natural as possible; anything else is dishonest.
6. Prepare songs/arias of contrasting styles and languages together with music for the part for which you are auditioning, playing to your strengths.[1]

If the audition requires a tape or CD, it is advisable to choose an appropriate acoustic, avoiding anywhere with background noise. The tape must impress immediately, the piano and accompaniment must be acceptable, and it is a wise move to be very self-critical, bearing in mind that those listening have only a disembodied sound on which to base their judgement. It also pays to have the tape made professionally, after getting several price quotations, and checking whether or not the company keeps the tape or CD (some companies have been known to produce additional tapes later for commercial purposes). It should have appropriate fade up and fade down, and it is vital to have previously heard other recordings made by the company. A cheap price for making a recording generally means a cheap job. Since some competition administrators decry editing it is well to make several performances and choose the best. It is important to check the competition rules precisely to be certain of what is required and which formats are acceptable.

Radio and Television

Being on radio or television is a great opportunity to perform to a large number of people and can make a big difference to a performing career, given that the opportunity is used well. Because television is such an expensive medium the most welcome singers are those who can get it right first time, hence no retakes. However getting it right first time in a television studio is not as easy as it seems – there are many distractions, one being moving cameras. Another difficulty sometimes encountered is beginning on cue when recording.

Clothing for the small screen has to be thought out carefully, bearing in mind that it is generally said that television adds 3kg/10lbs to the average physique. Stripes and checks can be problematic for cameras. Studio lighting is very hot – this should be considered when choosing clothes; one does not want to appear to be sweating. Makeup must be discreet as the director may take a close-up and false eyelashes may then appear grotesque. Movement should be minimized: extraneous movement will appear exaggerated and distracting to the viewer. If being interviewed then the same thing will apply. Material should be well prepared in advance, time will be short and the message needs to come across crisply. Of course the editor will have the final say about content.

In a radio interview it is advisable keep to the point, and not speak over anyone else, eliminating 'umm-ing' and 'ah-ing'. One-word answers should be avoided wherever possible. It is useful to be aware of the time allowed to your interview to aid with your preparation.

Note

1   See further, Legge, Anthony (1988), *The Art of Auditioning*, London: Rhinegold Publishing; Fisher, Jeremy and Gillyanne Kayes (2002), *Successful Singing Auditions*, London: A&C Black.

Appendix 4

Illustrations

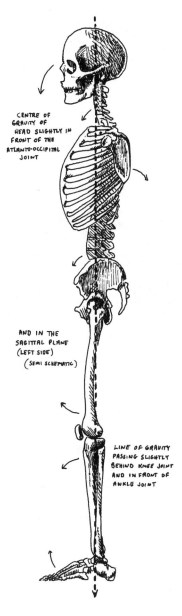

CENTRE OF
GRAVITY OF
HEAD SLIGHTLY IN
FRONT OF THE
ATLANTO-OCCIPITAL
JOINT

AND IN THE
SAGITTAL PLANE
(LEFT SIDE)
(SEMI SCHEMATIC)

LINE OF GRAVITY
PASSING SLIGHTLY
BEHIND KNEE JOINT
AND IN FRONT OF
ANKLE JOINT

Illustration 1 Schematic drawing of skeleton with a line showing the centre of gravity of the body

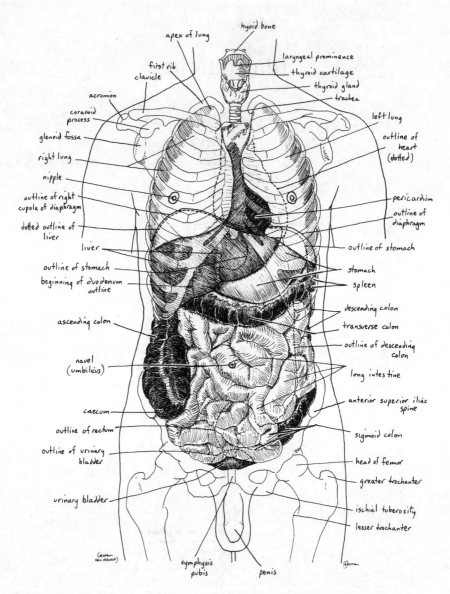

Illustration 2 Front view of the thoracic and abdominal viscera inside the skeleton

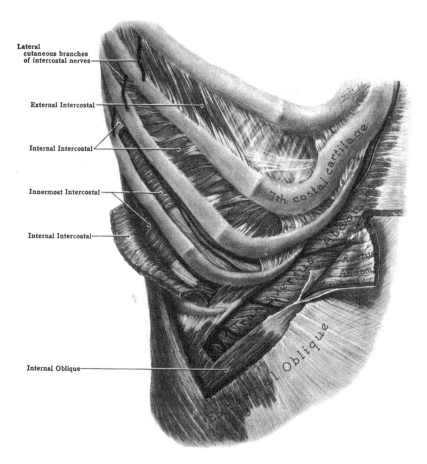

Illustration 3 Intercostals, lower ribs and muscles of the abdomen

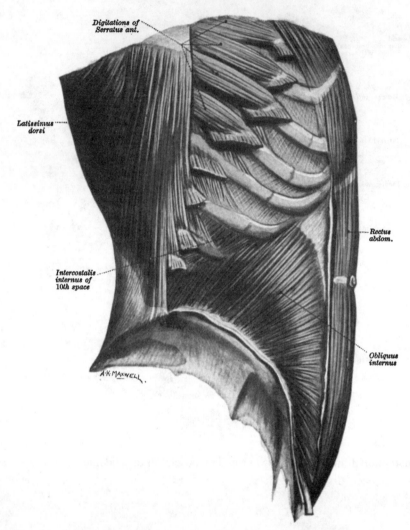

Illustration 4 Dissection of the muscles of the right side of the trunk

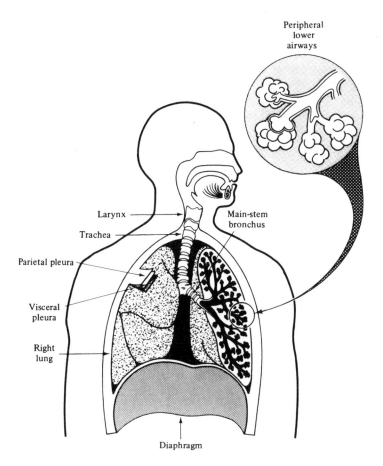

Illustration 5 Front view of the major structures of the pulmonary system. From Daniloff, Raymond in Minifie, Flexon and Williams (eds), 'Normal Articulation Processes', in *Normal Aspects of Speech, Hearing and Language*, published by Allyn and Bacon, Boston, MA. Copyright © 1973 by Pearson Education.

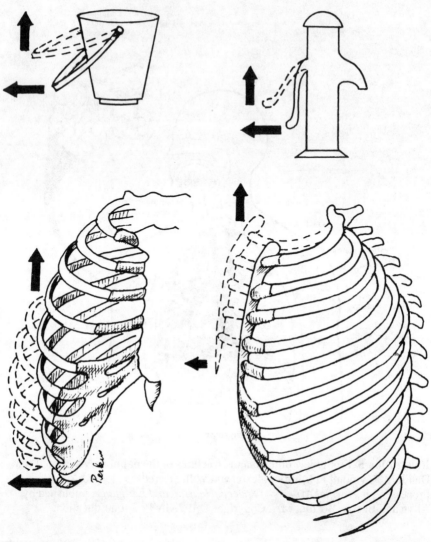

Illustration 6
Lateral thoracic expansion   Anteroposterior thoracic expansion

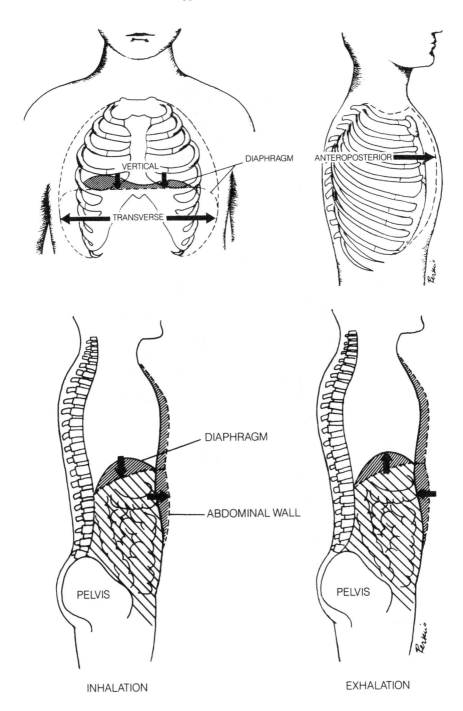

Illustration 7 Diaphragm and abdominal movement

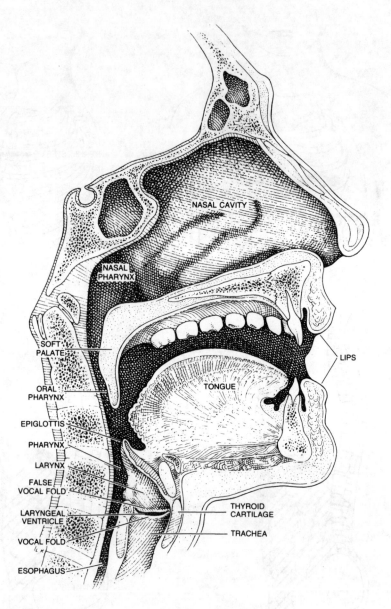

Illustration 8 Voice organ

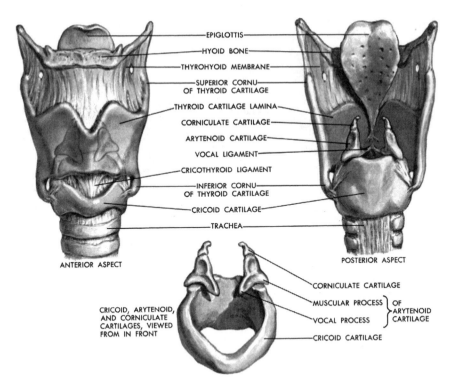

Illustration 9 Cartilages of the larynx

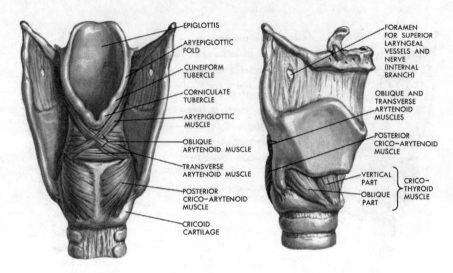

Illustration 10 Intrinsic muscles of the larynx

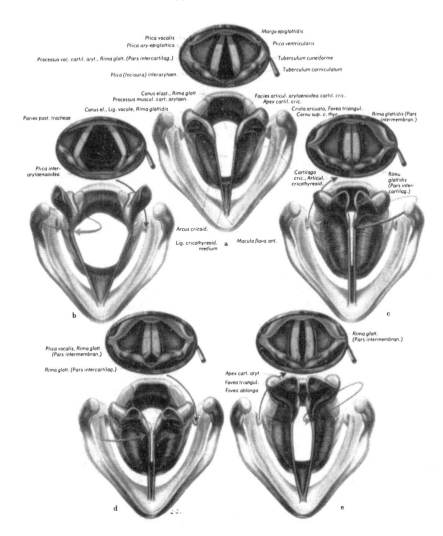

Illustration 11 Vocal folds viewed by laryngeal mirror, with a schematic design beneath, in (a) quiet breathing, (b) deep inhalation, (c) normal phonation, (d) one form of whispering, (e) falsetto

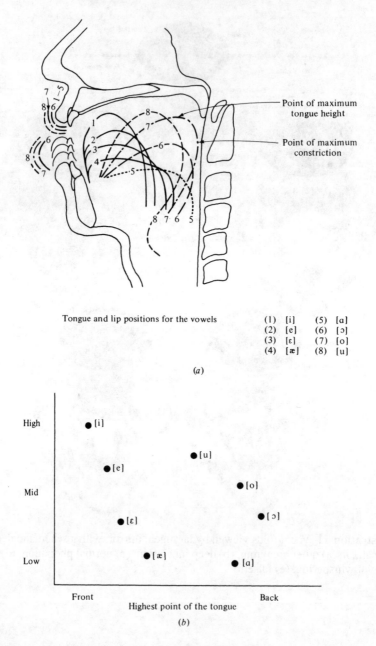

Tongue and lip positions for the vowels

(1)	[i]	(5)	[a]
(2)	[e]	(6)	[ɔ]
(3)	[ɛ]	(7)	[o]
(4)	[æ]	(8)	[u]

(a)

(b)

Illustration 12 Schematic drawing of tongue and lip positions for certain vowels. From Daniloff, Raymond in Minifie, Flexon and Williams (eds), 'Normal Articulation Processes', in *Normal Aspects of Speech, Hearing and Language*, published by Allyn and Bacon, Boston, MA. Copyright © 1973 by Pearson Education.

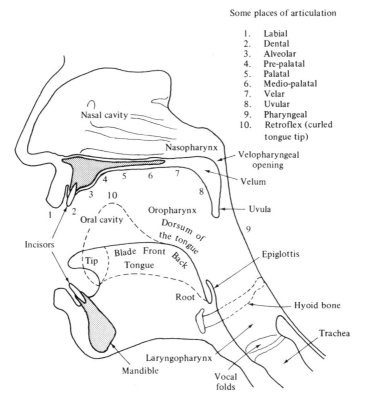

Some places of articulation

1. Labial
2. Dental
3. Alveolar
4. Pre-palatal
5. Palatal
6. Medio-palatal
7. Velar
8. Uvular
9. Pharyngeal
10. Retroflex (curled tongue tip)

Illustration 13 Schematic view of articulators, vocal tract cavities, and places of articulation. From Daniloff, Raymond in Minifie, Flexon and Williams (eds), 'Normal Articulation Processes', in *Normal Aspects of Speech, Hearing and Language*, published by Allyn and Bacon, Boston, MA. Copyright © 1973 by Pearson Education.

Bibliography

Abaza, Mona M., and Robert T. Sataloff (1999), 'Sore throats in singers', *Journal of Singing*, **16** (1), September/October, 33–8.

Ackland, Lesley (1997), *15-Minute Pilates*, London: Thorsons (HarperCollins).

Adler, Kurt (1907), *The Art of Accompanying and Coaching*, rep. (1965), New York: Da Capo.

Adorno, Theodor (1992), 'The philosophy of modern music', in Sim, Stuart (ed.), *Art: Context and Value*, Milton Keynes: The Open University.

Agricola, Johann Friedrich (1995), *Introduction to the Art of Singing*, trans. Julianne C. Baird, *Cambridge Musical Texts and Monographs*, Cambridge: Cambridge University Press.

Åhlberg, Lars-Olof (1994), 'Suzanne Langer on representation and emotion in music', *British Journal of Aesthetics*, **34** (1), January, 69–80.

Alcantara, Pedro de (1997), *Indirect Procedures: A Musician's Guide to the Alexander Technique*, Oxford: Clarendon Press.

Alexander, Frederick Matthias (1910), *Man's Supreme Inheritance*, rep. (1988), Long Beach: Centerline Press.

—— (1923), *Constructive Conscious Control of the Individual*, rep. (1987), London: Victor Gollancz.

—— (1932), *The Use of the Self*, rep. (1985), London: Victor Gollancz.

—— (1941), *The Universal Constant in Living*, rep. (1986), Long Beach: Centerline Press.

Allen, Rose L. (2000), 'The effects of preventive vocal hygiene education on the vocal hygiene habits and perceptual vocal characteristics of training singers', *Journal of Voice*, **14** (1), March, 58–71.

Allen R.T. (1990), 'The arousal and expression of emotion by music', *The British Journal of Aesthetics*, **30** (1), January, 57–61.

Amtmann, Inger-Marie (1997), 'Music for the unborn child', *International Journal of Music Education,* **29**, 66–72.

Anderson, Margaret (1996), 'A study of motivation and how it relates to student achievement', *Canadian Music Educator*, **38** (1), Fall, 29–31.

Andress, Barbara (1980), *Music Experiences in Early Childhood*, New York: Holt, Rinehart and Wilson.

Andrews, Moya, and Anne Summers (1988), *Voice Therapy for Adolescents*, Boston: College-Hill.

Appelman, D. Ralph (1967), *The Science of Vocal Pedagogy, Theory and Application*, Bloomington, IN: Indiana University Press.

Aristotle, *De Audibilius*, trans. T. Loveday and E.S. Foster (1913), *The Works of Aristotle*, 12 vols, Ross, W.D. (ed.), Vol.VI, Oxford: Clarendon Press.

—— *De Anima*, trans. J.A. Smith (1931), *The Works of Aristotle*, 12 vols, Ross, W.D. (ed.), Vol. III, Oxford: Clarendon Press.

Armin, Georg (1932), *Die technik der Breitspannung: In Beitrag über die horizontal-vertikalen Spannkräfte beim Aufbau der Stimme nach dem 'Stauprinzip'*, Berlin: Verlag der Gesellschaft fur Stimmkultur.

Austin, Stephen F. (2000), 'Nasal resonance – fact or fiction?' *Journal of Singing*, **57** (2), November/December, 33–41.

Bacilly, Bénigne de (1668), *Remarques curieuses sur l'art de bien chanter*, Paris, trans. Austin B. Caswell (1968), Brooklyn, New York: Institute of Mediaeval Music.

Bailey, Todd (2000), 'Proof that babies don't miss a trick', *The Times Higher Education Supplement*, 15 September, 2.

Balk, H. Wesley (1985), *The Complete Singer-Actor*, Minneapolis: University of Minnesota Press.

—— (1985), *Performing Power*, Minneapolis: University of Minnesota Press.

Bamberger, J. (1982), 'Revisiting children's drawings of simple rhythms: a function of reflection-in-action', in Strauss, S. (ed.), *U-shaped behavioural growth*, New York: Academic Press, 191–226.

Banfield, Stephen (1985), *Sensibility and English Song*, Cambridge: Cambridge University Press.

Barefield, Robert (1999/2000), 'The beginning voice teacher', *American Music Teacher*, **49** (3), December–January, 28–31.

Barkway, Ann (2002), 'Music and movement', *Classical Music*, 16 February, 15.

Bartlett, J.C., and W.J. Dowling (1980), 'The recognition of transposed melodies: a key-distance effect in developmental perspective', *Journal of Experimental Psychology: Human Perception and Performance*, **6** (3), 501–15.

Barwell, Ismay (1986), 'How does art express emotion?' *The Journal of Aesthetics and Art Criticism*, **35** (2), Winter, 176–81.

Bassini, Carlo (c. 1857), *Bassini's Art of Signing: An Analytical Physiological and Practical System for the Cultivation of the Voice*, Storrs Willis R. (ed.), Boston: O. Ditson and Co.

Battaille, Charles (1861), *Nouvelles recherches sur la phonation: Mémoire présenté et lu à l'Académie des sciences le 15 Avril 1861*, Paris: Victor Masson et fils.

Battisti, Frank (1996), 'The art of interpretation', *The Instrumentalist*, **50** (7), February, 12–15.

Bean, Matt (1998), 'Manipulate the accompanist', *Journal of Singing*, **54** (3), March/April, 41–3.

Behnke, Emil (1880), *The Mechanism of the Human Voice*, London: Curwen.

—— (1890), with Lennox Browne, *Voice, Song and Speech*, New York: G.P. Putnam's Sons.

Benade, Arthur H. (1976), *Fundamentals of Musical Acoustics*, 2nd revised edn (1990), New York: Dover.

Benedetti, Jean (1990), *Stanislavski: An Introduction*, London: Methuen.

Beniston, Keith (2001), 'Annual review', *Forte*, Winter, 2–6.

Benton, Rita (1970), *French Song from Berlioz to Duparc*, trans. Frits Nose, New York: Dover.

Bérard, Jean-Baptiste (1755), *L'art du chant*, trans. Sydney Murray (1969), Milwaukee: Pro Musica.

Berenson, Frances (1994), 'Representation and music', *British Journal of Aesthetics*, **34** (1), January, 60–68.

Bernac Pierre (1978), *The Interpretation of French Song*, New York: W.W. Norton.

Berry, Cecily (1994), *The Actor and His Text*, London: Virgin.

Blakemore, Colin, and Sheila Jennet (2001), (eds), *The Oxford Companion to the Body*, Oxford: Oxford University Press.

Blanchet, Joseph (1756), *L'art, ou les principes philosophiques du chant*, Paris: A.M. Lottin.

Bonynge, Richard (1995), 'Let's hear it for bel canto', *Opera Now*, June, 16.

Boone, Daniel R., and Stephen C. McFarlane (1988), *The Voice and Voice Therapy*, Englewood Cliffs, NJ: Prentice-Hall.

—— (1997), *Is Your Voice Telling on You?*, London: Whurr.

Borden, Gloria J., and Katherine S. Harris (1984), *Speech Science Primer*, Baltimore: Williams & Wilkins.

Bosanquet, Caroline R. (1987), 'The Alexander principle and its importance to music education', *British Journal of Music Education*, **4** (3), 229–42.

Bowman, Robin (2000), 'Pierre Bernac – the artist and teacher', *Singing* (38), Summer, 12–16.

Boyd, James (2001), 'Embracing Alexander', *Communicating Voice*, **1** (3), Errata, June, n.p.n.

Boytim, Joan (1999), 'Choosing repertoire', *Inter Nos*, **37** (1), January/February, 8–9.

Brandfonbrener, Alice G. (2002), 'Assessment of performing arts medicine in the new millenium', *The Journal of the British Performing Arts Medicine Trust* (3), Spring, 38–47.

Bridger, Michael (1996), 'Performance as narrative – notes towards a theory of the performing arts', *Performing Arts International*, **1** Part 1, 53–66.

Bridges, V.A. (1965), 'An exploratory study of the harmonic discrimination ability of children in kindergarten through grade three in two selected schools', unpublished PhD thesis, Ohio State University.

Brodnitz, Friedrich S. (1988), *Keep Your Voice Healthy*, Boston: College-Hill.

Brower, Harriet, and James Francis Cooke (1920), *Great Singers on the Art of Singing,* rep. (1996), New York: Dover Publications.

Brown, Howard Mayer (1980), 'Performing practice', in Sadie, Stanley (ed.), *The New Grove Dictionary of Music and Musicians*, 20 vols, London: Macmillan, Vol. XIV.

—— (1989), with Stanley Sadie, *Performance Practice: Music before 1600,* London: Macmillan.

Brown, James Murray (1972), *A Handbook of Musical Knowledge,* 2 vols, London: Trinity College of Music.

Brown, Maurice J.E. (1967), *Schubert Songs,* London: BBC.

Brown, Oren L. (1996), *Discover your voice,* San Diego: Singular Publishing.

Brown, W.E. (1931), *Vocal Wisdom: Maxims of Giovanni Battista Lamperti,* enlarged edn (1957), New York: Taplinger.

Browne, Lennox, and Emil Behnke (1890), *Voice, Song and Speech,* New York: G.P. Putnam's Sons.

Bruscia, Kenneth (1989), 'Building effective, relationships in the private music studio', *American Music Teacher,* **39** (2), October/November, 12–15, 56.

Bunch, Meribeth (1995), *Dynamics of the Singing Voice,* Wien: Springer-Verlag.

—— (2000), *A Handbook of the Singing Voice,* London: Meribeth Dayme (formerly Bunch).

Burney, Charles (1789), *A General History of Music, II,* Frank Meyer (ed.), (1957), New York: Dover.

Butcher, Peter; Annie Elias, and Ruth Raven (1993), *Psychogenic Voice Disorders and Cognitive Behaviour Therapy,* London: Whurr.

Caccini, Guilio (1601/2), *Le nuove musiche,* Florence, trans. O. Strunk (1981), *Source Readings in Music History,* London: Norton.

Caire, Jill Bond (1991), 'Understanding and treating performance anxiety from a cognitive-behaviour therapy perspective', *The NATS Journal,* **47** (4), March/April, 27–30, 51.

Caldwell, Robert (1991/2), 'Imagining the performance', *American Music Teacher,* **41** (3), December/January, 20–25, 79.

Campbell, Murray, and Clive Greated (1987), *The Musician's Guide to Acoustics,* Oxford: Oxford University Press.

Capell, Richard (1957), *Schubert's Songs* London: Pan Books.

Capestro, Susan (1989), 'Sales techniques for the IMT', *American Music Teacher,* **39** (1), 31.

Carlin, Francis (2000), 'Double Act', *Opera Now,* May/June, 37–8.

Carlsson, G., and J. Sundberg (1992), 'Formant frequency tuning in singing', *Journal of Voice,* **6** (3), 256–60.

Carner, Mosco (1982), *Hugo Wolf Songs,* London: BBC.

Caruso, Enrico and Luisa Tetrazzini (1909), *Caruso and Tetrazzini on the Art of Singing,* rep. (1975), New York: Dover.

Caswell, Austin B. (1968), *Bacilly: A Commentary upon the Art of Proper Singing (Musical Theorists in Translation Service: Vol 7),* Brooklyn, NY: Institute of Medieval Music.

Catford, J.C. (1990), *A Practical Introduction to Phonetics,* Oxford: Clarendon Press.

Celletti, Rodolfo (1991), *A History of Bel Canto,* trans. F. Fuller, Oxford: Clarendon Press.

Child, Dennis (1973), *Psychology and the Teacher*, London: Cassell.

Ching, James (1947), *Performer and Audience*, London: Keith Prowse.

Chorley, Henry F. (1926, posthumous), *Thirty Years' Musical Recollections,* New York: Alfred A. Knopf.

Chosky, Lois; Robert M. Abramson, Avon Gillespie, and David Woods (1986), *Teaching Music in the Twentieth Century*, Englewood Cliffs, NJ: Prentice Hall.

Chryssides, George D., and John H. Kaler (2001), *An Introduction to Business Ethics*, London: Thomson Learning.

Clarke, Sophie (1997), 'Our project will "prepare and equip" young singers', *Classical Music*, n.p.n.

Clement of Alexandria *Stromateis*, trans. William Wilson (1867) in *The Works of Clement of Alexandria*, Edinburgh: T. & T. Clark.

Cleveland, Thomas F. (2000), 'Voice rest for singers: "twelve things I've learned while being mute"', *Journal of Singing*, **56** (3), January/February, 65.

Clingman, Allen E., and Dennis R. Vincent (1993/4), 'Community music education study: attitudes and preferences of Canadian Registered Music Teachers', *Bulletin of the Council for Research in Music Education* **19**, Winter, 65–75.

Cockburn, Jacqueline, and Richard Stokes (1992), *The Spanish Song Companion*, London: Victor Gollancz.

Coffin, Berton (1981), 'Vocal pedagogy classics: practical reflections on figured singing by Giambattista Mancini', in Miller, Richard (ed.), *The NATS Bulletin*, **37** (4), 47–9.

—— (1989), *Historical Vocal Pedagogy Classics*, Metuchen, NJ: Scarecrow.

Cohen, Madelyn (2001), 'Glittering prizes', *Scholarships* (supplement), *Classical Music*, 6.

Collins, Stewart (2000), 'Lesson time', *Classical Music*, 26 August, 26–7.

Colorni, Evelina (1970), *Singers' Italian*, New York: Schirmer.

Comins, Jayne (1996), 'Making the break', *The Singer*, August/September, 14–15.

—— (1996), 'Let's get physical,' *The Singer*, October/November, 15.

Cooksey, John M. (1993), 'Do adolescent voices "break" or do they "transform"?' *Voice*, **2** (1), 15–39.

—— (1998), with Graham F. Welch, 'Adolescence, singing development and national curricula design', *British Journal of Music Education*, **15** (1), 99–119.

Cooper, David E. (1992), (ed.), *A Companion to Aesthetics*, Oxford: Blackwell.

Cornford, Francis Macdonald (1951), *The Republic of Plato*, Oxford: Clarendon Press.

Corri, Domenico (1810), *The Singer's Preceptor*, London: Chappell.

Cottingham, C.M. (1996), 'Pricing policy', *The Singer*, February/March, 7.

Cox, Richard G. (1970), *The Singer's Manual of German and French Diction*, New York: Schirmer.

—— (1990), *Singing in English*, Lawton, OK: American Choral Directors Association.

Critchley, Macdonald (1983), 'The secret world of the singer', in Falkner, K. (ed.), *Voice*, London: Macdonald.

Croy, Elizabeth (1998), 'Collaborative arts presentations: an holistic approach to the art song recital', *Journal of Singing*, **54** (5), May/June, 15–17.

Crutchfield, W. (1989), 'The 19th century: voices', in Brown, H.M., and S. Sadie (eds), *Performance Practice: Music after 1600*, New York: Norton.

Cunningham, Sara (2003), 'Judge and jury', *Classical Music: Competitions Supplement*, 9.

Daniloff, Raymond G. 'Normal Articulation Processes', in Minifie et al., Q.V., pp. 169–209.

Dart, Thurston (1967), *The Interpretation of Music*, London: Hutchinson.

Davidson, L., and L. Scripp (1988), 'Young children's musical representations: window on music cognition', in Sloboda, J. (ed.), *Generative Processes in Music: The Psychology of Performance, Improvisation and Composition*, New York: Oxford University Press, 195–230.

Davidson, Jane W., Michael J.A. Howe, Derek G. Moore, and John A. Sloboda (1996), 'The role of parental influences in the development of musical performance', *British Journal of Developmental Psychology*, **14** (4), 399–412.

Davies, D. Garfield, and Anthony F. Jahn (1995), 'Acid reflux and vocal disorders', *Performing Arts Medicine News*, **3** (3), Autumn, 36–7.

—— (1999), *Care of the Professional Voice*, Oxford: Butterworth-Heinemann.

Davis, Richard (1996), 'Making the tape', *Journal of Singing*, **5** (2), November/December, 13–6.

—— (1998), *A Beginning Singer's Guide*, Lanham, MD: Scarecrow.

Davis, Robert and Mark Pulman (2001), 'Raising standards in performance', *British Journal of Music Education*, **18** (3), November, 251–9.

De'Ath, Leslie (2002), 'The hazards of reflex: caveats of a voice coach', *Journal of Singing*, **59** (1), November/December, 155–9.

DeBellis, Mark (1999), 'The paradox of musical analysis', *Journal of Music Theory*, **43** (1), Spring, 83–99.

DeGeorge, Richard T. (1999), *Business Ethics*, Upper Saddle River, NJ: Prentice Hall.

Dejonckere, P.J., Minoru Hirano, Johan Sundberg (1995), *Vibrato*, San Diego: Singular.

Delle Sedie, Enrico (1885), *L'estetica del canto e dell' arte melodrammatica*, Livorno: The author.

Deutsch, D. (1982), (ed.), *The Psychology of Music*, New York: Academic Press.

Diagram Group (1999), *Collins Gem Body Language*, London: Collins.

Dickie, George (1992), 'Art and the aesthetic', *Art: Context and Value*, in Sims Stuart (ed.), Milton Keynes: The Open University.

Diggle, Keith (1996), 'Marketing yourself', in Ford, Trevor (ed.), *The Musician's Handbook*, London: Rhinegold Publishing.

Dodd, Julian (2000), 'Musical works as eternal types', *British Journal of Aesthetics*, **40** (4), 424–40.

Donington, Robert (1980), 'Interpretation', in Sadie, Stanley (ed.), *The New Grove Dictionary of Music*, 20 vols, London: Macmillan, Vol. IX.

—— (1982), *Baroque Music: Style and Performance*, London: Faber Music.

Doscher, Barbara M. (1994), *The Functional Unity of the Singing Voice*, Metuchen, NJ: Scarecrow.

Dowling, W. Jay (1982), 'Melodic Information Processing and Its Development, in Deutsch, Diane (ed.), *The Psychology of Music*, New York: New York Academic Press, pp. 413–27.

Duey, Philip A. (1951, repr. 1980), *Bel Canto in its Golden Age*, New York: Da Capo.

Dunn, Robert E. (1999), 'The phenomenon of the voice', *Canadian Music Educator*, **40** (3), Spring, 23–7.

Dunn, Sinclair (1893), *The Solo Singer*, London: Curwen.

Edgar, Andrew (1990), 'An introduction to Adorno's aesthetics', *British Journal of Aesthetics*, **30** (1), January, 46–56.

Edidin, Aron (2000), 'Artistry in classical music performance', *British Journal of Aesthetics*, **40** (3), July, 317–25.

Eliade, Mircea (1954), *The Myth of the Eternal Return*, trans. Willard R. Trask, Princeton, NJ: Princeton University Press.

Elkin, Susan (1996), 'Connections – words which sing and songs which speak', *Singing*, **30**, Summer, 47–50.

Elliott, David J. (1993), 'On the values of music and music education', *Philosophy of Music Education*, **1** (2), 81–93.

Emmons, Shirley, and Stanley Sonntag (1979), *The Art of the Song Recital*, New York: Schirmer.

—— and Alma Thomas (1998) *Power Performance for Singers*, New York: Oxford University Press.

Eshelmann, D. (1992), 'Leading a renaissance in training adolescent boy singers', *Choral Journal*, **32** (3), 25.

Evans, Colin (2000), 'Keeping track of progress', *Music Teacher*, May, 22–3.

Falkner, Keith (1983), (ed.), *Voice*, London: Macdonald.

Fawkes, Richard (1996), 'All in the mind', *Classical Music*, 27 April, 25.

—— (2000), 'Stand and deliver', *Classical Music*, 12 August, 27.

Feil, Arnold (1988), *Franz Schubert: die schöne Müllerin, Winterreise*, trans. Ann C. Sherwin, Portland, OR: Amadeus Press.

Ferrari, Jacapo (1818), *A Concise treatise on Italian Singing*, trans. W. Shield, London: Schultz and Dean.

Ferrein, Antoine (1741), 'De la formation de la voix de l'homme', *Histoire de l'académie royale des sciences de Paris*, **51**, 409–32.

Fields, Victor Alexander (1984), *Foundations in the Singer's Art*, New York: The National Association of Teachers of Singing.

Fillebrown, Thomas (1911), *Resonance in singing and speaking*, Boston: Oliver Ditson.

Fisher, Jeremy and Gillyanne Kayes (2002), *Successful Singing Auditions*, London: A&C Black.

Flind, Louise (2001), 'Clouds over Cardiff?' *Opera Now*, September/October, 95–6.

Flusser, Victor (2000), 'An ethical approach to music education', *British Journal of Music Education,* **17** (1), March, 43–50.

Fontana, David (1981), *Psychology for Teachers,* Basingstoke: Macmillan.

Ford, Trevor (1996), 'Income tax and national insurance', in Ford, Trevor (ed.), *The Musician's Handbook,* London, Rhinegold Publishing.

Fox, Donna Brink (2000), 'Music and the baby's brain', *Music Educators Journal,* **87** (2), September, 23–7, 50.

Freed, Donald Callen (2000), 'Imagery in early twentieth-century American vocal pedagogy', *Journal of Singing,* **56** (4), March/April, 5–12.

Fuchs, Viktor (1963), *The Art of Singing and Voice Technique,* rep. (1973), London: Calder and Boyars.

Fujimura, Osamu, and Minoru Hirano (1995), *Vocal Fold Physiology,* San Diego: Singular.

Garcia, Manuel (1847 and 1872), *A Complete Treatise on the Art of Singing, Parts I and II,* collated, trans. and ed. Donald V. Paschke (1975), New York: Da Capo.

—— (1894 and 1911), *Hints on Singing,* trans. Beata Garcia, ed. Hermann Klein, London: Ascherberg, Hopwood and Crew.

Garcia, Manuel del Popolo Vincente (1868), *340 Exercises composés pour ses Elèves,* Paris.

Garden, Mary (1920), 'The Know How in the Art of Singing', in Brower and Cooke (1920), Q.V., pp. 62–7.

Gardner, H. (1973), *The Arts and Human Development,* New York: Wiley.

—— (1979), 'Developmental psychology after Piaget: an approach in terms of symbolization', *Human Development,* **22,** 73–88.

Gardner, P.A.D., and R.W. Pickford (1944), 'Relation between dissonance and context', *Nature,* **154,** 274–5.

Gellrich, Martin (1991), 'Concentration and tension', trans. Richard Parncutt, *British Journal of Music Education,* **8,** 167–79.

Giustiniani, Vincenzo (c. 1628), *Discorso sopra la musica,* trans. Carol MacClintock, Musicological Studies and Documents, 9, Middleton, WI American Institute of Musicology.

Goehr, Lydia (1998), *The Quest for Voice: Music, Politics, and the Limits of Philosophy,* California: University of California Press.

Goetze, Mary (1989), 'A comparison of the pitch accuracy of group and individual singing in young children', *Bulletin of the Council for Research in Music Education,* 99, Winter, 57–73.

Goldovsky, Boris, and Arthur Schoep (2002), *Bringing Soprano Arias to Life,* London: Shelwing.

Gorman, David (nd.), *The Body Moveable,* Guelph, Ontario: Ampersand.

Gould, Coral (1998), 'The singing teenager', *Singing,* **35,** Winter, 25–7.

Gray's Anatomy (1980), Robert Warwick and Peter Williams (ed.), Edinburgh: Churchill Livingstone .

Greene, Harry Plunket (1914), *Interpretation in Song,* London: Macmillan.

Greenhead, Karin (1991), 'Eurhythmics', *Singing*, **20**, Summer, 15–16.

Greer, R.D. (1981), 'An operant approach to motivation and affect: ten years of research in music learning', paper presented at the National Symposium for the Application of Learning Theory to Music Education, Reston, Virginia: MENC.

Gregg, Jean Westerman (1999), 'Maintaining high standards in the teaching of singing', *Journal of Singing*, **55** (4), March/April, 1–2.

—— (2001), 'Resonation and articulation – a new concept', *Journal of Singing*, **58** (2), November/December, 167–9.

Grindea, Carola (1982), *Tensions in the Performance of Music*, London: Kahn and Averill.

—— (2000), 'The phenomenon of "Peak Experience" or "The Flow" in musical performance', *ISSTIP Journal* (10), November, 7–11.

Grout, Donald Jay (1978), *A History of Western Music*, London: J.M. Dent.

Günter, Horst (1992), 'Mental concepts in singing: a psychological approach, Part I', *The NATS Journal*, **48** (5), May/June, 4–9, 46.

—— (1997), 'Singing and pedagogy from 1562–1854: What do the books tell us?' *Singing* (33), Winter, 9–12.

Gurnee, Robert T. (nd.), (ed.), *In Memoriam: Selected Articles from the writings of William Vennard*, National Association of Teachers of Singing.

Guthrie, D., A. Milner, R. Paget, R. Curry, and C. Horsford (1938), 'Discussion on functional disorders of the voice', *Proceedings of the Royal Society of Medicine*, **32**, pp. 447–54.

Hagberg, Garry L., Book Review: Lydia Goehr (2000), 'The quest for voice: music, politics, and the limits of philosophy', *The Journal of Aesthetics and Art Criticism*, **58** (1), Winter, 85–8.

Haid, Karen (1999), 'Coping with performance anxiety', *Teaching Music*, **7** (1), August, 40–41, 60.

Hammond, Mary (1995), 'Vocal class', *The Singer*, October/November, 11–12.

Hanfling, Oswald (1995), (ed.), *Philosophical Aesthetics*, Oxford: Blackwell.

Hanslick, Eduard (1891), *On the Musically Beautiful*, trans. and ed. Geoffrey Payzant (1986), Indianapolis: Hackett Publishing.

Hargreaves, David (1986), 'Developmental psychology and music education', *Society for Research in Psychology of Music and Education*, **14**, 83–96.

—— (1992), with M.P. Zimmerman, 'Developmental theories of music learning', in Colwell, R. (ed.), *Handbook of research on music teaching and learning*, New York: Schirmer.

—— (1996), 'The developmental psychology of music', in Spruce, Gary (ed.), *Teaching Music*, London: Routledge.

—— (1997), with A. North (eds), *The Social Psychology of Music*, New York: Oxford University Press.

—— (1999), *The Developmental Psychology of Music*, Cambridge: Cambridge University Press.

Harries, M.Ll., Maggie Griffiths, S. Walker, and S. Hawkins (1996), 'Changes in the male voice during puberty: speaking and singing voice parameters', *Logopedics Phoneatrics Vocology*, **21** (1), 95–100.

Harris, Ellen T. (1989), 'The Baroque era: voices', in Brown, H.M. and S. Sadie (eds), *Performance Practice: Music after 1600*, New York: Norton.

Harris, Lee D. (1993), 'An investigation of selected vocal characteristics in young male singers at various stages of maturation', *Texas Music Education Research*, 15–22.

Harris, Paul, and Richard Crozier (2000), *The Music Teacher's Companion*, London: ABRSM.

—— (2001), 'Simultaneous learning – teaching pupils to think musically', *Libretto* (3), 14–15.

Harris, Sandra R. (1998) 'A study of musical performance anxiety', *American Music Teacher*, **37** (4), February/March, 15–16.

Harris, Tom, Dinah Harris, and Joseph Liebermann (1994), 'Voice clinics and the care of the professional voice', *Voice*, **3** (2), 108–9.

—— (1997), with Sara Harris, John S. Rubin, and David M. Howard, *The Voice Clinic Handbook*, London: Whurr.

Hartford, Robert (1995), 'Taking the mike', *Classical Music*,' 4 November, 12–13.

Haunch, Bernard (2001), 'Girls and choirs', *Music Teacher*, April, 18.

Hayes, John (1999), (ed.), *Dictionary of Biblical Interpretation*, 2 vols, Nashville: Abingdon Press, Vol. II.

Hayes, Nicky (2000), *Foundations of Psychology*, London: Thomson Learning.

Helfgot, Daniel, and William Beeman (1993), *The Third Line: The Opera Performer as Interpreter*, New York: Schirmer.

Helm, Rebecca Norton (1996), 'The development of vocal pedagogy to 1700', *Journal of Singing*, **52** (4), March/April, 13–20.

Heman-Ackah, Yolanda D. (2002), 'Who takes care of voice problems? A guide to voice care providers', *Journal of Singing*, **59** (1), November/December, 139–46.

Hemsley, Thomas (1998), *Singing and Imagination*, Oxford: Oxford University Press.

Henderson, William James (1906), *The Art of the Singer. Practical Hints about Vocal Techniques and Style*, New York: G. Scribner's Sons.

Herbert-Caesari, E.G. (1936), *The Science and Sensations of Vocal Tone*, London: Dent.

Heriot, Angus (1956), *The Castrati in Opera*, London: Secker and Warburg.

Hewer, Reinhardt J., Cheryl Hoover, Margaret Baroody, Rhonda K. Rulnick, and Robert T. Sataloff (1993), 'The role of the speech-language pathologist in the treatment of the vocally-impaired singer', *NATS Journal*, **49** (5), May/June, 25–6.

Hewitt, Graham (1980), *Learn to Sing*, London: Independent Television Books.

Higgins, Tom (1996), 'Setting the standard', *Classical Piano*, March/April, 27.

Hiller, Johann Adam (1774), *Anweisung zum musikalisch-richtigen Gesange*, Leipzig: J.F. Junius.

—— (1780), *Anweisung zum musikalisch-zierlichen Gesange*, Leipzig: J.F. Junius.

Hines, Jerome (1988), *Great Singers on Great Singing*, New York: Limelight.

Hixon, T.J. (1987), *Respiratory Function in Speech and Song*, Boston: College-Hill.

Hold, Trevor (2002), *Parry to Finzi: Twenty English song-composers*, Woodbridge: Boydell Press.

Hollien, H. (1993), 'That golden voice – talent or training', *Journal of Voice*, **7** (3), 197–8.

Holmes, Gordon (1885), 'History of the progress of laryngology from the earliest times to the present', *The Medical Press*, London: July 15, 49.

Honderich, Ted (1995), (ed.), *The Oxford Companion to Philosophy*, Oxford: Oxford University Press.

Hoole, Ivor (1995) 'Once more with feeling', *Music Teacher*, September, 12–15.

Howard, David M., and James Angus (1996), *Acoustics and Psychoacoustics*, Oxford: Focal Press.

—— (2000), 'Discord greets hymns for her', *The Times Higher Education Supplement* (reported by Alison Utley), 15 December, 48.

—— 'Survey of Internet free – and shareware tools for voice analysis', support for paper presented at the 4th Pan European Voice Conference, Stockholm University, 23–26 August 2001, <http://www-users.york.ac.uk/~dmh8/dmh_pevocIV.htm>.

Howard, Vernon A. (1997), 'Virtuosity as a performance concept: a philosophical analysis', *Philosophy of Music Education Review*, **1**, Spring, 42–54.

Husler, Frederick and Yvonne Rodd-Marling (1965, revised 1983), *Singing: The Physical Nature of the Vocal Organ,* revised edn, London: Hutchinson.

Ivey, Donald (1970), *Song: Anatomy, Imagery and Styles*, New York: The Free Press.

Jander, Owen (1995), 'Singing', in Sadie, Stanley (ed.), *The New Grove Dictionary of Music,* 20 vols, London: Macmillan, Vol. XVII.

Jay, W. (1982), 'Melodic information processing and its development', in Deutsch, Diana (ed.), *The Psychology of Music*, New York: New York Academic Press.

Jeal, Erica (2000), 'Am I too loud', *Opera Now*, September/October, 32–5.

Jenkins, Lucien (2002), 'Marking schemes', *Music Teacher*, June, 5.

Johnson, Graham and Richard Stokes (2000), *A French Song Companion*, Oxford: Oxford University Press.

Joiner, James Richard (1998), *Charles Amable Battaille: Pioneer in Vocal Science and the Teaching of Singing,* Metchuen, NJ: Scarecrow.

Jones, Earl William (1989), *Sound, Self, and Song*, Metuchen, NJ: Scarecrow.

Jones, Merilyn (1979), 'Using a vertical-keyboard instrument with an uncertain singer', *Journal of Research in Music Education*, **17** (3), Fall, 173–84.

Jumilhac, Pierre Benoit de (1673), *La science et la pratique du plainchant*, Paris.

Juslin, Patrik N., and Guy Madison (1999), 'The role of timing patterns in recognition of emotional expression from musical performance', *Music Perception*, **17** (2), Winter, 197–220.

Kagen, Sergius (1950), *On Studying Singing*, rep. (1960), New York: Dover.

Kant, Immanuel (1987), *Critique of Judgement*, trans. Werner S. Pluhar, Indianapolis: Hackett Publishing Company.

Kay, Elster (1963), *Bel Canto*, London: Dennis Dobson.

Kay, Graeme (1996), 'Competitions', in Ford, Trevor (ed.), *The Musician's Handbook*, London: Rhinegold Publishing.

Kayes, Gillyanne (2000), *Singing and the Actor*, London: A&C Black.

Kemp, Anthony (1990), 'Kinaesthesia in music and its implications for developments in microtechnology', *British Journal of Music Education*, **7** (3), 223–9.

—— (2000), *The Musical Temperament*, Oxford: Oxford University Press.

Kennedy-Dygas, Margaret (2000), 'Historical perspectives on the "science" of teaching singing', *Journal of Singing*, **56** (4), March/April, 23–30.

Kennedy-Fraser, Marjorie (1929), *A Life of Song*, London, Oxford University Press.

Kent, Ray D., and Charles Read (1992), *The Acoustic Analysis of Speech*, San Diego: Singular.

Kimbell, David (1991), *Italian Opera*, Cambridge: Cambridge University Press.

Kimmel, Lawrence D. (1992), 'The sounds of music: first movement', *Journal of Aesthetic Education*, **26** (3), Fall, 55–65.

Kirkland, Henry Stuart (1916), *Expression in Singing: a practical study in means and ends*, Boston: R.G. Badger.

Kivy, Peter (1980), *The Corded Shell*, Princeton, NJ: Princeton University Press, rep. (1989), as *Sound Sentiment: An Essay on the Musical Emotions*, Philadelphia, PA: Temple University Press.

—— (1990), *Music Alone*, Ithaca, NY: Cornell University Press.

—— (1991), *Sound and Semblance: Reflections on Musical Representation*, Ithaca, NY: Cornell University Press.

—— (1994), 'Speech, song, and the transparency of medium: a note on opera metaphysics', *The Journal of Aesthetics and Art Criticism*, **52** (1), Winter, 63–8.

—— (1995), *Authenticities: Philosophical Reflections on Musical Performance*, Ithaca, NY: Cornell University Press.

—— (1999) 'Feeling the musical emotions', *British Journal of Aesthetics*, **39** (1), January, 1–13.

—— (2002), *An Introduction to a Philosophy of Music*, Oxford: Clarendon Press.

Klinger, Rita; Patricia Shehan Campbell, and Thomas Goolsby (1998), 'Approaches to children's song acquisition: immersion and phrase-by-phrase', *Journal of Research in Music Education*, **46** (1), Spring, 24–34.

Knieter, Gerard L. (1983), 'Aesthetics for arts' sake', *Music Educator's Journal*, **59** (7), March, 33–5, 61–4.

Kofler, Leo (1889), *Art of Breathing as the Basis of Tone Production*, New York: E.S. Werner.

Koster, Ré (1986), *The Commonsense of Singing*, London: Thames Publishing.

Lagdefoged, Peter (1962), *Elements of Acoustic Phonetics*, Chicago: University of Chicago Press.

Lamperti, Francesco (1890), *The Art of Singing,* trans. J.C. Griffith, New York: G. Schirmer.

Lamperti, Giovanni Battista (1905), *The Technics of Bel Canto,* trans. Theodore Baker, New York: G. Schirmer.

Langer, Suzanne (1957), *Philosophy in a New Key,* Cambridge, MA: Harvard University Press.

Lanza, Gesualdo (1813), *Lanza's Elements of Singing (in the Italian and English Styles),* London: The author.

Lasser, Johann Baptist (1805), *Vollständige Anleitung zur Singkunst so wohl für den Sopran, als auch für den Alt,* Munich: Gedrückt mit Hübschmannschen Schriften.

Lavender, Justin (1994), 'Society dos and don'ts', *The Singer,* August/September 26–7.

Lawrence, Van L. (1991), 'Sermon on hydration (the evils of dry)', *Vocal Health and Science* (eds) Sataloff, Robert T., and Ingo R. Titze, Jacksonville, FL: The National Association of Teachers of Singing.

LeBlanc, Albert; Young Chang Jin, Mary Obert, and Carolyn Siivola (1997), 'Effect of audience on music performance anxiety', *Journal of Research in Music Education,* **45** (3), Fall, 480–96.

Leden, Hans von (1997), 'A cultural history of the larynx and voice', in Sataloff, Robert T. (ed.), *Professional Voice: The Science and Art of Clinical Care,* San Diego: Singular.

Legge, Anthony (1988), *The Art of Auditioning,* London: Rhinegold Publishing.

Leenman, Tracy E. (1997), 'A closer look at DICTION', *Chorus* **5** (1), August, 34–5, 42.

Lehmann, Lilli (1924), *How to Sing,* New York: Macmillan.

Lehmann, Lotte (1945), *More than Singing,* rep. (1985), Mineola: Dover.

Leonhard, Charles (1971), 'Aesthetic education in a world of numbers', *The Canadian Music Educator,* **12** (4), Summer, 5–7.

Lippman, Edward A. (1992), *A History of Western Musical Aesthetics,* Lincoln, NE: University of Nebraska Press.

Lonergan, Bernard (1971), *Method in Theology,* London: Darton, Longman and Todd.

Lorince, Margaret (1990), 'The training of performance teachers – then, now and tomorrow', *American Music Teacher,* **39** (5), April/May, 23–5, 46.

Lovelock, William (1978), *Commonsense in Music Teaching,* London: Bell and Hyman.

Lovetri, Jeanette (2000), '"Alternative medical therapy" use among singers: prevalence and implications for the medical care of the singer', *Journal of Voice,* **14** (3), September, 398–409.

Luchsinger, Richard, and Godfrey E. Arnold (1965), *Voice-Speech-Language,* trans. Godfrey E. Arnold, and Evelyn Robe Finkbeiner, Belmont, CA: Wadsworth Publishings.

Lundin, R.W. (1967), *An Objective Psychology of Music,* New York: Ronald.

Lunn, Charles (1906), *The Philosophy of Voice*, London: Baillière, Tindall & Cox.

Lütgen, B. (nd.), *Hints to Students of Singing*, London: E. Donajowski.

Mabry, Sharon (2002), *Exploring Twentieth-Century Vocal Music*, Oxford: Oxford University Press.

McCallion, Michael (1988), *The Voice Book*, London: Faber and Faber.

MacClintock, Carol (1979), (ed.), *Readings in the History of Music in Performance*, Bloomington: Indiana University Press.

Macdonald, Glynn (1995), 'Alexander Technique and the singing voice', *Performing Arts Medicine News*, **3** (2), Summer, 26–8.

McGee, Timothy J. (1996), (ed.), A.G. Rigg and David N. Klausner, *Singing Early Music: The Pronunciation of European Languages in the Late Middle Ages and Renaissance*, Bloomington: Indiana University Press.

Mackenzie, Morrell (1890), *The Hygiene of the Vocal Organs*, New York: Macmillan.

Mackinlay, M. Sterling (1908), *Garcia the Centenarian and his Times*, New York: D. Appleton.

McKinney, James C. (1994), *The Diagnosis and Correction of Vocal Faults*, Nashville: Genevox Music Group.

Mackworth-Young, Lucinda (2000), *Tuning In: Practical Psychology for Musicians who are Teaching, Learning and Performing*, Swaffam: MMM Publications.

McNaughton, Elizabeth (2002), *Breathing for Singing and its Vocal Pedagogy*, London: Phoenix Again.

Maffei, Giovanni Camillo (1562), *Delle lettere … libri due, un discorso della voce e del modo, d'apparar di cantar Garganta senza maestro*, Naples: Apprò Raymuso Amato.

Mancini, Giambattista (1774), *Pensieri, e riflessioni practiche sopra il canto figurato*, Milano: Galeazzi.

Mandl, Louis (1876), *Hygiène de la voix*, Paris: Baillière et Fils.

Manén, Lucie (1974), *The Art of Singing*, London: Faber Music.

—— (1987), *Bel Canto*, Oxford: Oxford University Press.

Manfredini, Vincenzo (1797), *Regole Armoniche o sieno Precetti Ragionati per apprender la musica*, Venice: G. Zerlotti.

Manning, Jane (1986), *New Vocal Repertory*, London: Macmillan.

—— (1998), *New Vocal Repertory*, Vol. 2, Oxford: Clarendon Press.

Marafioti, P. Mario (1949), *Caruso's Method of Voice Production*, rep. (1981), New York: Dover.

Marchesi, Mathilde (1898), *Marchesi and Music,* New York: Harper.

—— (1970), *Bel Canto: A Theoretical and Practical Vocal Method*, rep. New York: Dover.

Mark, Desmond (1998), 'The music teacher's dilemma', *International Journal of Music Education*, **32**, 3–23.

Mark, Michael L. (1982), 'The evolution of music education philosophy from utilitarian to aesthetic', *Journal of Research in Music Education*, **30** (1), 15–21.

Marpurg, F.W. (1763), *Anleitung zur Musik überhaubt, und zur Singkunst besonders, mit Uebungsexempeln erläutert*, Berlin: A. Wever.

Marshall, Madeleine (1953), *The Singer's Manual of English Diction*, New York: Schirmer.

Martienssen-Lohmann, Franzisca (1923), *Das bewusste Singen: Grundlegen des Gesangstudiams*, Leipzig: C.F. Kahnt.

—— (1943), *Der Opensänger*, Mainz: B. Schott's Söhne.

Martin, B.J., S. Robinson, D.L. Wiegman, and L.H. Aulick (1975), 'Effect of warm-up on metabolic responses to strenuous exercise', *Medicine in Science and Sports*, **7** (2), 146–9.

Martini, Johann Paul Aegidus (c. 1792), *Mélopée moderne; ou L'art du chant, réduit en principes*, Paris: Chez Naderman.

Mason, David (2001), 'Real trouble', *Opera Now*, March/April, 6.

Matthay, T. (1926), *Memorizing and Playing from Memory*, London: Oxford University Press.

Mattheson, Johann (1739), *Der volkommene Capellmeister,* Hamburg, rev. trans., Ernest C. Harris (1981), Ann Arbor, MI: UMI Research Press.

Maurice, Glenda (1997), 'Some personal thoughts on artistry', *Singing* (32), Summer, 11–14.

Meister, Barbara (1980), *An Introduction to the Art Song*, New York: Taplinger.

Mengozzi, B. (1803), *Méthode de chant du Conservatoire de Musique*, Paris.

Merrill, James D. (2002), 'Musical growth through a singing apprenticeship', *Music Educators Journal*, **88** (4), January, 36–41.

Mersenne, Marin (1636), *Harmonie Universelle*, Paris: Cramoisy.

Metzger, Bruce M., and Michael D. Coogan (1993), (eds), *The Oxford Companion to the Bible,* Oxford: Oxford University Press.

Meynell, Hugo (1995), 'On Nietzsche, postmodernism and the New Enlightenment', *New Blackfriars*, **76** (889), January, 4–18.

Miller, L.B. (1989), 'Children's musical behaviors in the natural environment', in J.C. Peeryet (ed.) *Music and Child Development,* New York: Springer-Verlag.

—— (1990), 'The singing teacher as voice therapist', *Singing* (19), Winter, 60–62.

Miller, Niven (1998), 'That certain something', *The Singer*, October/November, 23.

Miller Richard (1986), *The Structure of Singing*, New York: Schirmer.

—— (1990), 'Movement and freedom', *The NATS Journal*, **47** (2), November/December, 20.

—— (1993), *Training Tenor Voices*, New York: Schirmer.

—— (1996), *On the Art of Singing*, Oxford: Oxford University Press.

—— (1997), *National Schools of Singing*, Lanham, MD: Scarecrow.

—— (1998), 'Historical overview of vocal pedagogy', in Sataloff, R.T. (ed.), *Vocal Health and Pedagogy*, San Diego: Singular.

—— (1999), *Singing Schumann*, New York: Oxford University Press.

—— (1999), 'Establishing or altering a tonal concept', *Journal of Singing*, **56** (1), September/October, 27–9.

—— (2000), *Training Soprano Voices*, New York: Oxford University Press.

—— (2002), '(1) Imaginative singing', *Journal of Singing*, **58** (5), May/June, 415–16.

—— (2004), *Solutions for Singers*, New York: Oxford.

Minifie, Fred D., Thomas J. Hixon, and Frederick Williams (1973), (eds), *Normal Aspects of Speech, Hearing, and Language*, Englewood Cliffs, NJ: Prentice-Hall.

Miriani, Dorothy (1992), 'Motivation and personality types', *American Music Teacher*, **41** (6), June/July, 18–21, 56.

Mitchell, Philip A. (1991), 'Adult non-singers: the beginning stages of learning to sing', *Psychology of Music*, **19**, 74–6.

Monahan, Brent Jeffrey (1978), *The Art of Singing,* Metuchen: Scarecrow.

Moog, H. (1976), *The Musical Experience of the Pre-School Child*, trans. C. Clarke, London: Schott.

Moore, Gerald (1975), *The Schubert Song Cycles*, London: Hamish Hamilton.

—— (1986), *Collected Memoirs*, Harmondsworth: Penguin.

Morgan, Rhian (2002), 'Young ears', *Music Teacher*, October, 38–9.

Morphew, Richard (1997), 'Let the children sing', *Singing*, **32**, Summer, 28–32.

Morrison, Murray, and Linda Rammage (1994), *The Management of Voice Disorders*, London: Chapman and Hall.

Moure, E.J. and A. Bouyer (1910), *The Abuse of the Singing and Speaking Voice*, London: Keegan Paul, Trench, Trübner.

Murphy, Judith (1980), 'Conflict, consensus, and communication', *Music Educators Journal*, **66** (7), Supplement, March, 1–32.

Mursell, James L., and Mabel Glenn (1938), *The Psychology of School Music Teaching*, New York: Burdette.

Mussen, Paul Henry; John Janeway Conger, Jerome Kagan, and Aletha Carol Huston (1990), *Child Development and Personality*, New York: HarperCollins.

Nair, Garyth (1999), *Voice-Tradition and Technology*, San Diego: Singular.

—— (1999), 'Vocal pharmacology: introducing the subject at Drew University', *Journal of Singing*, **55** (3), January/February, 53–63.

Netter, F. (1964), 'The larynx', *Clinical Symposia*, **16** (3), 70–71.

Newman, Ernest (1963), *Wagner as Man and Artist,* London: Gollancz.

Nivelon, Francois (1737), *The Rudiments of Genteel Behaviour*, London, cited by Joan Wildblood (1965), *The Polite World*, Oxford: Oxford University Press.

Northcote, Sydney (1966), *Byrd to Britten: A Survey of English Song*, London: John Baker.

Noske, Frits (1970), *French Song from Berlioz to Duparc*, trans. Rita Benton, New York: Dover.

O'Dea, Jane (1994), 'Authenticity in musical performance: personal or historical?' *British Journal of Aesthetics*, **34** (4), October, 363–75.

Osborne, Charles (1974), *The Concert Song Companion*, London: Victor Gollancz.

Osborne, Corrynne (2001), 'Encouraging confidence and self-esteem in young singers', *Singing*, **40**, Summer, 21–2.

Osborne, Harold (1972), (ed.), *Aesthetics*, Oxford: Oxford University Press.

Ottman, Robert W. (1986), *Music for Sight Singing*, Englewood Cliffs, NJ: Prentice-Hall.

Paddison, Max (1993), *Adorno's Aesthetics of Music*, Cambridge: Cambridge University Press.

Page, Christopher (1987), *Voices and Instruments of the Middle Ages*, London: J.M. Dent.

Perkins, William H. and Raymond D. Kent (1968), *Functional Anatomy of Speech, Language and Hearing*, Austin, TX: Pro-Ed.

Pernkopf, E. (1963), *Atlas of Topographical and Applied Human Anatomy*, vol. 1, Munich: Urban and Schwarzenburg.

Persson, Roland (1996), 'Brilliant performers as teachers: a case of common sense teaching in a conservatoire setting', *International Journal of Music Education*, **28**, November, 25–36.

Petty, Geoffrey (1993), *Teaching Today*, Cheltenham: Stanley Thornes.

Peyer, Adrian de (1994), 'The *passaggio* – conclusion', *Music Journal*, October, 153–6.

Phillips, Gerald L. (2002), 'Diction: a rhapsody', *Journal of Singing*, **58** (5), May/June, 405–9.

Piaget, J., and B. Inhelder (1969), *The Psychology of the Child*, London: Routledge and Keegan Paul.

Piatak, Jean and Regina Avrashov (1991), *Russian Songs and Arias*, Dallas: Pst ... Inc.

Picard, Andre (1999), 'Qualitative pedagogical inquiry into cognitive modulation of musical performance anxiety', *Bulletin of the Council for Research in Music Education*, **140**, Spring, 62–76.

Pickett, Philip (1996), 'A blast for the past', *BBC Music Magazine*, April, 41–2.

Pilkington, Michael (1989), *Campion, Dowland and the Lutenist Songwriters*, Bloomington and Indianapolis: Indiana University Press.

—— (1989), *Gurney, Ireland, Quilter and Warlock*, Bloomington and Indianapolis: Indiana University Press.

—— (2000), 'Some thoughts on recitative', *Singing*, **38**, Summer, 9.

—— (2003), *British Solo Song*, Norwich: Thames/Elkin.

Plato (1875), *Laws*, trans. B. Jowett, in *The Dialogues of Plato*, 5 vols, Oxford: Clarendon Press, Vol. V.

—— (1941), *The Republic*, trans. F.M. Cornford, Oxford: Clarendon Press.

Pleasants, Henry (1983), *The Great Singers,* London: Macmillan.

Plummeridge, Charles (1999), 'Aesthetic education and the practice of music teaching', *British Journal of Music Education*, **16** (2), July, 115–22.

Polunin, Tanya (1996), 'The independent teacher', in Ford, Trevor (ed.), *The Musician's Handbook,* London: Rhinegold Publishing.

Potter, John (1998), *Vocal Authority: Singing Style and Ideology*, Cambridge: Cambridge University Press.

—— (2000), (ed.), *The Cambridge Companion to Singing*, Cambridge: Cambridge University Press.

Praetorius, Michael (1619), *Syntagma musicum*, Willibald Gurlitt (ed.), (1958), Documenta Musicologica, Kassel: Bärenreiter.

Predelli, Stefano (1995), 'Against musical Platonism', *British Journal of Aesthetics*, **35** (4), October, 338–50.

Pringle, B., and E.G. Daniel (1993), 'Practical aspects of establishing a combined voice clinic in Wexham Park Hospital', *Voice*, **2** (2), 97–111.

Proctor, D.F. (1980), *Breathing, Speech and Song*, New York: Springer-Verlag.

Punt, Norman A. (1979), *The Singer's and Actor's Throat*, New York: Drama Book Specialists.

Putman, Daniel (1990), 'The aesthetic relation of musical performance and audience', *The British Journal of Aesthetics*, **30** (4), October, 361–6.

Quantz, Johann Joachim (1752), *On Playing the Flute*, trans. Edward R. Reilly (1966), London: Faber.

Radocy, R.E., and J.D. Boyle (1969), *Psychological Foundations of Musical Behavior*, Springfield, IL: C.C. Thomas.

Rainbow, Bernarr (1968), *Handbook for Music Teachers*, London: Novello.

Rameau, Jean Philippe (1760), *Code de musique practique ou Méthodes*, Paris.

Ramig, L., and Shipp, T. (1987), 'Comparative measures of vocal tremor and vocal vibrato', *Journal of Voice*, **10** (2), 162–7.

Read, Donald (1997), ' A pronouncement: ethics revisited', *Journal of Singing*, **53** (4), March/April, 27–30.

Reese, Sam (1976), 'How do your ideas about music affect your teaching?' *Music Educators Journal*, **62** (6), February, 84–8.

—— (1983), 'Teaching aesthetic listening', *Music Eductors Journal*, **69** (7), March, 36–8.

Reid, Cornelius L. (1950), *Bel Canto: Principles and Practices*, New York: Coleman Ross.

—— (1983), *A Dictionary of Vocal Terminology*, New York: Joseph Patelson.

—— (1995), *The Free Voice*, New York: Joseph Patelson.

—— (1999), *Voice: Psyche and Soma*, New York: Joseph Patelson.

—— (2000), with Donna S. Reid, 'Eighteenth-century registrational concepts', *Journal of Singing* **56** (4), 31–8.

Reinders, Ank (1998), 'Knowledge and practice hand in hand', *Logopedics Phoniatrics Vocology*, Supplement 1, 5–9.

Ries, N.L. (1987), 'An analysis of the characteristics of infant-child singing expressions: replication report', *Canadian Journal of Research in Music Education*, **29**, 5–20.

Robinson, Jenefer (1994), 'The expression and arousal of emotion in music', *The Journal of Aesthetics and Art Criticism*, **52** (1), Winter, 13–22.

Robinson, Lynne and Gordon Thomson (1997), *Body Control: The Pilates Way*, London: Pan Books.

Rodenburg, Patsy (1992), *The Right to Speak*, London: Methuen.

—— (1997), *The Actor Speaks*, London: Methuen.

Rose, Arnold (1962), *The Singer and the Voice,* rep. (1978), London: Scholar Press.

Rosen, Deborah Caputo, and Robert Thayer Sataloff (1997), *Psychology of Voice Disorders*, San Diego: Singular.

Rosenthal, Eleanor (1989), 'The Alexander Technique: what it is and how it works', *American Music Teacher*, **39** (2), October/November, 24–7, 57.

Ross, Stephanie A., and Jennifer Judkins (1996), 'Conducting and musical interpretation', *British Journal of Aesthetics*, **36** (1), January, 16–29.

Ross, W.D. (1930), *The Right and the Good,* Oxford: Clarendon Press.

Rowe, M.W. (1999), review of Scruton, Roger, *The Aesthetics of Music*, Clarendon Press in *British Journal of Aesthetics*, **39** (4), October, 423–9.

—— (2000), 'How do criticism and aesthetic theory fit together', *British Journal of Aesthetics*, **40** (1), January.

Rushmore, Robert (1971), *The Singing Voice,* London: Hamish Hamilton.

Rutkowski, Joanne (1999), 'The nature of children's singing voices: characteristics and assessment', *Canadian Music Educator*, **40** (3), Spring, 43–7.

Sadie, Stanley (1995), (ed.), *The New Grove Dictionary of Music and Musicians*, 20 vols, London: Macmillan.

—— (1989), *History of Opera*, New York: W.W. Norton.

Sams, Eric (1972), *Brahms Songs*, London, BBC.

—— (1983), *The Songs of Hugo Wolf*, London: Eulenburg.

Santley, Charles (1908), *The Art of Singing and Vocal Declamation*, New York: Macmillan.

Sataloff, R.T., Joseph R. Spiegel, Linda M. Carroll, Kathy S. Darby, Mark J. Hawkshaw, and Rhonda K. Rulnik (1990), 'The clinical voice laboratory: practical design and clinical application', *Journal of Voice*, **4** (3), 264–79.

—— (1991), (ed.), with Alice G. Brandfonbrener, and Richard J. Lederman, *Performing Arts Medicine* (1998), San Diego: Singular.

—— (1995), 'Rational thought: the impact of voice science upon voice care', *Voice*, **4** (2), 77–95.

—— (1997), (ed.), *Professional Voice: The Science and Art of Clinical Care*, San Diego: Singular.

—— (1998), (ed.), *Vocal Health and Pedagogy*, San Diego: Singular.

—— (2000), 'Performance anxiety: what singing teachers should know', *Journal of Singing*, **56** (5), May/June, 33–9.

—— (2000), 'Vocal aging and its medical implications: what singing teachers should know', *Journal of Singing*, **57** (2), November/December, 23–8.

—— (2001), 'Arts medicine: the state of the art', *Journal of Singing*, **58** (2), November/December, 153–60.

Saunders, William H. (1964), 'The Larynx', *Clinical Symposia*, **16** (3).

Saxon, Keith G., and Carole M. Schneider (1995), *Vocal Exercise Physiology*, San Diego: Singular.

Scherer, R.C. (1995), 'Laryngeal function during phonation', in Rubin, J.S., and W.J. Gould (eds), *Diagnosis and Treatment of Voice Disorders*. New York: Igaku-Shoin.

Schmidt, Charles P. (1989), 'An investigation of undergraduate music education curriculum content', *Bulletin of the Council for Research in Music Education*, **99**, Winter, 42–56.

Scott, Michael (1977, 1979), *The Record of Singing, Vol. I, to 1914*, and *Vol II, 1914–1925*, London: Duckworth.

Scruton, Roger (1980), 'Programme music', in Sadie, Stanley (ed.), *The New Grove Dictionary of Music and Musicians*, 20 vols, London: Macmillan, Vol. XV.

—— (1987),'Analytical philosophy and the meaning of music', *The Journal of Aesthetics and Art Criticism*, **46**, Special Issue, 169–76.

—— (1999), *The Aesthetics of Music*, Oxford: Clarendon Press.

Seashore, Carl E. (1938), *Psychology of Music*, rep. edn (1967), New York: Dover.

Seiler, Emma (1875), *The Voice in Singing*, Philadelphia: J.B. Lippincott.

Sell, Karen (1995), 'The training of the voice teacher: some observations', *Singing*, **18**, Summer, 37–42.

—— (1995/6), 'A question of choice', *The Singer*, December–January, 18–19.

—— (1996/7), 'The moral of the story', *The Singer*, December–January, 24–5.

—— (1997), 'The healthy mind in the healthy body', *Mastersinger*, **25**, Spring 2–3.

—— (1997), 'The environment and the voice', *Mastersinger,* **26**, August, 23.

—— (1997), 'Ailments, medications and early warning signs', *Mastersinger,* **27**, Winter, 5–6.

—— (1998), 'And so to sing,' *Mastersinger*, **28**, Spring, 2–3.

—— (2001), 'Ethics and the voice teacher (Part 1)', *Singing*, **41**, Winter, 8–10.

—— (2002), 'Ethics and the voice teacher (Part 2)', *Singing*, **42**, Summer, 8–10.

Senyshyn, Yaraslov (1996), 'Kierkegaard's aesthetic stage of existence and its relation to live musical performance', *Philosophy of Music Education Review*, **4** (1), Spring, 50–62.

—— (1999), 'Perspectives on performance and anxiety and their implications for creative teaching', *Canadian Journal of Education*, **24** (1), 30–41.

Shakespeare, William (1899), *The Art of Singing, Based on the Principles of the Old Italian Singing Masters*, London: Metzler.

—— (1924), *Plain Words on Singing*, London: G.P. Putnam's Sons.

Sherman, Joy, and Lawrence R. Brown (1995), 'Singing *passaggi*: modern application of a centuries-old technique', *Choral Journal*, **36** (1), August, 27–36.

Shuter-Dyson, Rosamund, and Clive Gabriel (1981), *The Psychology of Musical Ability*, London: Methuen.

Siepmann, Jeremy (2000), 'Editorial', *Piano*, May/June, 3.

Sim, Sheila (1996), 'Emotion and meaning in music', *Canadian Music Educator*, **38** (1), Fall, 25–8.

Sim, Stuart (1992), (ed.), *Art: Context and Value*, Milton Keynes: The Open University.

Slater, David D. (1911), *Vocal Physiology and the Teaching of Singing*, London: J.H. Larway (Edwin Ashdown).

Sloboda, John A. (1985), *The Musical Mind: The Cognitive Psychology of Music*, Oxford: Oxford University Press.

—— (1996), with Jane W. Davidson, Michael J.A. Howe, and Derek G. Moore, 'The role of practice in the development of performing musicians', *British Journal of Psychology*, **87** Part 2, May, 287–309.

Soloman, Judith (1981), 'The pianist as vocal accompanist: servant or partner?' *American Music Teacher*, **31**, September/October, 12.

Sparshott, Francis (1980), 'Aesthetics', in Sadie, Stanley (ed.), *The New Grove Dictionary of Music*, 20 vols, London: Macmillan, Vol. I.

—— (1994), 'Music and Feeling', *The Journal of Aesthetics and Art Criticism*, **52** (1), Winter, 23–35.

Spender, Natasha, and Rosamund Shuter-Dyson (1980), 'Psychology of music', *The New Grove Dictionary of Music and Musicians*, 20 vols, Sadie, Stanley (ed.), London: Macmillan, Vol. XV, 388–427.

Spruce, Gary (1996), (ed.), *Teaching Music*, London: Routledge.

Stambak, M. (1960), 'Trois épreuves de rhythme', in Zazzo, R. (ed.), *Manuel pour l'examen psychologique de l'enfant*, Paris: Delachaux and Niestlé.

Stanislavski, Constantin (1975), and Pavel Rumyantsev, *Stanislavski on Opera*, trans. Eliza Reynolds Hapgood, New York: Routledge.

—— (1989), *Building a Character*, trans. E.R. Hapgood, London: Methuen.

—— (1990), *Creating a Role*, trans. E.R. Hapgood, London: Methuen.

—— (1992), *An Actor Prepares*, trans. E.R. Hapgood, London: Methuen.

Stanley, Douglas (1929), *The Science of Voice*, New York: Carl Fischer.

—— (1933), *Your Voice, Its Production and Reproduction*, New York: Pitman.

—— (1945), *Your Voice: Applied Science of Vocal Art*, New York: Pitman.

Stark, James (1999), *Bel Canto. A History of Vocal Pedagogy*, Buffalo, NY: University of Toronto Press.

Steane, J.B. (1993), *The Grand Tradition*, London: Duckworth.

—— (2000), 'In recital: Birmingham and London', *Opera Now*, September/October, 94, 96.

Stecker, Robert (1999), 'Davies on the musical expression of emotion', *British Journal of Aesthetics*, **39** (3), July, 273–81.

Stein, Jack (1971), *Poem and Music in the German Lied from Gluck to Hugo Wolf*, Cambridge, MA: Harvard University Press.

Stemple, Joseph C. (2000), *Voice Therapy: Clinical Studies*, San Diego: Singular.

Stendhal (Henri Beyle), (1824), *Life of Rossini*, trans. Richard N. Coe (1970), London: Calder and Boyars.

Steptoe, Andrew (1989), 'Stress, coping and stage fright in professional musicians', *Psychology of Music*, **17**, 3–11.

Stevens Denis (1960), *A History of Song*, rep. (1971), London: Hutchinson.

—— (1997), *Early Music*, London: Kahn and Averill.

Stewart, Andrew (nd.), 'Ear change', *Music Teacher*, 12–15.

Stockhausen, Julius (1884), *Method of Singing*, trans. Sophie Löwe (1886), London: Novello.

Stollak, Mary Alice, and Lois Alexander (1998), 'The use of analogy in the rehearsal', *Music Educators Journal*, **84** (6), May, 17–21.

Strouse, Lewis H. (1991), 'What do we teach when we teach interpretation?' *American Music Teacher*, **40** (4), February/March, 18–19, 72–3.

Strunk, Oliver (1998), *Source Readings in Music History,* rev. and ed. Leo Treitler, London: Norton.

Stubley, Eleanor (1993), 'Musical performance, play and constructive knowledge: experiences of self and culture', *Philosophy of Music Education Review*, **1** (2), Fall, 94–102.

Sundberg, Johan (1977), 'The Acoustics of the Singing Voice', *Scientific American*, March, **236** (3).

—— (1987), *The Science of the Singing Voice*, Dekalb, IL: Northern Illinois University Press.

—— (1988), 'Vocal tract resonance in singing', *The NATS Journal*, **44** (4), March/ April, 11–20.

—— (1991), *The Science of Musical Sounds*, San Diego: Academic Press.

—— (2001), 'Consistency of inhalatory breathing patterns in professional operatic singers', *Journal of Voice*, **4** (3), September, 373–83.

Surmani, Karen Farnum (1995), *Teach Yourself to Sing*, Van Nuys, CA: Alfred.

Sutcliffe, Tom (2001), 'Centre Stage', *Opera Now*, May/June, 14.

Sutton, Alison Mary (1992), 'Singing technique: pain or pleasure?' *Singing*, **22**, Summer, 33–7.

Swanson, Frederick J. (1961), 'When voices change', *The Canadian Music Educator*, **2** (4), March, 29–35.

Swanwick, Keith (1986), *A Basis for Music Education*, Windsor: NFER-Nelson.

—— (1988), *Music, Mind and Education*, London: Routledge.

—— (1991), 'Musical criticism and musical development', *British Journal of Music Education*, **8**, 139–48.

—— (1999), *Teaching Music Musically*, London and New York: Routledge Falmer.

—— (2000), 'Why composing, why audience-listening?' *Libretto*, **2**, 10–11.

Tarry, Joe E. (1973), 'Music in the educational philosophy of Martin Luther', *Journal of Research in Music Education*, **21** (4), Winter, 356–65.

Tattersall, Norman (1991), *Singing in a Nutshell*, Colchester: Minim Books.

Taylor, David Clark (1914), *Self-help for Singers; a manual for self-instruction in voice culture based on the old Italian method*, New York: H.W. Gray.

Taylor, Eric (nd.), *A Method of Aural Training: Part 1*, London: Oxford University Press.

—— (1999), *The AB Guide to Music Theory: Part 1 and 2*, London: ABRSM.

Telfer, Nancy (1992), *Successful Sight Singing*, San Diego: Neil A. Kjos.

Thom, Paul (1990), 'Young's critique of authenticity in performance', *British Journal of Aesthetics*, **30** (3), July, 273–6.

Thurman, Leon, and Graham Welch (2000), *bodymind & voice: foundations of voice education*, 3 vols, revised edn, Collegeville, MN; Iowa City; London: The

Voice Care Network, National Center for Voice and Speech, Fairview Voice Center, Centre for Advanced Studies in Music Education.

Thyme-Frøkjaer, Kirsten, and Børge Frøkjaer-Jenson (2001), *The Accent Method: A Rational Voice Therapy in Theory and Practice*, Oxford: Speechmark Publishing.

Timberlake, Craig (1990), 'The case of Manuel Garcia II', *The Nats Journal,* **46** (3) January/February 1990, 26–7.

—— (1993), with Velia Baglio Williams, 'Maffei: Medico e Musico', *The Nats Journal,* **49** (5), May/June, 23–4.

—— (1995), 'Pedagogical perspectives, past and present, apropos of *appoggio*, Part II', *The Nats Journal,* **51** (3), January/February, 35–8.

Titze, Ingo R. (1992), 'Rationale and structure of a curriculum in vocology', *Journal of Voice,* **6** (1), 1–9.

—— (1994), *Principles of Voice Production*, Englewood Cliffs, NJ: Prentice Hall.

—— (1995), 'What's in a Voice?' *New Scientist,* no. 1996, 23 September, 38–42.

—— (1996), 'What is vocology?' *Logopedics Phoniatrics Vocology,* **21** (1), 5–6.

—— (2001), 'The five best vocal warm-up exercises', *Journal of Singing,* **57** (3), January/February, 51–2.

—— (2001), 'Phonation into a straw as a voice building exercise', *Journal of Singing,* **57** (1), September/October, 27–8.

—— (2001), 'Should vocal training follow vocal development in childhood?' *Journal of Singing,* **58** (2), November/December, 161–2.

Tomeoni, Florido (1799), *Théorie de la musique vocale*, Paris.

—— (c. 1800), *Le guide musical; ouvrage dont le plan s'étend sur toutes les parties de la musique*, Paris.

Tomlinson, John (2000), 'Taking the mike,' an edited version of a speech made to the Royal Philharmonic Society, *Classical Music,* June 17, 12–13.

Tosi, Pier Francesco (1723), *Opinioni de' cantori antichi e moderni o sieno osservazioni sopra il canto figurato,* trans. Johann Ernst Galliard (1743), rep. (1968), *Observations on the Florid Song,* New York and London: Johnson Reprint Corporation.

Trivedi, Saam (2002), 'Against musical works as eternal types', *British Journal of Aesthetics,* **42** (1), January, 73–82.

Truefitt, Alison (1994), 'Views on the teacher training programme', *Singing,* **27**, Winter, 12–22.

Utley, Alison (2000), 'Discord greets hymns for her', *The Times Education Supplement,* 15 December, 48.

Valentine, C.W. (1957), *Psychology and its Bearing on Education,* London: Methuen.

—— (1962), *The Experimental Psychology of Beauty*, London: Methuen.

Varcoe, Stephen (2000), *Sing English Song*, London: Thames Publishing.

Veldhuis, Anne H. (1984), 'Spontaneous songs of preschool children', *Arts in Psychotherapy,* **11** (1), Spring, 15–24.

Vennard, William (1967), *Singing: The Mechanism and the Technic*, New York: Carl Fischer.

—— (1997/8), 'The psychology of the pupil-teacher relationship', *American Music Teacher*, **47** (3), December/January, 24–7.

—— (nd.), *In Memoriam: selected articles from the writings of William Vennard*, National Association of Teachers of Singing.

Viadana, Lodovico (1592), *Cento certi Ecclesiastici*.

Vilkman, E., and A.M. Laukkanen (1995), 'Vocal-fold collision mass as a differentiator between registers in the low-pitch range', *Journal of Voice*, **9** (1), 66–73.

Wainwright, Gordon (1999), *Teach Yourself Body Language*, London: Hodder and Stoughton.

Walker, Robert (1993/4), 'Identifying cultural uniqueness in musical sounds', *Journal of Research in Music Education*, **119**, 77–84.

Wall, Joan (1989), *International Phonetic Alphabet for Singers*, Dallas: Pst … Inc.

—— (1990), with Robert Caldwell, Tracy Gavilanes, and Sheila Allen, *Diction for Singers*, Dallas: Pst … Inc.

Walls, Geoffrey (1994), 'Unpitched notes – 2', *Singing*, **26**, Summer, 23–32.

Walton, Kendall L. (1988), 'What is abstract about the art of music', *The Journal of Aesthetics*, **46** (3), Spring, 351–64.

Wapnick, Joel; Alice Ann Darrow, Jolan Kovacs, and Lucinda Dalrymple (1997), 'Effects of physical attractiveness on evaluation of vocal performance', *Journal of Research in Music Education*, **45** (3), 470–79.

Ware, Clifton (1998), *Basics of Vocal Pedagogy: The Foundations and Process of Singing*, Boston: McGraw Hill.

Warrener, John J. (1985), 'Applying learning theory to music development: Piaget and beyond', *Music Educators Journal*, **72** (3), November, 22–7.

Warwick, Robert, and Peter Williams (1980), (eds), *Gray's Anatomy*, Edinburgh: Churchill Livingstone.

Watson, Colin (1989), 'Bernouilli in perspective', *The Voice Research Society Newsletter*, **4** (1), August, 21–4.

—— (1992), 'Higher partial enhancement and glottal source manipulation by the trained opera singer', *Voice*, **1** (1), 1–18.

Watson, Monica (1986), 'Organizing pupils' concerts', *Music Teacher*, 29–31.

Watt, Lawrence (1996), 'The law of contract', in Ford, Trevor (ed.), *The Musician's Handbook*, London: Rhinegold Publishing.

Weait, Christopher, and John B. Shea (1978), 'Vibrato: an audio-video-fluorographic investigation of a bassoonist', *Canadian Music Educator*, **20** (1), Autumn, 56–9.

Weatherston, Martin (1996), 'Kant's assessment of music in the *Critique of Judgement*', *British Journal of Aesthetics*, **36** (1), January, 56–65.

Wegman, Rob C. (2002), '"Musical understanding" in the 15th century', *Early Music*, **30** (1), February, 47–66.

Welch, Graham F. (1979), 'Poor pitch singing: a review of the literature', *Psychology of Music*, **7**, 50–58.

—— (1985), 'A schema theory of how children learn to sing in tune', *Psychology of Music*, **13**, 3–18.

—— (1993/4), with Peta White, 'The developing voice: education and vocal efficiency – a physical perspective', *Bulletin of the Council for Research in Music Education*, (119) Winter, 146–56.

—— (1994), 'The assessment of singing', *Psychology of Music*, **22** (1), 3–19.

Wells J.C., and Greta Colson (1992), *Practical Phonetics*, London: Pitman.

White, E.G. (1909), *Science and Singing*, rep. (1969), Boston: Crescendo Publishers.

—— (1918), *The Voice Beautiful in Speech and Song*, London: J.M. Dent and Sons.

—— (1938), *Sinus Tone Production,* London: Dent.

White, Peta (2001), 'Long-term average spectrum (LTAS) analysis of sex- and gender-related differences in children's voices', *Logopedics Phoniatrics Vocology*, **26** (3), 97–101.

Whitton, Kenneth (1984), *Lieder: An Introduction to German Song*, London: Julia Macrae Books.

Wildblood, Joan (1965), *The Polite World*, Oxford: Oxford University Press.

Wilkinson, Robert (1995), 'Art, emotion and expression', in Hanfling, Oswald (ed.), *Philosophical Aesthetics*, Oxford: Blackwell.

Williams, Harry Evan (1920), 'How I Regained a Lost Voice', in Brower and Cooke (1920), Q.V., pp. 123–31.

Wilson, Glenn D. (2002), *Psychology for Performing Artists*, London: Whurr.

Wilson-Dickson, Andrew (1992), *The story of Christian Music*, Oxford: Lion.

Winspur, Ian, and Christopher B. Wynn Parry (1998), *The Musician's Hand: A Clinical Guide*, London: Martin Dunitz.

Witherspoon, Herbert (1925), *Singing – A Treatise for Teachers and Students*, New York: G. Schirmer.

Wlodkowski, Raymond J., and Judith H. Jaynes (1992), 'Overcoming boredom and indifference', *American Music Teacher*, **41** (6), June/July, 12–17, 56.

Wohl, Miriam A. (1996), 'Alexander Technique for performers', *Performing Arts Medicine News*, **4** (1), 33–4.

Wolf, George Frederick (1784), *Georg Friedrich Wolf's Unterrict in der Singkunst*, Halle in Sachsen: J.C. Hendel.

Wood, David (1988), *How Children Think and Learn*, Oxford: Blackwell.

Wyke, B.D. (1974), 'Laryngeal neuromuscular control systems in singing: a review of current concepts', *Folia Phoniatrica*, **26** (1), 295–306.

Yarbrough, Cornelia; Judy Bowers and Wilma Benson (1992), 'The effect of vibrato on the pitch-matching accuracy of certain and uncertain singers', *Journal of Research in Music Education*, **40** (1), 30–38.

Yuktanandana, Aksak (1995), 'Musical beauty and levels of hearing', *British Journal of Aesthetics*, **35** (1), January, 49–60.

Zacconi, Lodovico (1592), *Prattica di musica utile et necessario si al compositore*, Venice: Girolamo Polo (1996), rep. Bologna: Forni.

Zarlino, Goiseffo (1573), *Institutioni Harmoniche*, Venice.

Zemlin, Willard R. (1988), *Speech and Hearing Science*, Englewood Cliffs, NJ: Prentice Hall.

Zenatti, A (1976), 'Jugement esthétique et perceptive de L'enfant, entre 4 à 10 ans, dans des épreuves rhythmiques', *Année Psychologique*, **76**, 185–90.

Zielinski, Shirley, and Paul Kiesgen (2002), 'To listen or not to listen', *Journal of Singing*, **59** (2), November/December, 133–8.

Zimmerman, Marilyn Pflederer (1970), 'Percept and concept: implications of Piaget', *Music Educators Journal*, **56** (6), February, 49–50, 147–8.

Index of Persons

Select Index of Subjects